THE VIRGIN
GUIDE TO
VOLUNTEERING

Also published by Virgin Books:

The Virgin Travellers' Handbook
The Virgin Guide to Working Abroad
The Virgin Travel Health Handbook
The Virgin Alternative Guide to British Universities

THE VIRGIN GUIDE TO VOLUNTEERING

REBECCA HARDY

First published in Great Britain in 2004 by
Virgin Books Ltd
Thames Wharf Studios
Rainville Road
London
W6 9HA

A catalogue record for this book is available from the British Library.

ISBN 0-7535-0857-5

Typeset by Phoenix Photosetting, Chatham, Kent
Printed and bound in Great Britain by Mackays of Chatham, Chatham, Kent

CONTENTS

ACKNOWLEDGEMENTS

There is a long list of people whom I would like to thank for their help and support while writing this guide. Thanks loads to all the volunteers who willingly gave up their time to talk to me about their experiences, as well as those who put me in touch with them: Ruth Asher, Rosie Barnes, Marco Van Belle, Simon Bowen, Theo Cresser, Katharine Dennison, Lucy Dixon, Charlotte Duck, Ruth Eslin, Jon Finch, Charlotte Goddard, Maria Gold, Nicky Goodchild, Karen Harrison, Chris Hern, Iain Hook, Maria Jacovides, Clare Lewis, Ryan McBirney, Pamela McLean, Paolo Maroni, Kate Marshall, Kathy Miller, Ben Moor, Lynne Moor, Alison Neighbour, Bob Randall, Rosie Rayner, Ellie Sandercock, Andrew Schofield, Hugh Burnham Slipper, Jessica Sutton and Alison Tapp. Thanks too to all the people who contacted me whose stories I didn't use.

Thanks to Angela and Mark at the National Centre for Volunteering who took the time to talk to me about this guide and also allowed me to use their extensive library. The following organisations were also extremely helpful and provided much-needed research and information: BSES Expeditions, Business in the Community, Concordia, Gap Activity Project, JustDoSomething.net, The Neem Tree Trust, Net Aid, Planning Aid, Project Trust, RSVP, Scene and Heard, Student Volunteering UK, Time Bank, Voluntary Service Overseas (VSO), World Service Enquiry and Youth Net UK. Acknowledgements too to Richard Dawood at the Fleet Street Clinic for the information he compiled on food hygiene in the health section, Jason Gibbs from the Nomad Travel Clinic, the website Netbackpacker.com, and Katherine Gaskin and Justin Davis Smith for their study and research into European volunteering.

Thanks too to my original editor Mark Wallace, who came up with the idea for this book, my new editor Barbara Phelan, Becke Parker and Gareth Fletcher for keeping me posted, and all the team at Virgin Books for putting the book together.

I'd also like to pass on a general thank you to all the people who have gone out of their way to help promote this book and *The Virgin Guide to Working Abroad*: Kate Marshall, Tracey Smith, Juliet Giles, Denton Brown, Damon Syson, Stefan Melzak, Alex Rayner, Ester Dixon and all the staff at Books etc. Sincere apologies to anyone whose name I have missed out.

Thanks loads to all my lovely friends who kept me sane by making me laugh and entertaining me. Big thanks to Lara, Sarah, Stella and her amazing circular list, Dan for being so goddamn chuffed with me, Gill and Bob Whittaker, Lucia for long lunches and Cava, Maria for being my big sis, Karen for mutual mischief-making, my beautiful cats Daffodil and the dear departed Henry, who kept me company in the long hours spent writing, and most of all my mum and dad and my loving partner Andrew. Thank you everybody!

INTRODUCTION

The world of voluntary work is changing. Gone is the traditional image of the little old lady in elasticated slacks helping out behind a charity shop counter. Welcome to the new face of volunteering: the virtual volunteer who puts technological skills to good use translating documents for an NGO in Africa; the entrepreneur who provides business expertise to community groups; the lawyer who gives legal advice for free to people who can't afford to pay; the Human Resource manager who listens to children read each week; the grandmother of two grandchildren who works part-time in a hospice; the actor who helps underprivileged children to write plays. In fact, the voice of contemporary volunteering is about as far from 'little old lady' as you can get. Employers are increasingly recognising the benefits of volunteer work in helping to build staff morale and teach important transferable skills. Studies show that volunteering can provide that much-needed leg-up into a new career and employers are more likely to take you on if you have voluntary experience. There is even evidence to suggest that volunteering can make you healthier. No surprise then that more and more people see giving a couple of hours a week not just as helping a worthy cause, but also as an interesting way of winding down after a tough and hectic week.

And it doesn't stop there: gap years and eco-tourist holidays are booming. No longer just the preserve of students and gappers, successful professionals are just as likely to take career breaks to load up their backpacks and help out on international development projects. Retired people, fitter and healthier than ever before, are increasingly drawn to travelling overseas and using their new-found free time to broaden their horizons and put their lifetime skills to good use. Whatever the motives, there is plenty of opportunity. The gap between the developing and industrialised countries is deepening and assisting on sustainable development projects can allow you the chance to engage with the world and to do work that actually means something.

The aim of this guide is to provide an informative and inspiring look into this new world of volunteering, ranging from recent social developments such as employee-volunteer schemes and virtual volunteering, to the mixed blessings of overseas development work. The first section covers local volunteering, whether it's helping at the local hospice or mentoring refugees by email. The second section looks at international volunteering with travel advice and details of resources to find projects worldwide and schemes that apply to a range of countries. Finally, the third section offers region-by-region information on worldwide volunteer opportunities. Whatever you want to do, whether it's residential or non-residential, at home or overseas, this guide will provide all the information you need.

As this book will testify, volunteering brings huge opportunities for personal growth. Whether you're volunteering in the local school down the road, working in an orphanage in Bulgaria or sitting at home and sending emails to prisoners, what you stand to gain from volunteering is immense. Without wishing to be too slushy, I have been awed, humbled and shamed while researching this guide. The fact is that there are hundreds of people out there we rarely hear about who are working tirelessly to build and strengthen communities. But the great thing is that this so rarely comes from a spirit of do-gooding. All of the people I spoke to derived a tangible pleasure from their work. Volunteering is about so much more than helping other people in a dreary spirit of Victorian philanthropy. Instead it is a two-way street, where the volunteers gain just as much as the people they are supposed to be 'helping'. Some of this comes from learning new skills and branching into new areas, but it is also about feeling that they are doing 'good' and making time to do what they want to do.

The fact is that people can and do change their lives through volunteering. Whether it is gaining a new career or discovering a fresh outlook on life, the case studies in this book prove that, given the motivation, voluntary work can be the key to revitalising your life. As Anaïs Nin once said, 'Life shrinks or expands in proportion to one's courage.' Whatever you are drawn to, take steps today – you never know, it could be the start of something wonderful.

Rebecca Hardy

August 2003

PART ONE: HOME
LOCAL VOLUNTEERING

1. GETTING STARTED

Volunteering can be a life-changing experience. Whether you are a highflying business man, or an overstretched mother, whether you're unemployed, retired, itching for new horizons or on a burning mission to help the poor and dispossessed, voluntary work could be the key to transforming your life. The fact is that, no matter who you are, where you live, what your job is, whether you're earning a hundred grand a year or you've been on the dole for eighteen months, there is something out there waiting for you.

If you've picked up this book, the chances are that you're thinking about a way to change your life. Perhaps you're looking for a new direction, a fresh stimulus or something to give a welcome kick to your routine. Congratulations – you've come to the right place. Volunteering can do all that, and more. If you don't believe me, have a look at the case studies in this guide. Each and every one talks about their experience in terms of personal growth. Yes, they are providing a much-needed service. Yes, they are helping people and communities in a way that previously might not have existed. But the fact is that what really starts to emerge is how positive it makes them feel. Volunteering can leave you feeling good – really good. In the course of researching this guide, I have spoken to countless people who have done some really interesting things for some very worthwhile causes. But perhaps the biggest visible benefit is in how happy it has made them. 'I've never felt so alive', said one person about volunteering for a telephone counselling line. 'I'd be doing it now if I could be paid to,' said another. 'I realised there was so much to life,' was a common response. 'It stretched me, gave me confidence, and changed the way I saw myself.'

WHY CHOOSE TO VOLUNTEER?

Volunteering can help if you . . .

Want to learn new skills to bring to your present job

Fancy a change in direction

Can't get a job

Feel stuck in a rut

Need new skills to break into a new career

Have free time on your hands and would like to fill it in an interesting, challenging way

Feel passionate about a particular cause

Want to live in a new culture or environment

Would like to meet new people

Like the idea of learning new undiscovered aspects of yourself

Want to 'give something back'

WHAT DO YOU STAND TO GAIN?

Rest assured that not all volunteers are the saintly, altruistic kind, gladly giving their free time to help the infirm and needy. Maybe you're one of the few who are genuinely like that – and, if so, good for you, the world is crying out for you rare enlightened souls. But the chances are that, like most of us, you're looking for what it can do for you. Am I right? You're thinking about giving up your time, and in your hard-wired, calculating little brain, you're thinking: right, hmm, so far so good, but what exactly do *I* get out of this? The short answer is . . . well, there is no short answer. Volunteering comes in a myriad different forms and has a myriad different advantages. But rest assured you will get something out of it.

Like what? How about the chance to meet new people and broaden your experiences; do things you never knew you could do before; pick up vital new skills that will surely boost your appeal to employers; live and work in cultures or workplaces you wouldn't have access to otherwise; see the fruits of your labour flourish and yes, get that warm, saintly glow that comes from helping other people.

Take a look at this list – all these words were frequently mentioned by volunteers when I asked what they had gained from voluntary work:

People skills
Courage
Initiative
Confidence
The chance to learn about new technology
A new job
Promotion
New friends
Sense of achievement
Training
Networking
Adventure
Understanding and insight
A new lease of life

CONFIDENCE

One of the most commonly quoted benefits is that mysterious, elusive quality – confidence. Some volunteers positively exude it. It's not surprising: they have thrown themselves into challenging situations and emerged on the other side radiating a new-found self-belief. Believe it or not, voluntary work can get you out of your comfort zone and challenge you in fresh, unexpected ways. You may be called on to use new skills you didn't have before or you may discover new aspects to yourself you never even knew existed in your old life of plodding familiarity.

NEW SKILLS

Many volunteering posts come with training and orientation where you can pick up transferable skills that will put you in good stead in the job market. Even those that don't are bound to throw up opportunities to learn new skills on the way – be it in technology, negotiating, team building or leading groups of people. Such is the need of many of these projects, people who have little or no experience may find themselves being elevated to positions of responsibility they would never have been granted in a typical work environment. Jon spent four years volunteering for BTCV and found himself managing and training people despite never having done it before. The whole experience taught him new skills with which he could impress future employers, and radically improved his self-esteem. As serial volunteer Ruth Asher says, 'I didn't go into volunteering to get a job out of it, but I've realised that I've learned loads of skills that employers really value, such as teamwork, leadership and interpersonal skills. I also get a lot of enjoyment out of it. Volunteering has given me dreams, motivation and confidence. Volunteering is addictive – it's not about do-gooding. There's so much more you get out of it.'

IMPROVE YOUR EMPLOYABILITY

None of this is to be sniffed at. In these competitive times, employers are looking for more than the ability to just show up and get on with the job in hand. Employers like people with drive and initiative, which voluntary experience proves you have. They want people who don't resent getting out of bed in the morning. Volunteering shows that you're the kind of person who actually enjoys working. Most of all they like people who have skills and a wide range of experience to draw on.

Volunteering is also a great way to shoulder your way into a new career or industry. We all know that vicious circle: no experience, can't get work – can't get work, no experience. Voluntary work can lift you out of that hole. Want to get into drama teaching? Help out at the local youth group. Fancy yourself as a promoter and fundraiser? How about setting up a project yourself? Want to be a counsellor? Offer your skills in mentoring. And so on . . .

Most application forms and interviewers will ask you to say why you're suitable for the job, and what relevant experience you have. Here unpaid work counts just as much as paid work. In fact, it's even more impressive if you've chosen to do it without the cash incentive. So hold your head high, and shout about your achievements. You'll have a lot to be proud about.

THE PROS

As mentioned before, voluntary work can bring huge rewards and challenges. Most of us operate in a tightly operated comfort zone – we know who we are and we know what we're good at. Volunteering can blast you out of that comfort zone, and trigger radical personal transformations. When Maria Jacovides was working in a magazine publishing company, she never thought that fours years later she'd be training to be a National Park Ranger in South Africa after an animal conservation project in Zambia.

That's the funny thing about voluntary work – it can introduce you to a whole new way of looking at the world, yourself included.

THE CONS

Of course, voluntary work has its shadow side too and, before you commit to a project, it's well worth considering how you are likely to deal with the cons. The most obvious con is the fact that you won't get paid and, if you're engaged in mind-numbingly monotonous tasks with no immediate reward, you may question your sanity for giving up your time for free. Some work also may be menial and 'beneath you'; working on community projects, for example, can involve a sweeping range of duties such as cleaning toilets or making beds. Watch out for organisations that exploit you as cheap labour. Many have policies not to use volunteers when they can pay someone to do the job, but it's best to be aware. You may be voluntary but it doesn't mean you're there to be exploited.

Many voluntary projects tend to draw a diverse range of backgrounds and personalities and, if you're working to a common goal, it's important you rub along. Of course, group dynamics are a funny thing, and it's worth noting that teamwork in voluntary work can bring up exactly the same frictions that paid employment can bring.

SO WHAT KIND OF VOLUNTEERING CAN YOU DO?

With around 200,000 voluntary bodies in the UK, you can be sure that whatever your circumstances there are literally hundreds of opportunities out there waiting for you. This could include anything from helping out with the local football team or cat-sitting for Cats Protection while their owners are on holiday to working as a Samaritan or fundraising for Greenpeace. You could be looking at:

Local volunteering in community groups

Volunteering from home via the Internet

Setting up your own scheme

Voluntary service overseas

Aid work

Eco-tourism holidays

Volunteering through work

Giving professional services for free

Maybe there's something you've never done before but would always like to do. Fancy yourself as a budding actress? How about offering your services at a local drama school? Always wanted to try your hand at social work? There are community groups worldwide dying to hear from you. Think you've got good people skills that have never been fully developed? Maybe you could try your hand as a mentor. Are you a good, non-judgemental listener? Try the Samaritans. The list goes on . . .

IS VOLUNTARY WORK RIGHT FOR YOU?

Perhaps the most crucial point in trying to match yourself to voluntary work is the old adage 'know thyself'. You may have a million good causes in the world, and a vast array of exciting, cutting-edge skills you'd like to develop, but make sure you know what you're letting yourself in for. Opting to volunteer isn't to be taken lightly. Yes, it can offer you the chance to test the waters before you dive in to a full-blown career, but it still requires a level of commitment. Speak to any volunteer manager, and they'll tell you that they want reliable people who they can trust to commit. In short, don't make any promises you can't keep.

Before you sign yourself up to anything, ask yourself the following questions: how important is money to you? Do you think you will be happy working for no financial recompense, or do you think you may start to resent it? Are you passionate about the cause you will be working for? How important is that to your motivation?

How much free time do you have? How much me-time do you need before you start to go mad?

MAKING THE RIGHT CHOICE

So, how do you choose which type of volunteering is right for you? Before you choose, ask yourself the following questions:

HOW MUCH TIME CAN I GIVE?

One of the great things about volunteering is the flexibility it allows. Basically, you call the shots and, unlike the rigours of most paid work, you can decide just how much time you have to give and when you would like to do it. Whatever your commitments and responsibilities, you should be able to find something for you.

Day-time

Evening

Weekends

'Whenever'

Work out how much time you can feasibly give to the project. If you're integrating it with work, picture yourself arriving home from the office. How do you think you'll feel if you've signed up to volunteer every evening? How much time do you feasibly think you'll be able to offer without it becoming a chore? Is it easy to get to? Does it involve unsociable hours? Are you a night-time or day-time person? Can you give time regularly as part of your weekly schedule, or would it be more suitable to opt for a volunteer holiday? If the answer is the latter, there are plenty of schemes both local and overseas that offer the chance to give a set period of time to a project, often involving travel. If you are not sure how easily you can integrate volunteering into your life, a short volunteer holiday may be the best option. Meanwhile if you're a 'whenever' person, fundraising activities are ideal if you can only give time in regular but arbitrary spurts, when an event is up and running.

WHERE DO I WANT TO DO IT?

With so many voluntary organisations in the UK, you should be able to volunteer pretty much wherever you fancy. Your local area is bound to throw up plenty of opportunities – contact your local Volunteer Bureaux to find out what's available in your area. There are also likely to be countless causes that haven't yet been catered for and, if you're really pro-active, you could start your very own project. Volunteering overseas is also a growing area – read the International Section for more details.

WHAT DO I WANT TO GAIN FROM THE EXPERIENCE?

Focusing on what you have to gain from the experience can help you narrow down the choices available to you. If adventure is top of the list, then choose an overseas project or opt for one of the more cutting-edge and challenging projects. If you're looking specifically to develop a certain skill, check that you will have the opportunity, although expect that you may have to do other things too. If you want to break into a specific industry or gain skills as a foundation to a further career, such as in teaching or nursing, look out for volunteering opportunities in the same area.

WHAT SKILLS DO I HAVE TO OFFER?

Think carefully about what you can offer an organisation and who might be interested. Don't assume that, just because you will be working for free, they'll be eager to snap you up. Voluntary organisations can be hugely professional. Maybe you are a good cook and could help in the kitchens of a refugee council, or maybe you have counselling skills. There are plenty of professions that can find voluntary placements.

Here's a small list of the kind of things you could do:

Fundraising

Campaigning

Rescuing

Training

Building

Restoring

Gardening

Nursing

Teaching

Cooking

Driving

Befriending

FINDING VOLUNTARY WORK

The secret to finding voluntary work is to cast your net wide. At the beginning, be prepared for inspiration to come from anywhere.

THE MEDIA

Look in the *Guardian* jobs section on Wednesdays, which often features a selection of about a hundred volunteering opportunities. Also keep an eye open for local newspapers which may have stories about new community projects requiring volunteers, or give you ideas for projects you could start yourself. The radio can also be a good starting point – there may be special programmes about voluntary work.

WORD OF MOUTH

Tell everyone you meet that you are interested in getting into volunteering and ask them if they know of any opportunities. You never know what leads people may come up with.

PUBLIC LIBRARIES

Ask if they have a notice board or a file of information on voluntary work or, even better, one of the published directories on voluntary work such as *The Voluntary Agencies Directory*.

PROFESSIONAL ORGANISATIONS

Some trade or professional organisations run their own volunteer schemes or will have details of ways in which they can help. See chapter two for more details.

LOCAL HOSPITALS

Local hospitals often take volunteers, particularly if you are looking to start a career in one of the caring professions. Contact them by letter first. It may also be worth contacting the Social Services Departments. They should have details of local schemes in your area such as mentoring.

ASK YOUR EMPLOYERS

Many employers are keen to see their staff volunteer as it can develop vital skills such as in team building and communication. Speak to your boss about your plans. Some companies have employee volunteering programmes which you can join, or at the very least you may be able to persuade them to lend you support with time off or money. Don't assume that your boss won't be interested – many employers now take an enlightened interest in supporting their staff and allowing them to develop their talents. See chapter three.

COLD CALL FOR WORK

If the organisation is a small one, such as a local animal sanctuary, for example, it may be in your interests to knock on the door and ask about working for them. In general, however, your best bet is to phone or write first. Voluntary organisations are by their nature overstretched and they may not want to give up precious time and staff to deal with you.

USE THE VOLUNTEER PLACEMENTS SERVICES

There are plenty of agencies and organisations which will match volunteers to opportunities. Here are the main UK resources:

Volunteer bureaux can tell you what voluntary work is available locally and put you in touch with local organisations. You can also discuss with them what you want to do and get advice. Most areas have a volunteer bureau – look up your nearest bureau in the phone directory under 'V' or phone Volunteer Development England on 0121 633 4555. You can contact the National Association of Volunteer Bureaux (NAVB) for details of your local volunteer bureau by writing to NAVB, New Oxford House, 16 Waterloo Street, Birmingham B2 5UG, Tel: 0121 633 4555 or 0121 633 4043, Email: info@vde.org.uk or visit the website **www.vde.org.uk**.

Millennium Volunteers is a Government-funded initiative which encourages 16- to 24-year-olds to volunteer through over 200 projects. To get an information pack, visit the website **www.millenniumvolunteers.gov.uk** where you can also search by geographical area to find local contact details for projects, or write to MV Unit, Department for Education and Skills, Room E4, Moorfoot, Sheffield S1 4PQ.

Student Volunteering UK gives information about volunteering opportunities within students unions. Visit **www.studentvol.org.uk** or freephone 0800 0182146. You can also get hold of a copy of its quarterly magazine *Grapevine* and booklet *The Art of Crazy Paving* (£10 or free to students) which has advice on using volunteering to get on in the job market.

National Association of Councils for Voluntary Service is the umbrella body for 300 local Councils for Voluntary Services. Go to **www.nacvs.org.uk** to find your local CVS and volunteering opportunities in your region. Alternatively, contact the NACVS at 177 Arundel Street, Sheffield S1 2NU, Tel: 0114 278 6636, Fax: 0114 278 7004.

You can also get a full list at the website for **YouthNet UK (www.Do-it.org.uk)**. This is an Internet database of local volunteering opportunities in the UK and is searchable by postcode, type of work and type of organisation.

If there is no local bureau, you can also try the **Councils for Voluntary Service**. They are sometimes known by a different name, so look in the telephone book or Yellow Pages under 'Council', 'Volunteers' or 'Voluntary'. If you live in a rural area try the **Rural Community Councils**.

You can also register with **Timebank**, which will match your interests and skills with volunteering opportunities in your area. It also produces a volunteer guide and newsletter, as well as regular updates about volunteering opportunities. To register call 0845 601 4008 or for general enquiries call 0207 401 5438. Alternatively, register online at **www.timebank.org.uk.**

Also try the **National Centre for Volunteering**, Regent's Wharf, 8 All Saints Street, London N1 9RL, Tel: 020 7520 8900, Fax: 020 7520 8910, Email: Volunteering@thecentre.org.uk, website: **www.volunteering.org.uk**. As well as a volunteer magazine, it has a searchable database of local opportunities by area and can provide information for employee volunteering.

Voluntary Sector, published by NCVO Publications, contains news and information on those working for voluntary agencies. Contact NCVO Publications, Regent's Wharf, 8 All Saints Street, London N1 9RL, Tel: 020 7713 6161.

JOB CENTRES

Don't neglect job centres – they might not officially deal with voluntary jobs, but there may still be news of any local schemes you can join so it's well worth paying them a visit.

THE INTERNET

Several websites have databases of voluntary opportunities. The website **www.charitypeople.co.uk** is a searchable datebase of paid and unpaid opportunities in the not-for-profit sector. Another useful website is **www.jobsincharities.co.uk** which has a job search and a volunteer search area.

The website Going Green has a directory of voluntary organisations and campaigns you can get involved with, as well as details of eco-tourism projects overseas. Go to **www.goinggreen.net**.

If you have already decided on an area you would like to work for voluntarily (say, animals, for example), doing a search on a big search engine such as Google is bound to throw up plenty of ideas.

Also look out for **Volunteers' Week**, which runs in June each year. It is hosted by the National Centre for Volunteering and lists events going on around the UK to celebrate volunteering.

OLDER VOLUNTEERS

Older volunteers can contact **RSVP** (Retired and Senior Volunteer Programme), c/o CSV, 237 Pentonville Road, London N1 9NJ, Tel: 020 7278 6601.

REACH (REACH, Bear Wharf, 27 Bankside SE1 9DP, Tel: 020 7928 0452) specialise in finding voluntary schemes for retired professionals and executives.

DO YOUR RESEARCH

Once you've found an organisation you're interested in, a brief, polite phone call should allow you to shed light on any preliminary questions you have. Before you apply for work formally, make sure you know a little about the history of the organisation and the culture behind it. For example, who benefits from their help and how do they organise their fundraising? Are they a large organisation or a small, locally run one? How many staff and volunteers are working for them? How flexible are they and what kind of volunteers are they looking for? What activities are involved? Do they have a minimum requirement of hours spent volunteering per week/month or are there certain shifts expected of them?

It's also a good time to ask if it's possible to come along and visit one of their projects. Sometimes it takes seeing a scheme in the flesh to get a real sense of whether you can commit to it or not. It wasn't until my friend had visited a cat sanctuary to adopt a cat that she discovered she had a mad passion for cats, and pretty soon she was giving her services for free. Many voluntary organisations also have open days/evenings where you can go along and see the kind of work they do, and ask any questions. If you're happy with what you hear, you can then set about contacting them in writing. Find out who to address the application to and, if you're asking to receive further information, send an SAE.

THE APPLICATION PROCESS.

Applying for voluntary work is no different to writing an application for paid work – make sure your letter is as professional, concise and attractively presented as possible. Typewritten is best, and make sure you enclose a CV, unless the organisation requires you to fill out an application form instead.

There is plenty of good advice about writing a good CV and it's well worth taking the experts' advice. There are also a lot of conflicting ideas, however, but most experts agree on the following things:

Your CV should include:

Your name and address, telephone number and email address

Your work history

Your education history

Details of any special skills or interests

Make sure your CV is relevant to the work you are applying for. However, be aware of the value of 'transferable skills'. The fact that you directed a college play might not be directly relevant to applying for work on an archaeological dig, but it does show you enjoy being a leader and are creative.

- **Be concise and don't overelaborate – save that for the interview**
- **Keep the CV short – either one or two pages**
- **Don't include references, although if you have room you can say 'references available on request'**
- **Type or word process it in black ink on one side of the paper**
- **Keep to the same font throughout**
- **Make sure your spelling and grammar is good and check for any inconsistencies in spelling, titles, etc.**
- **Avoid using jargon**

THE APPLICATION FORM

Many voluntary organisations have their own application forms. Don't send a CV instead as you are risking it being ignored. Before you fill out the form, read through it carefully from start to finish and take note of any special instructions, such as whether to use block capitals or black ink. It's a good idea to make a few photocopies so you can fill it in rough first, and write the original one last. Before you begin, take a while to think about all the information you have to sell yourself and what sections it belongs.

Once you begin writing, make sure it is neat and easy to read. Don't eat or drink, and take your time and concentrate. Check spellings and grammar, and don't cram too much information into a small box. After you have filled in the first photocopy, review what you have written. Do your answers fit with the questions? Could the information work better in another section? Is it concise? Does it demonstrate you are suitable to work for this organisation?

APPLYING ON SPEC

When you write a spec letter to an organisation, draft it in the same way you would a normal spec letter for paid employment. If possible, address it to a named person – phone up beforehand and ask who deals with voluntary applications. Make sure you state right at the beginning your reasons for writing, and demonstrate that you have done some research into the company. If possible, try to find a topical peg. For example, if you first heard of the organisation through a feature on the local news or an article in the paper, mention it.

TIPS ON WRITING THE PERFECT SPEC LETTER

- Address it to a named person
- Keep it short and concise
- Enclose a CV
- State your reasons for writing – say what you want from the start e.g. I am writing to enquire about volunteering opportunities with your organisation.
- Highlight your relevant skills/appropriate qualifications, and why you think you would be suitable to work for them
- Give your reasons for applying to this particular organisation

THE SELECTION PROCESS

Some voluntary organisations require you to attend an interview before accepting you as a volunteer. Don't presume that, just because the position is unpaid, the organisations will take anyone. You should still aim to create a professional image and dress smartly for the interview. Some organisations are fiercely competitive and take only a very small proportion of applicants. If you are likely to be working with vulnerable people, such as children, the elderly or people with learning disabilities, don't be surprised if they want to run criminal record checks on you. Other organisations may ask you to sit an assessment test to see whether you are suitable. This doesn't happen often but it might, if the position is particularly demanding. In these cases, the best tactic is to be yourself and don't attempt to shape your answers to fit what you may think are their expectations. Assessment tests are designed to see how suitable you are for the job and are as much use to you as they are to the organisation.

Above all, approach an interview for voluntary work in the same way you would for a paid position. Make sure you:

- Show an interest in the company – ask questions and demonstrate that you have done some research into the kind of work they do

- Do some preparation beforehand. Read up on the cause they aim to benefit so you have some background knowledge. For example, if you hope to work for Greenpeace, make sure you know about the latest environmental issues

- Be positive about your achievements. Highlight relevant skills and think about what you genuinely have to offer the organisation

- Listen

- Be professional, smart and punctual

- Take your CV even if you have sent it on first

So what could be a typical question? Again, think what would happen in a normal job interview situation. Questions such as 'What made you particularly interested in our organisation?' and 'What do you think you have to offer us?' are standard fare in most interviews. Also expect probing questions about your motivation and ability to deal with stress. It's a good idea to think up examples of scenarios that have tested you in the past, with positive conclusions on how you dealt with the situation.

BEFORE YOU COMMIT

Once you have found the right scheme for you, you might feel tempted to rush in straight away and sign up to volunteer. However, it's wise to take it slowly. Before you commit make sure you have found out as much about the organisation as you can, and checked the following details:

- **How long will it take to travel to do the work? Is it a journey you can make easily?**

- **Does the work involve any outgoings of your own? If it does, will you get out-of-pocket expenses paid?**

- **If you are receiving any kind of state benefit, will volunteering affect your eligibility? Contact your local benefit office and read chapter two for more information.**

- **If you are doing any difficult tasks or working with special cases, will you get training?**

- **Will the organisation arrange any necessary insurance?**

TRANSFERABLE SKILLS

If you've been working in the same area for a while, it may be difficult to view your skills afresh and assess just what you have to offer an organisation. We all get used to seeing ourselves in little boxes but thinking about your volunteer alter ego can help you to see yourself from another perspective. If you're having problems working out what skills and strengths you can offer, it helps to break down and analyse your present job. For example, if you think you're a good computer programmer, ask yourself why. You might conclude, well, I'm good at computer programming because I'm good at thinking systematically and I like solving problems. Maybe you're a good sales manager because you enjoy working in a team, reaching targets and motivating people.

If you've just left college or university, spend some time thinking about the areas you enjoyed and did well in. Yes, even spending all your time down the student union can have its pluses . . . it shows you enjoy being part of a community and are probably good at communicating!

VOLUNTEERS' STORIES

Ben Moor works as a volunteer actor/writer for an after-school project that brings children from the area together with drama professionals. 'My advice for people thinking about volunteering is give it a go. It'll be harder work than you expect, but the rewards will be surprising. Not only will you make fine friends, but you'll learn something about yourself that you'll never know if you're just sat in front of the TV or behind a pint of beer every day. It's changed my life in the sense that I've made some great friends among the adult volunteers and it's reminded me that, within every rough kid, there's an artist of some sort wanting a little bit of attention and recognition. At the end of the day, that's important to know.'

17

SKILLS AND OPPORTUNITIES WHAT KIND OF VOLUNTARY WORK IS FOR YOU?

2. SKILLS AND OPPORTUNITIES

So, you've decided you'd like to try volunteering, but you have no idea what to do. You've checked out the available resources, thought about what you have to offer and you're still none the wiser. Faced with the bewildering array of choices on offer, even the most decisive of us can flounder at the first hurdle. But it's only natural that you need to take your time – after all, by working for no money you are opting to work without one of the biggest motivators. So there has to be some other factor strong enough to boot you out of bed in the morning. Like what? How about belief, vision, purpose – that enviable sense that you are moving towards something you really want to do and shaping your future to fit an image that actually motivates you. Besides, taking the pay packet out of the equation can grant a certain amount of freedom. Remember that old saying 'work like you don't need the money' – well, volunteering can actually give you the chance to do what turns you on, rather than always opting for the sensible option. As Theo Cresser, who started a career working for an NGO after volunteering one day a week, says, 'My advice to other volunteers is to look around at what issues you think are relevant to you and find out what you are passionate about. Then, once you have chosen, accumulate as much experience as possible even if it's only a basic level of administration.'

So, the first question to ask yourself is *what do I feel passionate about?*

WHAT KIND OF VOLUNTARY WORK IS FOR YOU?

The next question to ask yourself is, what do you want to learn? Where do you want this voluntary experience to take you? Maybe you want to launch a new career as a counsellor or teacher. If so, you know exactly the kind of areas you should be looking into. Or maybe your intentions are more nebulous than this and you only have a vague, muddled sense that you want to do something different that will somehow open up new opportunities. Are there any skills you would like to develop? Are there any missing areas to your CV, any neglected shadowy areas? Again Theo opted to volunteer on the French desk at Prisoners Abroad, so he could resurrect his diminishing French. Jon led a team of people on conservation trips after three years on the dole. He said it gave him back his confidence and taught him how to manage people.

A good way to select the most appropriate work is to ask yourself the following questions: *what skills would I like to learn? What skills do I have? What do I have to offer a voluntary organisation?*

QUALIFICATIONS

Of course, once you've found a cause that inspires you and you have an idea of what you want to achieve, you may have to temper your bright and fiery enthusiasms. Visions are fine – they're the welcome boost to motivate you to take action – but, after that, it's time to get down to some serious thinking. Never mind the fact that you're not getting paid, the world of volunteering can be as tough and demanding as the rough and tumble of paid employment. So, once you've decided the things that rock your world, think about what you are actually qualified to do.

WHAT QUALIFICATIONS DO YOU NEED?

The broad answer is that it depends on what you do – skilled jobs, such as in nursing, medicine, law, teaching and social work, for example, will require vocational training and expertise, while working in a charity shop will not. Generally, however, *most voluntary jobs will not require specific qualifications*, although they may stipulate at least five GCSEs (above C grade, including Maths and English), and some may employ only graduates. As yet, there is no general qualification in voluntary work.

When it comes to assessing what qualifications will be required, use your judgement. Obviously there's no point in applying for work as a vet if you've had no formal training. That said, some of these organisations may be looking for, say, veterinary assistants, which can be a useful foundation if you're hoping to train to be a vet at university.

Working in specialised areas with vulnerable people is more likely to require vocational qualifications than helping out with fundraising. Childcare work may require a nursing/childcare qualification such as the NNEB (Nursery Nurses Examination Board), while some conservation projects ask for people with related university degrees such as Environmental Studies, Ecology, Zoology or Biology. Archaeology projects often take only trained archaeologists or graduates of a related university degree such as Ancient History or Archaeological Studies.

HAVE VOCATION – WOULD LIKE TO HELP?

If you're a trained professional, you can be sure that there are plenty of organisations out there that are willing to use your expertise. This can be done in two ways: the first is through encouraging your company to take part in an employee-volunteer scheme. This is becoming increasingly popular as many enlightened companies are now realising that, through working on volunteer projects, staff can update and expand their skills base and become happier, more productive workers. (See chapter three for advice on how to get involved.)

The second way is through contacting the national body or organisation that represents your profession. Some sectors, such as accountancy, are actively encouraging their members to give time to voluntary schemes. For example, in 1999, the Institute of Chartered Accountants in England and Wales (ICAEW) launched the Everybody Counts initiative to match its members to voluntary work with charities. With their expertise in business planning and financial management, accountant volunteers can be crucial in getting a community-based project up and running.

Other workers in demand include medics, nurses, teachers, social workers, childcare specialists and lawyers. But, whatever your profession, you can be sure that there are plenty of projects willing to hear from you.

VOLUNTEERS' STORIES

Chris Hern received an MBE for his voluntary work for Planning Aid. Chris had been a Planning Aid volunteer for ten years and during that time undertook more than a hundred cases, including a dozen inquiries. Some have required his involvement for many months, taking him to the High Court, whilst others just required a friendly phone call to put the client on the right course.

Chris says, 'So many people just need a little bit of help to understand what's going on and how they can take part in decision-making. It's gratifying to see people grow in confidence and realise that they can improve their own environments.'

RESOURCES FOR VOLUNTEERING PROFESSIONALS

Professionals can volunteer their services on the website **www.professionals4free.org.uk**, which also carries details of brokers of free professional services.

ProHelp is a national network of professional firms who give their time and expertise for free to voluntary and community groups. For more information go to **www.prohelp.org.uk**.

The Cranfield Trust is a national charity providing free consultancy to small and medium-sized charities across the UK in a variety of management areas. They hold a register of 400 volunteers from the commercial sector that all hold professional qualifications such as MBAs and accountancy. Visit its website **www.cranfieldtrust.org.uk**.

Planning Aid recruits volunteer town planners to give their expertise to community groups. For more information call the co-ordinator on Tel: 0121 766 5282.

The Law Centres Federation promotes voluntary legal services to clients, individuals and communities. Call 020 7387 8570, or go to **www.lawcentres.org.uk**.

The Citizens Advice Bureaux also provide free legal help (**www.citizensadvice.org.uk**), as does the organisation Free Representation Unit, call 020 7831 0692 or go to **www.fru.org.uk** for more information.

The Chartered Surveyors Voluntary Service (CSVS) recruits volunteer surveyors to provide professional assistance on a voluntary, unpaid basis. For more information write to the CSVS Secretary at 12 Great George Street, Parliament Square, London SW1P 3AD, or Email: csvs@rics.org.uk.

You can also try Volunteers in Technical Assistance (VITA), which aims to empower those in developing countries through helping them with technological assistance. Visit **www.vita.org/**.

The UK project IT4 Communities recruits IT experts to volunteer their skills for charities and community groups. Visit **www.it4communities.org.uk**.

Engineers Without Borders is a not-for-profit organisation that organises overseas placements for Engineering students. Contact Engineers Without Borders, 29 Trumpington Street, Cambridge CB2 1QA, Fax: 01223 765625, or visit the website: **www.ewb-uk.org**.

The Prince's Trust requires volunteer business mentors to help young people, targeting 14- to 30-year-olds who are unemployed, in or leaving care, educational underachievers and ex-offenders. The mentor meets regularly with the young person to provide business advice, guidance, monitoring and counselling. Go to **www.princes-trust.org.uk** for more information.

TRAINING

For those of you who will be volunteering for work for which you are not necessarily qualified, however, you may have to undertake training. This depends, of course, on the kind of work you will be volunteering to do but, before agreeing to any voluntary work, it's a good idea to make sure you know if you will receive any training and, if so, what this will involve. Training varies from organisation to organisation but, if you are working in a particularly challenging area, you are bound to receive some sort of orientation course. This can range from a few hours of group work to fairly in-depth training spread over several days. Working with young offenders, for example, will require at least one full day's training, often run by the police, while mentors for young offenders with drugs or sex crimes will be given ongoing training. The Samaritans provide rigorous training for their counselling service, while organisations such as Crisis run courses in dealing with drugs problems, covering topics such as how to recognise specific drugs and what to do if you find a needle etc. Many of these courses can put you in good stead if you wish to follow a related career in healthcare or social work.

USING VOLUNTEERING TO GAIN QUALIFICATIONS

Volunteering is also a great opportunity to update any rusty skills you may have – if your knowledge of computers needs bringing into the twenty-first century, volunteering can be a great opportunity to get up on the latest software. Some work with voluntary organisations may lead to qualifications – some even do NVQs. If you are looking to improve specific skills or training, make sure you know exactly what your work will involve before making any commitment.

The Voluntary Sector National Training Organisation (VSNTO) provides training within the voluntary and community sectors for paid staff, volunteers and trustees. It has offices across Great Britain. For more information go to **www.voluntarysectorskills.org.uk.**

VOLUNTEERS' STORIES

Paolo Maroni was given rigorous training before she worked as a telephone counsellor for Childline. First she had to sit through a stringent selection process. She says, 'It started with a two-hour interview where they asked a lot of very in-depth questions about our childhoods and relationships with our parents, and so on. Basically, it was geared to seeing how open we were and whether we were suitable for the kind of work we would be doing – we might be too sensitive, for example. After that, we had ten weeks of training for three hours a week. This involved role-plays as if we were answering calls, where we talked about different "difficult" subjects such as sex. We also had to shadow a child for an afternoon and afterwards write a report about them. Two trainers assessed us all the way through. After that, we were put on the phone. At the beginning, we were partnered with an experienced counsellor. They listened in to the way we handled the calls, and then, after a couple of sessions, left us on our own. It was nerve wracking at first but we soon got used to it.'

UNEMPLOYMENT AND VOLUNTARY WORK

Contrary to popular thought, you *are entitled to benefits while doing voluntary work*. If you are claiming Job Seeker's Allowance, make sure that you tell the Job Centre straight away. If they query your eligibility for JSA, stick to your guns – as long as you are available for and actively seeking work you are still entitled to JSA. If they insist you are not, contact your local volunteer bureaux and ask them to back you up.

JOB SEEKER'S ALLOWANCE (JSA)

To claim JSA you must be available for and actively seeking work. This means that you must be able to go to a job interview or start a job at one week's notice. Providing you are still available for work and can stop or rearrange the voluntary position at short notice, you can volunteer and still claim JSA. However, if you commit to volunteer for a fixed period of time that stops you from being available for work, you may risk having your JSA stopped. Although there is no stated limit as to the number of hours a week you can volunteer when claiming JSA, if you are volunteering full-time you are not likely to meet the requirement to be actively seeking work. However, you can volunteer at a residential work camp in the UK for up to two weeks a year.

You can also claim out-of-pocket expenses from your voluntary organisation (including travel to and fro, meals while volunteering and childcare costs). Providing you don't receive more than your actual expenses, your benefit shouldn't be affected.

So, to sum up, if you are claiming JSA:

- **Tell the Job Centre straight away if you are volunteering**
- **Make sure you meet the requirements of being available for and actively seeking work**
- **Tell the Job Centre what skills you are learning and developing through volunteering**
- **Provide them with a letter from the organisation saying what you do, what skills you are developing and confirming that you are still available and contactable for paid work**
- **If the Job Centre queries your eligibility to JSA, contact your local volunteer bureaux**

You should also:

- **Inform your volunteer organisation that you are claiming JSA**
- **Tell them that you may be asked to attend an interview or start work with one week's notice**
- **Make sure you are contactable for paid work during your time in voluntary work. Ask them to pass on any messages to you or make sure you carry a mobile**

VOLUNTEERS' STORIES

Jon Finch volunteered for British Trust Conservation Volunteers (BTCV) in Leicestershire for three years while he was unemployed. Throughout that time, he was claiming unemployment benefits, which he was entitled to as long as he could prove he was actively seeking work and available for paid employment. Jon says, 'I had just finished doing a PhD in Physics and, after seven years in academia, wanted to do something completely different. I had always been interested in conservation work and kept seeing a BTCV van driving around town, so decided to find out about volunteering for them. So I phoned them and they told me just to turn up. So I went one day and loved every minute of it.'

Jon was soon volunteering three days a week, working in general woodland management, which included coppicing (cutting trees to stimulate growth), dry stone walling, building footpaths and hedge laying. He didn't need conservation experience but received job training from voluntary officers and occasionally professional dry stone wallers.

Jon loved the work and, after only one year, was made voluntary officer. This required more commitment and, although unpaid, Jon worked a 30 to 40-hour week. 'Working as a voluntary officer was demanding but satisfying. I had to visit the sites before we started conservation work there and run health and safety checks. I also had to plan the work in advance, making sure we had enough wood, or do other tasks like designing fences or writing reports. I was also responsible for the team of fifteen people, which could be quite a responsibility. The work could be dangerous, felling trees for example, and, because people could just turn up to work, it attracted a range of people – including students, unemployed people and those who couldn't work for health reasons, as well as potentially difficult people, such as schizophrenics or alcoholics. This carried its own stresses – I once had to fish a drunk out of a pond – but it certainly opened my eyes.'

Jon stayed for two more years as voluntary officer before finally landing a job in computers. Although he now earns a good salary, he says those three years volunteering were the best working years he has had. 'It was very stressful at times, doing a full-time job for no money, but I loved it. I loved working outside and I'd still be doing it now if it weren't for the fact it is unpaid. My only regret is that I didn't look harder to find paid work in conservation. Because I'd done a Physics degree, I didn't think it would be easy for me to find paid work in that field, but I know plenty of people from the BTCV who have gone on to work for the National Trust.'

GAINS AND REWARDS

Volunteering is a great opportunity to:

Update existing skills

Gain new ones

Improve your confidence

Try out a new job

Get training

Build new networks

USING YOUR EXPERIENCE TO UPDATE YOUR CAREER

Whether you're entering the workplace for the first time, are changing careers or have been out of work for a while, you can be sure that volunteering will provide you with plenty of scope to change your situation. Experience gained during volunteering is bound to improve your chances in the workplace. Not only does it show commitment and initiative, but it also shows you're not afraid of hard work and are engaged in your community. So, whenever you're selling yourself, don't denigrate what you have achieved. Think about what you have gained from the experience and sell yourself accordingly:

What did you do?

What were your responsibilities?

What projects did you work on?

What new skills did you develop?

What did you learn about yourself?

What was the most challenging aspect about your work and how did you meet it?

PRESENTING YOUR VOLUNTARY EXPERIENCE ON CV

In today's competitive job market, employers want to be sure that their staff have the necessary skills needed to do their job with as little intervention from them as possible. Voluntary work can show them that you have the relevant skills even though you may not have previous paid employment in that area. Therefore, it's up to you to really sell those experiences. Think about what attracted you to the project in the first place. The same things that sold it to you can also sell it to your prospective employer. Don't leave your voluntary experience to the hobbies and interests section at the end, but list it under your Work History or Relevant Experience section. Make sure you highlight your areas of responsibility and what training it covered. It's a good idea to adapt your CV to every job you apply for, so think carefully about what projects and skills have particular relevance to the job you are applying for. If you want to get into PR, for example, and helped out with fundraising at university, or wrote press releases to advertise forthcoming events, state this clearly. Include any training you received in your Education and Training section.

VOLUNTEERING TO GET OUT OF UNEMPLOYMENT

Ruth Eslin used volunteering as a way of switching careers from a lucrative post in the City to a more fulfilling role in the public sector. She says, 'I originally started volunteering when I was between jobs as a Human Resources director. Having worked in London but living in Hove, I wanted to do something that would connect me to the community. I began as an Appropriate Adult working with the Sussex police and the Brighton and Hove Youth Offending team, and since then I have become a business mentor for the Prince's Trust and recently trained as a Community Panel member for the Brighton and Hove Youth Offending team again. I also trained to be a mentor to young people.'

When Ruth found work again, she decided to carry on volunteering, pushing it back into the weekends and evenings. Six months later, she was made redundant again, but soon found another job, this time in the public sector. Ruth says, 'To my delight, I was appointed as Regional HR manager for the Environment Agency in Worthing. It was a great opportunity to combine my career with a job that means something and is a valuable part of the community.'

It was her voluntary experience that helped her make the cross-over. 'I was a wild card having never worked in the public sector before but my new boss said that one of the reasons I was appointed was that my voluntary work demonstrated that my core values fitted in with those of the Environment Agency. My volunteer work with the Prince's Trust also demonstrated that I had the skills needed for the post, such as understanding and setting business-related objectives.' Ruth is now a passionate advocate of the benefits of voluntary work: 'As an HR professional, I am always encouraging people to work in the voluntary sector as a way to learn new skills and learn about different things. I value the fact that people choose to do this in their own time and it would certainly play a part if there was a head-to-head employment decision.'

3. NEW DIRECTIONS

One of the greatest benefits in volunteering lies in its capacity for self-transformation. On the surface that may seem like a grandiose statement but, in the course of writing this guide, I have been amazed at the amount of people I have met who have genuinely discovered new aspects of themselves through broadening their sense of identity by volunteering. So, if you are stuck in a rut, and long for another life, volunteering can provide that long-desired kick up the ass you've been looking for.

Many of us reach crossroads where we have no idea where we're heading. We may feel that we're fading in the safe familiar routines of a long-established career, or turning up to the same place every day, running over the same old tasks on the same ploddingly productive routine. For those of us stuck in this place, a change of career may seem too daunting to achieve. We may feel we don't have the money, the time, the youth, the energy, the drive or the commitment. As much as we may long for a change, we may fear taking the risk to discover a new life, a new sense of the self or simply a change of routine.

The good news is that there are plenty of tales of people who have been in such a position and, through volunteering, found the will to make a move. Stories abound of people who have managed to change their working lives through getting involved in some kind of volunteering project. Many were amazed at the impact it had. Some fulfilled long-neglected ambitions, while others found that just giving up a few days a week gave them a new vision of who they were and triggered a major life overhaul. So, whatever your circumstances, wherever you are, volunteering can bring about the change of perspective you have been looking for.

Voluntary work can help if you:

Feel stuck in a rut, want to change things but have no sense of what you want to do instead.

Have a sense of what you would like to do but lack the resources or certainty to jump right in and launch a new career.

Are happy in your present job but feel you want to add new strings to your bow.

Feel you are wasting away and crave fresh challenges and new adventures.

MAKING A CAREER CHANGE

Working voluntarily can be a great way of testing out the waters of a new career. Many voluntary bodies allow for a flexible workforce, where you can choose to work part-time or job share to see how much you like the work first. Many jobs, particularly in the caring and social sector, demand voluntary experience first.

VOLUNTEERS' STORIES

Journalist Rosie Barnes volunteered for Saneline, a telephone help-line for people with mental health problems, when she decided she wanted to launch a career in counselling.

'I chose the work because I had suffered with bulimia for several years and found that there was no one suitable to talk to; I liked the idea of providing the service I had missed to someone else. I also needed counselling experience to apply for a course, and wanted to see whether I enjoyed it or not.'

The training started with a selection evening in which she was told what the volunteering involved and invited on to a selection weekend. 'This was very intensive,' says Rosie. 'It ran over two full weekends and we had to do role plays with volunteers on the phone, and learn about the most common mental health problems, legal information and details of local services and drugs. Many people opted out at this stage but it was amazing how much the rest of us wanted to do it. They made it sound so rewarding – it felt as if we would be really helping people.'

Once Rosie was volunteering on the telephone lines, she worked one four-hour shift every week. In two years, she received her fair share of strange calls. The lines were always busy, and would include a variety of callers, ranging from mundane requests for information to more bizarre incidents such as regular callers delivering streams of consciousness or men masturbating – 'it happens a lot because they know women are on the line.'

The worst calls were the silent ones. Rosie says, 'They could be quite hard to deal with – we had to be calm and accept that they wanted us to speak. Most people worried about suicidal callers and I had my fair share. One caller was on the verge of killing herself and I had no way of knowing if she went ahead with it or not. Sometimes it didn't hit me straight away but later I would find I couldn't stop thinking about it. It touched personal buttons of course, but luckily, I had support from my coordinators.'

After two years, Rosie decided to move on and start her training as a counsellor. 'I felt that talking to someone on the phone wasn't the whole story and I wanted to work with people face to face. But it stood me in good stead for my counselling course. I already knew a lot about mental health and law, and had vast experience of talking to people in distress. Some trainees were scared of strong emotions, but I knew that I was a good listener and could handle difficult stuff. And my counselling background has also helped me become a better journalist.'

WHAT KIND OF INDUSTRIES AND SECTORS REQUIRE VOLUNTEERING FIRST?

Voluntary work can help you with all kinds of employment, but there are some sectors and professions that require volunteer experience first. These include:

Teaching

Caring

Counselling

Charity work

Nursing

Drama/music/art or occupational therapy

Social work

Childcare

USING VOLUNTARY WORK TO FURTHER YOUR CAREER

Gaining new skills can be the key to furthering your present career or gaining promotion. In many companies the pressure and pace of work mean that too few bosses are ready to take a chance and give you a job that they feel you're not qualified or ready for. Voluntary work can be a great place to develop your skills and focus on the areas in which you would like to improve. More and more employers are coming round to this way of thinking and starting their own volunteer projects, after they've seen how much they benefit their workers.

Some organisations offer fixed-term contracts where you will be working for a set time, often on a particular project. This can be a useful way of testing the water first. Check with your present employer whether you can take a leave-of-absence to take part in some voluntary work.

Before you commit to voluntary work, however, try to work out how likely the experience is to meet your goals. Be clear about what you want to get out of it. Make sure the voluntary organisation you intend to volunteer for will be providing you with the opportunity to get all the skills you need.

It's also a good idea to try to find out how your present employer regards voluntary work before committing yourself. Even though many companies are becoming increasingly interested in the gains of volunteering, some still may hold the view that volunteers are nothing more than do-gooders. Check to see how much your work will be valued and considered before you make any serious changes.

CHARITY WORK

Of course, with all this talk of volunteering, you may just decide to bite the bullet and get a paid job in charity work. And why not? Working in the voluntary sector may not grant you the same financial perks that working in the private sector brings, but there are many other benefits. Like what? Like . . .

Working in a vibrant and fast-moving sector.

Giving your time and energy to a cause you feel passionate about.

Enjoying the sense of achievement that comes from knowing your work has gone to a good purpose and seeing your project flourish.

Feeling you are doing something worthwhile.

Voluntary sector work can come with other perks too. Many jobs within the voluntary sector involve ongoing career development. Fundraising can also involve ongoing assessment and training leading to diplomas, NVQs and MBAs. There are also good chances of mobility and promotion. The voluntary sector is small enough for talented people to be recognised for good work and chances of promotion can be better than slaving away in some faceless giant multi-national in the private sector.

Of course, like private companies and sectors, charities have to survive and flourish and make difficult decisions about money and recruitment. It's wise then not to go into the sector with a head full of ideals – I've met several charity workers who come out the other side disillusioned by the knowledge that working in the voluntary sector can involve long business-orientated meetings, deadlines and budgets just like any other profession. Working for a charity may require tough decisions about personnel and allocation of resources. Charities are by their nature cash-strapped and pushed to their limit, so working conditions can be tough and pressurised, and managers may be surprisingly hard-headed. There are other downsides too, such as lack of job security – what was all the rage last season may be old discarded news only a few months later. Think of the changing fortunes of the anti-fur campaign – one year lauded by the fashionistas, the next year treated with boredom and contempt. Like fashion and food fads, popular causes can come and go like the weather.

WHAT IS A CHARITY?

In order to be classed as a charity, an organisation must meet a number of requirements. These cover a wide range of things, but here are the most important definitions. In order to be classed as a charity, an organisation must do one of the following things:

Relieve poverty, disability and/or distress

Advance education

Advance religion

Do other charitable things that benefit the community

Organisations that do not meet the criteria are more likely to be classed as voluntary bodies: the definition of a voluntary body is that it is non-profitable and uses volunteers for some of its activities. A voluntary body, unlike a charity, can also promote political views, which is why Greenpeace and Amnesty International are classed as voluntary bodies and not charities.

WHAT OPPORTUNITIES ARE THERE?

So what kind of work can you do? There is such a huge range of jobs available in the voluntary sector that it is impossible to summarise. Around 12,000 new charities are added to the Charity Register every year, and around 10,000 are removed. Many projects arise and decline, and positions change as the organisation evolves. However, the voluntary sector is a significant employer within the UK economy, and the scope for employment is immense. According to the organisation Working For A Charity, there are about 141,000 general charities within the UK employing 563,000 paid workers (210,000 of them part-time).

In order to stay afloat, charities and voluntary organisations need to operate as professional, efficient businesses, and as such require a huge range of expertise – with experience in marketing, administration, publicity, research, finance and IT particularly in demand. In addition, employers are looking for people who learn quickly, communicate well, can manage people and work well in a team.

The important thing to bear in mind is that formal experience in the voluntary sector counts less than adaptability and transferable skills. That's not to say finding work in this area is easy – it isn't, and competition can be fierce, particularly in the big national charities. It's just that employers are often more interested in skills that can be adapted to their needs. By their very nature, charities and voluntary bodies have to be very resourceful in order to survive, and this attitude can spill over into their recruitment tactics. Managers in this sector are often very clued up on how to get the best out of people.

If you are really serious about working in charity, it might be a good idea to contact one of the charity organisations first, or read up on the subject.

FUNDRAISING

One of the fastest-growing jobs within the voluntary sector over the last ten years has been in fundraising. Fundraising is paramount to the success of a voluntary organisation because it both raises awareness and drums up that much-needed money. Traditionally, many fundraisers worked for charities purely on a voluntary basis, but the voluntary sector is now awash with people who have previously worked in PR, finance or administration. And with more and more charities feeling the squeeze, fundraising is becoming a popular move for the newly recruited graduate. It is also becoming increasingly professionalised. In these fickle days of celebrity worship, causes have to come with a hefty dollop of glamour in order to attract the necessary attention to fill their coffers. Cue an influx of bright young things.

You only have to think of the huge success behind operations such as Red Nose Day or the rise of celebrity-driven charity events to appreciate the canny thinking behind these schemes. Think of the rise of the dash-for-cash sponsored bike rides through China or Nepal – all in the name of charidee, of course.

SO HOW CAN YOU GET INTO FUNDRAISING?

Fundraisers are drawn from a wide variety of sectors so, whatever your background, you should be able to find a way in – although you may have to volunteer or take training first. Broadly speaking, fundraising is split into four sections: trusts, corporate, major gift and community fundraising, and most large charities will have a fundraiser for each area.

Obviously, you will stand a much better chance of finding work as a fundraiser if you come from a marketing background. You can also take a related degree or training. A few universities offer diplomas and degree programmes in fundraising. Southbank University in London does a post-graduate diploma and an MSc in Charity and Fundraising.

The Institute of Fundraising offers a Certificate in Fundraising Management (check out the website **www.institute-of-fundraising.org.uk** for more details). There is also talk of a setting up an NVQ in Fundraising, so keep your eye open in the charity press such as *Third Sector* (published by the Haymarket Group) and *Professional Fundraising*.

Many of the big charities such as Cancer Research UK take on a number of graduate trainees. Check out their websites for more details.

Then there's the traditional route of volunteering first. Fundraising has a notoriously high turnover: in London the typical fundraiser lasts an average of eighteen months – so opportunities can open up when people move on. Fundraising is increasingly more likely to be outsourced to agencies, so it may be worth contacting them first.

FUNDRAISING AGENCIES

Institute of Fundraising, Tel: 020 7627 3436.

Charities Aid Foundation, Tel: 01732 520 000.

Brakeley Ltd, Tel: 020 7287 3361.

VOLUNTEERS' STORIES

Simon Bowen describes his work as a charity fundraiser for the Tim Lilley Fundraising Consultancy. The work consists of six-week campaigns for charities such as Shelter, Victims of Torture and Amnesty International, cold-calling houses and asking people to donate. He found the agency on the Internet.

'The work started with a briefing in which they explained the company's philosophy and how they operate. If we were interested, we then started in a two-week training group.' Despite having no previous experience or qualifications in fundraising, Simon was then invited to join the group. Since then he has been working around 22 hours a week, working when he wants in the evenings.

'Basically, each fundraiser is given a postcode in London or Brighton and then we hit the road ourselves, knocking on doors and asking people to donate money, or "gift aids". First, we ask people to take a leaflet and we go back later to ask them if they will sign up for a donation.'

Simon says it is not suitable for everyone, a fact that is reflected in the high dropout rate. 'It's not for everyone – it's quite hard in a way; you're knocking on doors, maybe asking eighty people a night, so you have to be quite confident. You rarely get a bad reaction but you do get a lot of refusals. It can be soul destroying so we have regular support group meetings to off-load our frustrations.'

These weekly support groups draw on the agency's distinct philosophy, and consist of communication and relaxation exercises. Simon says, 'The idea is to be more relaxed on the doorstep so you avoid being aggressive. It's about getting into the moment so you are relaxed and friendly, and can also pick up signs about how the people are feeling.'

Simon values the work for its flexibility and says it is ideal for people who want to take time out to travel and start again when they come back. 'Basically I enjoy it and it's good to feel that my job is raising money for a good cause. It also allows me to do a part-time job and earn a living wage without work taking up my life.'

FINDING WORK IN CHARITY

So how can you find work? Volunteering for the charity you would like to work for can be a good way of getting your foot in the door. Not only will it introduce you to its culture, but it can also put you in touch with any vacancies that may arise. Many jobs are only advertised internally, so look out for newsletters, websites and in-house notices. There are also recruitment websites which advertise voluntary sector jobs. Try **www.jobsincharities.co.uk** and **www.jobsunlimited.co.uk**. The local and national press also carries some adverts. Alternatively try the charity recruitment agencies. It might be worth phoning them first to see whether they recruit for your area.

CHARITY RECRUITMENT AGENCIES
Charity Action Recruitment, 207 Waterloo Road, London SE1 8XD, Tel: 020 7928 2843.

CF Appointments, Lloyds Court, 1 Goodman's Yard, London E1 8AT, Tel: 020 7953 1190.

Charity Connections, 15 Theed Street, Waterloo, London SE1 8ST, Tel: 020 7202 9000.

Charity People, 38 Bedford Place, London WC1B 5JH, Tel: 020 7636 3900.

Charity Recruitment, 40 Rosebery Avenue, London EC1R 4RX, Tel: 020 7833 0770.

LOCAL AND NATIONAL PRESS
Guardian (Monday – PR and marketing; Wednesday – public sector and general charity; Saturday – general)

The Times (Thursday – executive & amp; senior management)

Independent (Monday – media; Thursday – general; Sunday – management)

Daily Telegraph (Thursday – general)

The Economist

Evening Standard (Monday – Just the Job supplement; Wednesday – Public & Community) for London based charities

Metro (Wednesday – Public and Community)

CHARITY PRESS
Third Sector (Haymarket Group)

Charity and Voluntary Sector Appointments (DP Media)

ICFM Recruitment Update (DP Media)

Professional Fundraising (Brainstorm Publishing)

TRADE PRESS
PR Week, *Marketing Week* and *Campaign*

TRAINING
Working For A Charity (The Peel Centre, Percy Circus, London WC1X 9EY, Tel: 020 7833 8220, Fax: 020 7833 1820, website: **workwww.wfac.org.uk**) runs training courses for people wishing to work in the voluntary sector. The website has plenty of good advice about finding work.

Directory of Social Change (24 Stephenson Way, London NW1 2DP, Tel: 020 7209 5151) is a publishing and training organisation for the voluntary sector. It also has a library, a bookshop and runs the annual three-day Charityfair event each spring.

Institute of Fundraising (Market Towers, 5th floor, 1 Nine Elms Lane, London SW8 5NQ, Tel: 020 7627 3436) offers training, information and advice to fundraising professionals and those wanting to become fundraisers.

National Council for Voluntary Organisations (NCVO) (Regent's Wharf, 8 All Saints Street, London N1 9RL, Tel: 020 7713 6161) also provides training.

USEFUL ORGANISATIONS

Charities Aid Foundation (CAF) (King's Hill, West Malling, Kent ME19 4TA, Tel: 01732 520 000) provides services to help donors make the most of their giving and charities make the most of their resources in the UK and overseas; it publishes an extensive range of reports and directories on the voluntary sector and runs the annual charities conference each autumn.

Charity Commission (Harmsworth House, 13–15 Bouverie Street, London EC4Y 8DP, Tel: 0870 333 0123) is a central regulatory body for charities in England and Wales.

Northern Ireland Council for Voluntary Action, 61 Duncarin Gardens, Belfast BT15 2GB, Tel: 02890 877 777.

Scottish Council for Voluntary Organisations (SCVO), 18–19 Claremont Crescent, Edinburgh EH7 4QD, Tel: 0131 556 3882.

Wales Council for Voluntary Action, Llys Ifor, Crescent Road, Caerphilly, Mid Glamorgan CF8 1XL, Tel: 01222 869 224.

To find details of charities to apply to, go to **www.charitychoice.co.uk**, a searchable directory of over 8,500 UK charities.

The website **www.charitypeople.co.uk** is a searchable database of paid and unpaid opportunities in the not-for-profit sector. Another useful website is **www.jobsincharities.co.uk** which has a job search area and a volunteer search area.

EMPLOYEE VOLUNTEERING

One of the fastest-growing areas in the voluntary sector is now employee volunteering, where companies arrange for their staff to volunteer in community-based projects, either in their own time or during work hours. Virtually unheard of ten years ago, employee-volunteering schemes are growing increasingly popular: the organisation Time Bank last year reported a massive 30 per cent increase in companies signing up. So what's in it for them? Well, on the one hand, it's all part of the government drive towards Corporate Social Responsibility, a wide-ranging movement that encourages business and the public sector to be more socially aware and accountable. The theory is that supporting community projects can also boost a company's image and help develop brand loyalty, but there is also a deepening awareness of the benefits volunteering can bring. Enlightened employers are increasingly recognising that through encouraging staff to volunteer they can build their skills base, and give workers the opportunity to develop skills such as team building, negotiating, problem solving, communication and coaching. And time off from the daily routine makes for a happier and more productive workforce – or so the theory goes.

WHAT DO EMPLOYEE-VOLUNTEERING SCHEMES INVOLVE?
Employee-volunteering schemes cover a huge range of projects from designing websites for voluntary organisations to painting youth clubs to working on out-reach programmes for homeless people. Many schemes encourage staff to use their professional skills, such as accounting, business planning, legal advice or IT. Others focus on interpersonal skills including mentoring or giving talks at schools or hospitals. There are also projects that draw on skills that may not be part of the volunteer's paid job, such as organising a special one-day event to raise money for an elderly people's home or renovating a community centre. Then there are the projects that venture out into the underworld of the poor and dispossessed. It may sound far-fetched, but the most forward-thinking companies think nothing of allowing staff to take time out from the office to help on drugs rehabilitation programmes or set up awareness campaigns with the police.

WHAT COMPANIES RUN THEM?
Employee volunteering is so popular now that, if you think of a big-name corporation, the chances are they will take part in some kind of voluntary scheme. Marks and Spencer, Boots, Barclays, Nokia, Waitrose, Unilever and Capital One all have employee-volunteering schemes, to name but a few. Many companies see these schemes as an important part of working life, where staff can broaden their skills base and actually be promoted on the strength of it. Some companies have introduced accreditation schemes where employees can chalk up points based on their voluntary experience. One such company is Boots the Chemist, which has introduced a Certificate of Recognition as a Community Associate, a formal accreditation acknowledging employee-volunteering activities during company time. So the benefits of employee volunteering are clear – not only will it introduce you to new challenges and new skills, but it could also move you forwards in the workplace.

VOLUNTEERS' STORIES

Ryan McBirney is one employee who took part in a volunteer scheme through work, and was promoted on the strength of it. Working one day a week for three months, Ryan's role was to provide figures for a campaign by Action Cancer, Northern Ireland's largest cancer-prevention charity, to raise awareness of the risks of testicular or prostate cancer among men. With 200 young men dying every year in Northern Ireland as a result of undetected testicular or prostate cancer, the aim was to find out the levels of awareness among young males of how to do a self-examination.

Ryan, 24, a planning technician in Belfast, knew that a high-impact direct approach would be needed and developed the 'Know your Bits' survey. Using an email-based questionnaire, Ryan found that 60 per cent of men pee in the shower and 70 per cent have peed without using their hands.

While the survey produced some amusing 'waterworks' trivia, it also revealed that one-third of NI men don't know where their prostate is; almost 50 per cent don't know how to do a testicular self-examination, and 75 per cent of 18- to 24-year-olds – and 50 per cent of NI men overall – don't know the symptoms of prostate and testicular cancer. The results were used to create a mini-movie, *Talking Balls*, a straight-talking video to tell young men exactly how it is.

Ryan himself says he gained valuable experience, in networking, report writing and communication. Perhaps the most challenging aspect, he says, was in mastering his time management. 'Time was a major factor and I had to learn to effectively timetable myself, so I could get everything done. I had one day less a week for my normal job, and only twelve days to work on this project, so it was a very hectic period. There were other challenges too – you don't realise how much you get into a comfort zone in your normal job so it was quite strange to go into a new place and start on your feet running straight away.'

Ryan succeeded, however, and a month later was promoted, a triumph he attributes partly to his volunteering experience. 'As part of my application I had to attend a criteria-based interview which had sections on resource management, time management, communication and interpersonal skills. Thanks to my time with Action Cancer, I could give good examples for each area; it certainly gave me the edge.'

PERSUADING YOUR COMPANY TO RUN AN EMPLOYEE-VOLUNTEER SCHEME

If your workplace doesn't run a volunteer scheme, it may be in your interest to persuade them to get involved. Arrange to see your community affairs manager, if you have one, or speak to the marketing people. They should be able to appreciate what clout a few community-spirited articles in the press can bring. Point out the benefits, such as:

- **Improved morale and motivation in the workplace**
- **Allowing staff to develop a wider skills base**
- **Improving the company's image**
- **Earning brownie points for helping out in the community**

You can even highlight financial considerations – in these times of economic uncertainty, many companies are keen to offer volunteers instead of signing large charity donation cheques.

If you can, cite examples of successful projects organised by other companies. Arm yourself with plenty of ideas for useful resources and contacts. Many volunteer schemes are set up through 'brokers', i.e. agencies and consultants who specialise in matching community projects to companies. These can be particularly useful if your employers are stretched for time and lack the resources and knowledge to set up a project themselves. Taking a few names and addresses can mean the difference between your idea being ignored or looked into.

Brokers include volunteer bureaux, Community Service Volunteers, Business Community Connections and Education Business Link Consortia.

Other useful organisations are:

Good Business: **www.goodbusiness.co.uk**, Tel: 020 7494 0565.

Business in the Community: **www.bitc.org.uk**, Tel: 020 7566 8697.

Common Purpose: **www.commonpurpose.org.uk**, Tel: 020 7608 8100.

Time Bank: **www.timebank.org.uk**, Tel: 0207 401 5438.

The website **www.employeevolunteering.org.uk** has plenty of useful advice on setting up your own employee-volunteering scheme.

USEFUL PUBLICATIONS
Employee Volunteering: The Guide by Liza Ramrayka, published by National Centre for Volunteering.

Employees in the Community: a global force for good published by The Center for the Study of Philanthropy in New York. The publication costs €23.00 and can be ordered from the Corporate Citizenship Company. For more details Tel: 020 7945 6130 or email mail@corporate-citizenship.co.uk.

Good Practice Guide published by National Centre for Volunteering, for new and experienced volunteer managers, 2002, £12.50. It covers the basics of setting up volunteer projects such as the latest information on criminal records screening and changes to the benefit rules, and can be used as a training tool kit for those training volunteers.

VOLUNTEERS' STORIES

Charlotte Goddard volunteered on a nine-month youth mentoring programme for the US organisation Youth At Risk. She signed up for the work through her company Haymarket Publishers, when the company approached them looking for volunteers. Charlotte says, 'I had been thinking of doing voluntary work for a while so, as soon as this came up, I went for it. After an evening's introductory session, we had a training weekend which was pretty tough and weeded a lot of people out. Then we started on the mentoring programme.'

The programme was aimed at young people 'at risk', which included young offenders and problem children. Many of the students had troubled family histories with parents who were either absent, in jail or alcoholics or drug addicts. Most were either expelled or in a pupil referral unit, and had been recommended to attend by the police. Others had sent themselves. The kids were sent on a five-day residential course that included assault courses and physical challenges, as well as courses designed to lead them into exploring their behaviour, looking at their future plans and family history.

Charlotte worked as an education mentor, which involved running drop-in sessions one evening a week, with access to computers and revision groups. Students could practice reading or writing, do homework or receive help in writing CVs and interview practice. Charlotte says, 'The work could be very stressful and there were some hairy moments. I didn't have any discipline problems but other volunteers did if they were trying to get them to give up drugs, for example.'

The general experience was rewarding, however. Charlotte says, 'One week we looked at role models, discussing who their role model was and why. The only problem was that most of them didn't have anyone they looked up to. Many of the parents were on drugs or in jail, or the students had a negative perception of their teachers. That's half the reason the programme was set up. Some of the students might not even know anyone in their normal lives who had a job – this way, they could meet people in their community who actually worked for a living.'

Through the course of the programme the students had to pick three goals to work on through the nine-month period. These could range from 'getting back into school' to 'coming off drugs' or 'staying out of prison', and the volunteers were there to help them achieve these goals.

Charlotte says the programme was a fascinating experience. 'I learned loads. First I learned practical skills such as coaching, but there were other benefits too. I felt more connected to kids I normally wouldn't know anything about – before I might have seen them on the bus and presumed they were just layabouts. Now I feel they're part of my community. I also learned a lot about relating and management skills because I had managed the education session. I did a lot of public speaking too.'

SETTING UP YOUR OWN PROJECT

Of course, if you can't get the backing of your employees, you could always start one up yourself. Maybe you've got time on your hands and long to do something 'useful'. Maybe you live in an area where you feel the council is falling short of its duties to provide civic help and protection. Some very successful volunteer projects have started this way where local people have grown sick of waiting for other people to take action and have organised something themselves. This can include starting an amateur football club or organising sponsored walks to raise money for a much-needed community centre. 'Speedy' Angela Gonzales was a nurse in a local hospital when she heard that the hospital authorities were trying to cull the legions of wild cats that were loose in the grounds. Already a firm cat lover, Speedy was shocked at the decision and took it upon herself to rescue the animals and give them a home. After several meetings with the authorities, she persuaded them to give her six months to clear the cats herself. Alone with only a large net, she then prowled the grounds. Using her own money, she built a shed in the grounds costing over £1,000, where she put the cats once they had been caught. Six months later, every one of them had been caught and were safely housed in the shed. Another six months later and they had all been found homes.

Setting up your own project can be easy if you have the determination and motivation. But the one thing it requires is an unwavering belief. Speedy never faltered from her mission to save each single cat from being killed. Maybe there's something on your doorstep that similarly demands your attention: a disused church or building that has so much more potential, elderly neighbours who feel cut off and alone, or a piece of common ground which could be cleared and renovated into a community green zone.

The first port of call if you want to find out more is the excellent website **www.justdosomething.net**. Aimed at people who want to make a difference to other people's lives, this website contains plenty of good advice and inspiring case studies to give you the know how to go and do it, as well as information on gaining funding and organising your own projects and campaigns.

ATTRACTING OTHER VOLUNTEERS

Of course, all the best ideals in the world are no good if you don't have the support of other people. Any project, no matter how big or small it is, requires that a certain amount of people get involved, and the more people you can bring on board the more ambitious you can afford to be.

The first thing to say in drumming up support and attracting other volunteers is the importance of engaging their interest and imagination. That may sound like an obvious point, but it's amazing how people still insist on fighting campaigns based on dry political points highlighting 'us' and 'them' situations which only leave people feeling disempowered and drained. So the first rule is to exude positive can-do vibes and enthusiasm. Make sure you relate your goals to their own experiences and interests. You may be in it for the good of your health, but most people don't have the time to get involved with projects that don't directly benefit them, so point out what *they* stand to gain. This might include making the streets safer for their children, reducing crime, increasing property prices or giving them a local haven of support and relaxation.

At the start of your project, you will need to organise some kind of meeting, event or social gathering where you can draw together people to discuss your aims. This can be done through delivering leaflets, putting up notices or advertising in the local paper. You could also try to contact the local paper or radio station and drum up some media attention. Make sure all your literature is clear and easy to read, and avoid using jargon or overcomplicated sentence structures.

Try to bring together a diverse representation of your local community. Residents, parents and local businesses can all have different takes on the same situation and, as such, offer different skills and solutions. Make sure the venue is accessible and the meeting is held at a time when most people can attend, such as in the evening or weekend. Get their attention by personalising the cause and relating it to their own experience. Highlight how they will benefit from it.

Once you have brought people together, try to encourage debate and make sure everyone has their say. Nothing is more off-putting than meetings where the same two people continually hold the floor. Once you have gained the support from people, be flexible about the different ways in which people get involved in terms of skills, time, commitment, etc. Think about what they will get out of it, and their needs as well as yours. Decide who is going to make the decisions, and what each person's role will involve. Together, you can then work out a strategy about the next steps you will take in gaining funding and publicity etc.

FUNDING YOUR OWN PROJECT

The first thing you have to do if you want to set up a project is get some funding. This can come through a variety of ways. These typically involve:

Organising your own fundraising events

Gaining sponsorship from local companies

Applying for National Lottery funding

Securing funding from a local trust or council

Bear in mind that, in order to be legally allowed to go out on the streets and collect money, first you must apply for a licence from the local authority. Before applying for one, make sure you know what their criteria for eligibility are. Some local authorities only give licences to registered charities, for example. It's also a good thing to apply well in advance of the date you intend to start collecting as there can often be long waiting lists.

There are many local trusts or benevolent funds that may donate money to the right cause. The Directory of Social Change publishes a variety of directories of grant-making trusts. For more information visit its website: **www.dsc.org.uk**, or call 020 7391 4800. Alternatively, visit its London office, which has a bookshop and library, at Directory of Social Change, 24 Stephenson Way, London NW1 2DP. There is also a Liverpool office: Directory of Social Change, Federation House, Hope Street, Liverpool L1 9BW, Tel: 0151 708 0117.

Your local council may also be able to help. Although they are unlikely to provide funding themselves, they should have details of other funding opportunities. Many local councils have regeneration departments which encourage smaller grass-roots groups in community-minded projects. Your local volunteer bureaux can also be a good first port-of-call.

The government Voluntary and Community Sector Grants website, **www.volcomgrants.gov.uk**, provides information on the grants available from four Government Departments – Home Office, Department for Education and Skills, Department for Transport, Local Government and the Regions, and the Department of Health. It also includes a Grant Finder and Eligibility Checker. At the time of writing this website is only in its pilot stage, so if there are any problems go to the Home Office website: **www.homeoffice.gov.uk** and look under the Active Community section.

Other useful contacts are Basac and the Community Development Foundation.

Changemakers is an organisation that develops young person-led projects, while Young Advocates help initiate action among young people.

In rural areas, you can try the Countryside Agency. Write to The Countryside Agency, John Dower House, Crescent Place, Cheltenham, Glos GL50 3RA, Tel: 01242 521381, Fax: 01242 584270, Email: info@countryside.gov.uk, or at their London office: Dacre House, 19 Dacre Street, London SW1H 0DH, Tel: 020 7340 2900, Fax: 020 7340 2911, website: **www.countryside.gov.uk**.

The regeneration unit of The Civic Trust provides support and training to small grass-roots organisations. Contact: The Civic Trust, 17 Carlton House Terrace, London SW1Y 5AW, Tel: 020 7930 0914, Fax: 020 7321 0180; Northern Office: The View, Gostins Building, 32–36 Hanover Street, Liverpool L1 4LN, Tel: 0151 709 1969, Fax: 0151 709 2022, website: **www.civictrust.org.uk**.

THE NATIONWIDE FOUNDATION
The Nationwide Foundation makes charitable grants to UK-based organisations whose aim is to improve the quality of life and the range of opportunities for those in need, tackle social exclusion and achieve real and sustainable benefit to communities. It also has a long list of the type of projects that it will *not* support, so check out the website first to make sure your project is appropriate. Once you have established whether your project fits the guidelines, telephone 01793 655113 (Monday to Thursday between 9.30am and 1pm).

NATIONAL LOTTERY FUNDING
The Community Fund distributes Lottery money to charities and voluntary groups to help those in greatest need. Applying for lottery money can be a complicated procedure and there have been some complaints that the system is geared more towards large professional organisations than small grass-roots movements. That's because there is a strong emphasis on prospective projects having committees and funding structures in place, etc. Therefore the first thing is to get organised.

The website **www.community-fund.org.uk** has all the information you need to know about applying for funding and the different types of projects and grants it awards. You can download all of its leaflets and publications, including the 'Guidance for Eligibility' leaflet, which is essential reading for anyone intending to apply for funding. It also carries details of the 50,000 projects it has funded.

Gaining funding is a complicated affair and a lottery in itself. Deciding who is eligible is down to Charity Law, and tends to be a painstaking procedure. However, meeting the following criteria may mean you are eligible.

If your project or organisation:

- **Has constitutional documents or a set of rules that sets out your organisation's aims and ways of working**

- **Is set up for charitable, benevolent or philanthropic purposes**

- **Has a committee with at least three members**

- **Has its own bank or building society account which needs at least two signatures on each cheque or withdrawal**

- **Can give the Community Fund a copy of its most recent approved accounts, signed and dated by the Chair, Secretary or Treasurer, and where appropriate by an auditor or independent examiner**

- **If you are a new organisation, can give an estimate of income and spending plans instead**

There are several different types of grant programmes to suit different organisations and projects. These include grants for large projects (for groups whose total project costs more than £60,000 or more than £30,000 if it involves property); grants for medium-sized projects (for groups whose total project (not just in one year) costs less than £60,000, or the total cost of any building construction or refurbishment work is less than £30,000 excluding VAT); research grants programme (for voluntary organisations working in partnership with research institutions in the areas of social and medical research); The Awards for All Programme gives small grants to small groups. There are also grants available for UK organisations that want to set up projects abroad.

THE AWARDS FOR ALL PROGRAMME

If you are thinking of setting up a small locally based project, the Awards for All Programme is by far the most relevant. This is a lottery grants scheme aimed at local communities which awards grants of between £500 and £5,000 to projects that enable people to take part in art, sport, heritage and community activities, as well as projects that promote education, the environment and health in the local community. The application is designed to be short and simple and applicants should hear within three months whether their application has been successful. To enquire about applying for funding, call 0845 791 9191 or contact the appropriate office.

Corporate Office and UK Office: St Vincent House, 16 Suffolk Street, London SW1Y 4NL, Tel: 020 7747 5300, Minicom: 020 7747 5347, Fax: 020 7747 5214, Email: enquiries@community-fund.org.uk.

Wales Office, 2nd Floor, Ladywell House, Newtown, Powys SY16 1JB, Tel: 01686 611700, Minicom: 01686 610205, Fax: 01686 621534, Email: enquiries.wales@community-fund.org.uk.

Scotland Office, Highlander House, 58 Waterloo Street, Glasgow G2 7BD, Tel: 0870 240 2391, Minicom: 0141 223 8628, Fax: 0141 233 8620, Email: enquiries.scotland@community-fund.org.uk.

Office for Northern Ireland, 2nd Floor, Hildon House, 30–34 Hill Street, Belfast BT1 2LB, Tel: 028 9055 1455, Minicom: 028 9055 1431, Fax: 028 9055 1444, Email: enquiries.ni@community-fund.org.uk.

GAINING SUPPORT FROM BUSINESS

Corporate Social Responsibility is a huge driving force at the moment and most companies are well aware of the benefits a little positive PR and community involvement can bring. It's no surprise then that local and national businesses can provide a useful source of funding and support to projects. Bear in mind that a company doesn't only have to donate money, there are also other means of pledging support – such as offering staff expertise, assistance in fundraising appeals, grants, advertising or sponsorship. Some may even be interested in becoming partners in the project. They may not be in it for purely altruistic reasons, but there other reasons why they may be interested in getting involved, such as good PR, being linked to your name and being associated with good community-minded work.

Before approaching companies, work out who your project would appeal to and why. Maybe you are working in a common area or have a shared goal. Think of local contacts and company links that might have a particularly strong reason to fund your organisation or project, rather than sending out mass mailing lists to hundreds of companies. Be ready with a list of reasons why you think your target company should get involved and what they will get out of it. This also includes recognition from you. If they do decide to help you, what will you offer in return? Will you carry the company logo on your letterhead, for example? Will you mention their name in all your appeals? Be clear about exactly what you want (funding, expertise, sponsorship or venue, for example) and what you can offer in return.

Once you have a clear idea about your expectations, contact the company in writing first. Try to find the person who deals with community projects but, if you can't find an exact name, address the letter to a relevant person, making sure the name and title is spelled correctly. Having someone's name is much more likely to prove successful than sending out a general, impersonal letter addressed to 'Dear Sir or Madam'. The letter should include:

Details of your project

Why it will help them

What you want from them

What you can offer the company in return

OBTAINING SPONSORSHIP

Another way of gaining business support is organising sponsorship. Again be clear about what you are looking for from a sponsor and what kind of sponsor you want to be associated with. Then think again about what you can offer in return. What kind of perks could you offer a potential sponsor? This could include:

Naming your project or event after the sponsor

Space and/or airtime for your sponsor to promote its company

Free advertising in your brochure or pamphlet

Carrying its logo on your letterheads and/or literature

Good publicity and verbal acknowledgement when you are promoting your project/campaign

Make sure you can deliver whatever you promise – businesses will want to make sure that the sponsorship deal will bring solid rewards. Try to include a package of options so you can negotiate with your potential sponsor which deal most meets your and their needs. It may be that, in order to be recognised, you will have to turn your scheme into a fully fledged professional operation.

Kathy Miller decided to gain charity status for her fundraising work for a boys' home in South India in order to approach businesses for support. The decision has meant a lot of extra work. Kathy says, 'In order for The Neem Tree Trust to be registered as a charity, I have to prove to the Charity Commission in England and Wales that it is a bona fide charitable organisation. This involves setting up a trust, executing a Trust Deed and getting four trustees to make sure that the trust is being run properly. It has involved a lot of paperwork, but I am really excited because having a registered number will let people know that we are a proper charity and all the money is going to the boys' home. That way we can contact businesses and operate more extensively.'

SHOW US THE MONEY

The next thing to discuss is the money. Pricing your sponsorship deal can be a minefield so, if you know someone who has previous sponsorship experience, talk to them first. According to the website Just Do Something, one of the golden rules is that you are not looking for shortfall funding. So, if you have raised £8,000 towards a total cost of £10,000, then your sponsorship opportunity should not automatically be costed at £2,000. The pricing will also be affected by the particular package of benefits you are offering. Other factors include what kind of people you will be reaching through the sponsorship and how their profile fits the goals of your potential sponsors, as well as how much media coverage it will generate and your track record of sponsorship.

Steps to obtaining sponsorship

- **Think carefully about your project – what is its purpose? How much money does it need? What will a company gain from offering sponsorship? What can you realistically offer in return?**

- **Research and target companies that have a common link with the cause you are supporting/campaigning for. What companies most match the profile of the people your campaign will be reaching? Are there any companies you already have a relationship with who may be interested in getting involved? In looking for new potential sponsors, which businesses are expanding or making big profits? Which companies have a negative public image and are in need of an image makeover?**

- **Once you have drawn up a list of suitable companies to target, approach them by letter first. Address the letter to a named person. Find out before by phone who is in charge of sponsorship deals. This may be the head of marketing or corporate events or even the chief executive. Send them out together, not one at a time, otherwise you could be waiting a long time for your project to get off the ground.**

- **The proposal should say who you are and what your organisation does, and include details of the project for which you would like support, a list of the benefits you are prepared to offer and the price including VAT. Make sure the proposal is clear and concise, typewritten and doesn't exceed more than two A4 pages. Be professional and businesslike – remember you are not asking for a donation but aiming to strike a deal which will benefit both parties.**

- **Follow up the letter with a phone call about a week later. If they are interested, they may want you to send further information or arrange a meeting. If they say no, or ask you to call again later, make sure you are polite and respond gracefully. They may not be willing to get involved now, but who knows what the future might bring.**

- **If your proposal is successful, don't rely on a verbal agreement or handshake. Draw up a signed agreement with the company covering what the business will and won't receive, the amount of the sponsorship and details on how and when the payment will be made.**

- **For more information on obtaining sponsorship, go to www.justdosomething.net. The website for Time Bank also has some good advice about starting up your own project.**

VOLUNTEERS' STORIES

Ruth Asher is one example of someone who has turned volunteering into a way of life. Since beginning her voluntary vocation with gap years abroad, she got involved with Student Volunteering at Durham University. After doing a range of things, including helping the elderly and conservation work, she decided to set up a scheme herself. The first thing she did was apply for funding from Future Capital, an organisation that provides grants for people who have taken part in the European Voluntary Service to set up community projects. With the £3,000 she received, Ruth set up Kids Create, providing local children with creative workshops. She says, 'I decided to set up Kids Create because I feel that creativity is pushed too much to the sidelines in education today. Basically it consists of children's workshops for eight- to eleven-year-olds in Durham, run by a team of nine student volunteers. Our first project was photography; we gave each child a disposable camera and told them to take pictures around Durham. We then had a discussion about them, blew each one up to poster size, and had them on display in shop windows around the city centre. The children wrote poems to go with their photographs.'

Since then there have been a variety of projects, ranging from the big (a fashion show where children modelled clothes they had designed and made themselves) to smaller classes in pottery, drama, song writing and crafts. The group also bought a video camera with funding from Future Capital, so the children could try their hand at animation and make short films, which they entered into a local television festival.

Ruth is now on the board of directors of Student Volunteering England, and this year was a finalist for the Whitbread Young Achiever Award. Now she has left university, Ruth has no intention of stopping volunteering. 'Kids Create is still running even though I have left, and my aim is to introduce the concept to other groups across the UK.'

4. VOLUNTEERING FOR THE OVER-FIFTIES

We live, as we all know, in an ageing population. At the same time we are living longer, healthier lives. According to a report from the United Nations, there were 600 million older people at the start of this century, treble the number recorded fifty years ago. And, by the middle of this century, this number is set to treble again. You wouldn't know it, of course, by looking at the newspapers. Health scares aside, the cult of youth is hammered home to us every day. Of course, many more traditional societies than ours have found ways of honouring their elders and respecting their wisdom. But, here in the West, with our obsession with surface beauty we tend to overlook the contribution our elders can and do make. The result is a massive squandering of skills and a recent study showed that 76 per cent of over-fifties think that 'society undervalues their skills and experience'.

It doesn't have to be like this, of course. People now retire earlier, live longer and are more fit and active than their predecessors were. So no surprise that many are not ready to spend their days parked in front of Richard and Judy, sucking on tinned soup and worrying about their bowel movements. The over-fifties is a crucial demographic in terms of consumer power and it is also a key time of life when many people experience a kind of second youth. Whether it's through travelling or taking up new artistic hobbies, the retirement age is often seen as a new beginning, a time when people can review their lives and do what they always wanted to do but somehow never found the time. So whether your children have flown the nest, or you are leaving work after forty years of hard labour, the Third Age can be a time of huge readjustment. Volunteering can be the perfect antidote to the stresses and boredoms it can bring.

RETIREMENT

Of course, one of the most dramatic changes people over fifty have is reaching retirement. You may have spent a lifetime building up skills that, once you retire, can be left untouched, leaving a vague sense of stagnation. All this isn't to say that most retirees clear out the peace plant from the office desk, accept their gold engraved clock with pride and shuffle back home to a twilight zone life of munching McVities and watching Carol Vorderman. I know plenty of retired people – my parents included – and know for a fact that many of them lead more active and fulfilling lives than many of the rest of us. Many go travelling; some move abroad; others look after grandchildren or elderly neighbours. And others volunteer. And why not? Volunteering can promise many things, including stimulation, a sense of achievement, the opportunity to meet new people and network, the chance to put the skills you have accrued over a lifetime to good use and the chance to update existing skills or even learn new ones. It can also bring a social life, a renewed sense of purpose and the chance to get involved. In return, retired people can offer maturity, skills, availability, flexibility, loyalty and commitment, something that many organisations are increasingly recognising.

WHY VOLUNTEER?

So, what's in it for you? Retiring from work can be a bewildering time. After years of full-time work, even the more independent of souls can find the space and free time a disorientating experience. For those who find the transition harder to make, volunteering can be the perfect way to fill the void. Not only can it fill your time, get you out of the house and introduce you to new people, but it can also grant a welcome sense of satisfaction that you are still learning new skills and putting old ones gained from years of experience to good use. Many voluntary organisations target the over-fifties because they say it is crucial to get volunteers on board pre-retirement so that, by the time they leave work, volunteering is already firmly part of their consciousness. If you're over fifty and approaching the shock and transition of retirement, volunteering a few hours a week can be a seen as an investment. However difficult the retirement transition may be, you will at least have some familiar routine to give you purpose and continuity.

SO WHAT CAN YOU DO?

In recent years there has been a renewed interest in recruiting the over-fifties for voluntary work and there are literally thousands of charities who are waiting to hear from you. Never underestimate what you have to offer – you have spent a lifetime building up your skills, and now have the expertise and maturity to offer a wide range of people. Of course, unknown to the rest of us, many older people are already involved in community volunteering, and often in ways that go unrecorded and unnoticed. According to Time Bank, 45 per cent of people aged 65–74 and 35 per cent of those over 75 give time regularly across a whole spectrum of activities, including shopping for housebound neighbours, collecting for their favourite charity, setting up stalls at jumble sales, baking for local events, mentoring friends and families, and so on.

There are, however, other more stretching opportunities. If you have a profession or a trade, it may be a good idea to target the organisation representing your line of work to see if they have any schemes in place for retirees or know of any opportunities. Another good way of finding work is to contact the agency Reach, which specialises in matching retired professionals and executives (see useful contacts section). Even if you have no trade as such, you still have much to offer in the way of time and lifetime experience. Yes, some charities do have age limits, but many are increasingly recognising the contribution that retired people can bring. So cast your net wide and think about what you have to offer.

One obvious line of work is to help out with the charities geared at helping the elderly such as Help the Aged and Age Concern. This is so popular, some sources tell me, that some volunteers are older than the people they are actually aiming to help. While it's true that the age charities can be particularly clued-up to the qualities a retiree can bring, there are also plenty of other rewarding ways to offer help. You could mentor a mother, for example, or be an adopted grandparent to a family in need. If you are net-savvy but have problems with mobility, you could register as a virtual volunteer. If you have plenty of time on your hands, boundless energy and the will to enthuse other people and get them motivated to achieve goals, you could start up your own project.

ORGANISING YOUR TIME

The first thing you will have to consider before committing to voluntary work is how much time you can give. Many retired people lead active, demanding lives, often looking after grandchildren, travelling or enjoying a life of rich and varied interests. Don't bite off more than you can chew. If you're newly retired and are worried how you may adjust to the change, the temptation may be to commit to a gruelling schedule that is not far off the hours you worked before. It's best to take it slowly and not overreach yourself. You may be surprised at how busy you are during the day, even after you have given up full- or part-time work. Besides, once you have adjusted to your new daily routine, you can always agree to give more time.

UPPER AGE LIMITS

If you are contacting organisations and charities directly, the first thing you will have to check is whether they have an upper age limit. Although this practice appears to be declining, there is still evidence that a significant minority of volunteer-involving organisations operate an upper-age-limit policy. The primary reason for this, they say, is difficulty in obtaining insurance, particularly in relation to driving, as some insurance companies perceive older people as a high-risk group (despite the fact that, statistically, younger people are more likely to have car accidents). There is also concern that, after a certain age, older volunteers may not be physically strong enough to carry out their tasks.

HEALTH AND SAFETY ISSUES

Retired people now are fitter, more active and better educated than ever before. But, no matter how healthy you are, it is unlikely you have the same boundless energy as when you were young. Therefore, it is wise to think carefully about what particular strains volunteering may bring. All of this isn't to put you off, but there are still precautions you can take to avoid suffering from unnecessary strain. For example, some types of volunteering may involve carrying heavy objects or hard physical work, such as in conservation. Others may require lifting or supporting people, as in social and healthcare (working in hospices, etc.). Before you pledge your support, make sure you know exactly what the work will involve and think carefully about whether you have the strength to carry out the tasks. Also find out whether you have a certain degree of flexibility to work at your own pace, or to take time out to look after sick grandchildren or when they are off school. Some organisations have emergency volunteer teams who can step in at the last moment. Asking beforehand if the organisation has support like this in place could save unnecessary pressure and anxiety. Another good rule is to check you are covered by an insurance cover for driving and public liability claims.

To sum up, make sure:

- **You are covered by an insurance policy for driving and public liability claims**

- **You know exactly what type of tasks the work will involve and know that physically you are up to them**

- **The organisation has precautions set in place concerning physical activities such as lifting clients, when transporting sick people from hospice to home, for example**

- **You have the flexibility to determine your own working pace**

- **The organisation has an emergency volunteer team in place if you have to take time off during schools hours (if you are looking after grandchildren, for example)**

FINDING WORK

To find work, go through the usual sources of enquiry. Contact the usual volunteer brokerages and organisations, such as Time Bank, the Volunteer Bureaux, and read the *Guardian* Wednesday section.

There are also agencies that specifically cater for older volunteers. The **Experience Corps** is an independent, non-profit-making company, funded by the Home Office, set up to encourage all people aged fifty and over to offer their skills and experience to benefit others in their local communities. Its database has over 75,000 opportunities listed as well as features about people who have volunteered. Anyone interested in becoming a member of The Experience Corps can ring the information line on 0800 10 60 80 or go to **www.experiencecorps.co.uk**.

REACH, 89 Albert Embankment, London SE1 7TP, Tel: 020 7582 6543, Fax: 020 7582 2423, Email: info@reach-online.org.uk, website: **www.volwork.org.uk**, specialises in matching retired professionals and executives. Its database has around 3,000 interesting and often unexpected opportunities, and finds the right people for nationwide bodies including the National Trust, British Red Cross and Relate. Its website lists specific vacancies for volunteers, from book-keeping to archivist and marketing. The average age of volunteers is 57 and there is no age limit.

RSVP (Retired and Senior Volunteer Programme), c/o CSV, 237 Pentonville Road, London N1 9NJ (Tel: 020 7278 6601), organises projects including working in healthcare, on environmental projects or with people who have disabilities, knitting clothes for premature babies on maternity wards or assisting in primary schools. This can range from listening to children read to working in the school library one afternoon a week. RSVP volunteers also work with community partners such as doctors, teachers, social care workers and local authorities officers. Also look out for the Senior Volunteer Action Week, now called Get Active Week, held every year, usually in June.

Women's Royal Voluntary Service is one of the UK's largest voluntary services dedicated to tackling social isolation or deprivation. Tasks cover a wide range of skills, including retail, driving, customer service, communication, caring for older people, working with children, in a hospital environment, catering, event organising, fundraising and IT. The organisation also needs people to support teams in training, finance, health and safety, and volunteer recruitment. To find out more about vacancies near you, telephone 0845 601 4670, or write to WRVS Head Office, Milton Hill House, Milton Hill, Steventon, Abingdon, Oxfordshire OX13 6AD.

OVERSEAS OPPORTUNITIES

With all that time on their hands, many retired people now head for foreign shores in a bid for the adventure they feel they missed during years of nine-to-five drudgery. So it's no surprise that volunteering overseas is an increasingly popular option. No longer the province of gap-year students, more and more over-fifties are loading up their backpacks and venturing off to get down and dirty with voluntary programmes in developing countries around the world.

If volunteering overseas interests you, one of the first places to try is **Voluntary Service Overseas (VSO)**. In recent years, VSO has changed its focus from looking for pre- and post-university graduates to work on year-long placements to recruiting people who have taken early retirement and have professional qualifications and a wealth of experience (such as teachers, accountants and doctors). In terms of health and safety issues, VSO says that, as long as certain health standards are met beforehand, there is no difference in approach to the younger age groups. There is an upper age limit of 67 for applying (the application process takes between three and nine months). Placements last for a minimum of two years.

RSVP is a member of the **European Network of Older Volunteers (ENOV)**, a strong network with links to NGOs, governments and organisations involved with older volunteering throughout Western and Eastern Europe. Although it is not a brokerage as such, it does have links with RSVP programmes in America and Europe. Go to the website: **www.csv-rsvp.org.uk/enov.html** for more information.

The US, traditionally a pioneer in community volunteering, is particularly clued up to the qualities offered by the over-fifties and has a huge network of organisations and brokerages representing older volunteers. The website for The Centre for Communication and Consumer Services has many links and contact details, and if you are American is well worth a visit. Go to **www.aoa.gov/NAIC/Notes/volunteeradults.html**.

VOLUNTEERS' STORIES

Kathy Miller was 51 when she decided to work in a boys' home in South India, through the organisation Teaching and Projects Abroad. Driven by nothing more than a fleeting sense of dissatisfaction, she packed in her work teaching IT at a local college, left her teenage children and husband at home and set off to India. The experience proved to be life changing. Three months later she returned to the UK to carry on fundraising for the boys' home. Four years on, she is now applying to register her fundraising work as a charity, The Neem Tree Trust.

Kathy says, 'Sometimes you do something and have no idea what repercussions it may have. I arrived in India not knowing what to expect. It was the first time I had travelled alone or travelled in a developing country – before this I had never been out of Europe or America.'

Kathy knew only that the boys were disabled and most had polio. 'I didn't look after them as such, but I did projects with them. In the evenings, I taught them English songs, and played games, and they were always very keen to speak English. In India they are very strict on studies as they realise that by passing exams they are likely to get out of the poverty trap – so I provided a little light relief. It could be a humbling experience to see them all – they were always smiling, joking and laughing.'

When Kathy came home she was eager to continue helping and started organising ways to raise funds for the home. Instead of returning to teaching, she devoted more time to her fundraising. This mainly involved organising a '100 Club Lottery' every year, where 60 per cent of the funds go to the boys' home. This generates around £2,000–3,000 annually – a huge amount of money in India – and is supplemented by a Christmas raffle at her house, as well as selling cushion covers and drawstring bags made by the boys. The money is used to provide tools, such as sewing machines or carpentry equipment, which the boys can use to support themselves when they leave the home.

Kathy says the experience has broadened both her and her family's horizons. 'India has tremendous pulling power; it is changing dramatically at the moment but there are still villages in rural India where people are leading very simple lives. The last time I went I took my teenage daughter and it had a wonderful effect on her. My children see me in a different light now, and it has made them realise how comfortable we are and how much we take our privileged lives for granted.'

If you are interested in finding out more about The Neem Tree Trust, contact Kathy Miller on 01225 865 789.

5. VOLUNTARY WORK OPPORTUNITIES

CARING

Volunteering in the caring sectors covers a huge array of jobs and organisations. Some of these include:

Nursing and medical staff
Working with the elderly
Working with disabled people
Volunteering at hospitals or hospices
Befriending and mentoring
Counselling
Working with offenders, victims or people with drug/alcohol problems

Obviously the type of qualifications you need depend on the work you want to do. All nursing posts, for example, require nursing qualifications, while teachers and medical staff supporting the disabled will be expected to be professionals. However, there are a great many opportunities for people with no relevant experience or qualifications. Many organisations will provide training themselves (such as counselling on telephone help-lines or working with drugs offenders). The most important thing you can offer is an understanding of the issues surrounding the people you are working with and a cheerful and friendly attitude.

Typical kinds of work can include:

Visiting offenders in prison

Organising day trips for elderly people

Teaching disabled people how to horse-ride

Counselling people with mental illness on the telephone

Providing face-to-face guidance for the distressed and suicidal

Home visits to the housebound and disabled

Helping part-time in residential homes, day centres and hospices

HOSPITALS AND HOSPICES

Hospitals and hospices use a large number of volunteers in the day-to-day running of a hospital. This can range from bedside visiting, working on the hospital radio station, fundraising, art therapy or providing refreshments. Volunteering in a hospital is a good way to get experience before entering particular professions. Prospective occupational and art therapists may be able to organise voluntary work in hospitals to boost their application for vocational courses, while many fledgling radio journalists start their careers in hospital radio.

Find work by writing to the administrator of your local hospital. Explain why you want to work in a hospital, what you have to offer, and how much time you can give. Also mention any relevant experience you have.

For more information contact the National Association of Leagues of Hospital Friends and The National Association of Hospital Broadcasting Associations.

VOLUNTEERS' STORIES

Jessica Sutton volunteers on a local hospital radio. One of Jessica's friends had started volunteering for the radio some years before and had eventually become programme controller. Jessica says, 'I wanted to get some experience to be a journalist so I sent an application letter to my friend, who then invited me in one evening.' Much to Jessica's surprise, her big break came sooner than anticipated. 'One of the presenters couldn't do their show, so I was put on air that evening. I was so nervous – I hadn't expected it at all. My friend just turned on my mike and I had to introduce the song requests and mention the patients' names.'

After her initial session, Jessica volunteered once a week until, a month or so later, she asked if she could help at the kids' wards station. To her delight, the person who presented the children's radio show said he was on his own and needed some help.

Jessica started volunteering every Saturday morning, on the children's one-and-a-half-hour show. Jessica says, 'The work involves a lot of planning. We start off by visiting the children's wards, seeing the patients and asking them if they have any requests. We then go on air and play the requests we have. On air, we do a lot of talking. I spend a lot of time beforehand finding news stories on the web – anything that might interest them. This could be showbiz stuff or anything topical – when the Harry Potter book came out, we spent a lot of time talking about that. Some of it is planned but often we just go with the flow. There's no pressure to be witty, you just have to be natural.'

Jessica is now hoping to use the experience to launch a career in broadcast journalism, starting with a BA Hons in Journalism. Her radio voluntary work, she says, has been a brilliant starting point. 'It's given me confidence and taught me technical skills. It's also very satisfying to know that patients are listening and you hope that they are getting something from it too. At the end of the day it's great fun and very rewarding.'

WORKING IN MEDICINE AND HEALTH

Medical and health organisations work tirelessly to alleviate suffering around the world. Not surprisingly most of the work available requires solid experience and qualifications, particularly in overseas disaster settings. That said, there is also help needed back home, working in the charity shops, doing admin work or fundraising.

The following organisations require volunteers for overseas projects: ATD Fourth World, The Red Cross, Oxfam, The Salvation Army, UNICEF and UNHCR.

The following domestic organisations run projects in the UK:

Action Against Allergy, PO Box 278, Twickenham TW1 4QQ, Tel: 020 8892 4949, **www.actionagainstallergy.co.uk**.

Communities Against Toxics (CATs), PO Box 29, Ellesmere Port CH66 3TX, Tel: 0151 339 5473.

Eating Disorders Association (EDA), 103 Prince of Wales Road, Norwich, Norfolk N1 1DW, Tel: 01603 621414, **www.edauk.org.uk**.

Mind (National Association for Mental Health), 15–19 Broadway, London E15 4BQ, Tel: 020 8519 2122, **www.mind.org.uk**.

St John's Ambulance, 27 St John's Lane, London EC1M 4BU, Tel: 020 324 4000, **www.sja.org.uk**.

WORKING WITH DRUG AND ALCOHOL ADDICTION

Addaction, 67–69 Cowcross Street, London EC1M 6BP, Tel: 020 7251 5860, Email: info@addaction.org.uk, or visit **www.addaction.org**.

ADFAM National (The National Charity for Families of Drug Users), 32–36 Loman Street, London SE1 0EE, Tel: 020 7928 8898, **www.adfam.org.uk**.

ASH – Action on Smoking and Health, 102 Clifton Street, London EC2A 4HW, Tel: 020 7739 5902, **www.ash.org.uk**.

Chemical Dependency Centre Ltd, 11 Redcliffe Gardens, London SW10 9BG, Tel: 020 7352 2552.

WORKING WITH THE HOMELESS

With more and more people on the streets, the homeless are in dire need of people's support, particularly with their increased susceptibility to drug addiction. As such there are a wide range of ways you can help, from hands-on work, such as running soup kitchens and helping out at homeless centres, to working in charity shops or admin work. There is also a need for experienced people to provide advice on employment, education, rights and benefits. Like many homeless organisations, the Big Issue Foundation runs a whole gamut of services from providing clothing and housing advice to running poetry and art classes. The organisation Crisis runs the Crisis Open Christmas where for a week during Christmas homeless people can get shelter and take advantage of a huge range of services on offer from volunteers. This requires professions and assistance right across the board, including doctors, nurses, dentists, hairdressers and alternative therapists. There is also help needed in the clothing department and canteen. All trainers receive an induction, which includes advice on how to deal with drugs issues, such as finding needles and dealing with outbursts. Apply directly to the local hostels in your area or contact the national organisations.

The Big Issue Foundation, Fundraising, The Big Issue Foundation, 1–5 Wandsworth Road, London SW8 2LN (write explaining why you think you'd make a good volunteer), **www.bigissue.co.uk**.

Crisis, Warwick House, 25–27 Buckingham Palace Road, London SW1W 0PP, Tel: 0870 011 3335, **www.crisis.org.uk**.

Homes for Homeless People, Cyrenian House, 9–11 Union Street, Luton, Bedfordshire LU1 3AN, Tel: 01582 481 426.

Shelter, 88 Old Street, London EC1V 9HU, Tel: 020 7505 4699, **www.shelter.org.uk**.

Simon Community, PO Box 1187, London NW5 4HW, Tel: 020 7485 6639.

WORKING WITH THE ELDERLY

As in all forms of care work, the qualifications and experience required to work with the elderly vary greatly. Nurses and medical staff should obviously be qualified, but there is plenty of work to be found helping out in day centres or residential homes, or visiting people's homes to provide nothing more than companionship and support. Look up the addresses of local residential homes in the Yellow Pages or contact your local authority for a list of homes in your area that may be in need of volunteers.

Alternatively, try the following organisations:

Age Concern England, Astral House, 1268 London Road, London SW16 4ER, Tel: 020 8765 7200, **www.ace.org.uk**.

Age-Link, 9 Narborough Close, Brackenbury Village, Ickenham, Middlesex UB10 8TN, Tel: 01895 676689, **www.age-link.org.uk**.

Help The Aged, 207–221 Pentonville Road, London N1 9UZ, Tel: 020 7278 1114, **www.helptheaged.org.uk**.

WORKING WITH DISABLED PEOPLE

Volunteering with the disabled covers a wide range of organisations and institutions. Work can range from helping out at a local day centre to teaching disabled people how to use computers or practising yoga. With all organisations the emphasis is on practical guidance and support, helping the disabled how to live with their disabilities rather than doing things for them. Some posts will require qualifications, such as teaching and medical support, but there are many opportunities for people with no previous experience to provide assistance.

RADAR is an umbrella organisation with nearly 700 members including individuals, organisations of and for disabled people, and corporate and public-sector organisations. Its website, **www.radar.org.uk**, contains many links to other caring organisations. Contact RADAR, 12 City Forum, 250 City Road, London EC1V 8AF, Tel: 020 7250 3222, Fax: 020 7250 0212.

Look in *Community Care* and *Disability Now* journals.

ORGANISATIONS

British Council of Disabled People, Litchurch Plaza, Litchurch Lane, Derby DE24 8AA, Tel: 01332 295 551, **www.bcodp.org.uk**.

Gardening for Disabled Trust, Frittenden House, Frittenden, Cranbrook, Kent TN17 2DG, Tel: 01580 852249.

Leonard Cheshire, 30 Millbank, London SW1P 4QD, Tel: 020 7802 8200, **www.leonard-cheshire.org**.

Mencap, 123 Golden Lane, London EC1Y 0RT, Tel: 020 7454 0454, Fax: 020 7696 5540, **www.mencap.org.uk**.

Riding for the Disabled Association (RDA), National Agricultural Centre, Stoneleigh Park, Kenilworth, Warwickshire CV8 2LG, Tel: 02476 696510.

Royal National Institute for the Blind (RNIB), 105 Judd Street, London WC1H 9NE, Tel: 020 7388 1266, Email: rnib@rnib.org.uk, **www.rnib.org.uk**.

OFFENDERS AND VICTIMS

There are many organisations set up to offer advice and support to victims, offenders and their families. Some of these, such as Apex Trust, aim to help ex-offenders back into the job market. One particular area of growth recently has been 'prison visiting', where volunteers regularly visit someone in prison who has no other visitors, family or friends. This could be because they are far from home, they have no close relatives or their family is not interested in them. The National Association of Prison Visitors is looking for people who are good listeners and between the ages 21 and 70. You don't need any special qualifications, but you should be able to commit to visiting the same prisoner regularly (every week or so). If you speak or understand an ethnic-minority language, you could offer a lifeline for some prisoners. If you are interested in becoming a prison visitor, telephone the National Association of Prison Visitors on 01234 359763, E-mail: info@napv.org.uk or visit the website: **www.hmprisonservice.gov.uk/prisons/**.

Other organisations that organise prison visiting are Apex Trust, Independent Custody Visiting Association and National Association for the Care and Resettlement of Offenders (NACRO). Alternatively you can contact the prison governors of your local prison. Look in the Yellow Pages for addresses or check the Prison Service website.

ORGANISATIONS

Aftermath, PO Box 414, Sheffield S4 7RT, Tel: 0114 275 3883 (supports families of serious offenders).

Apex Trust, St Alphanage House, Wingate Annexe, 2 Fore Street, London EC2Y 5DA, Tel: 020 7638 5931, **www.apextrust.com** (helps ex-offenders improve their chances in the job market).

Independent Custody Visiting Association, 16–18 Whidborne Street, London WC1H 8EZ, Tel: 020 7837 0078, **www.icva.org.uk**.

NACRO (National Association for the Care and Resettlement of Offenders), 169 Clapham Road, London SW9 0PU, Tel: 020 7582 6500, **www.nacro.org.uk**.

Victim Support, Cranmer House, 39 Brixton Road, London SW9 6DD, Tel: 020 7735 9166, **www.victimsupport.org**.

COUNSELLING AND MENTORING

Many services in the voluntary sector involve mentoring, counselling and giving advice, sometimes face to face, and sometimes over the telephone. If you are giving specialist information, such as legal and benefit rights, you may be expected to be an expert in that area. However, many counselling/advice services provide training themselves and volunteers do not need previous experience or particular qualifications. That said, the selection procedure can be tough and not every applicant will succeed in finding a voluntary position. If you are interested in launching a career in counselling and therapy, volunteering in this area can be an ideal way of gaining the necessary experience first.

ORGANISATIONS

Befrienders International, 26–27 Market Place, Kingston Upon Thames, Surrey KT1 1JH, Tel: 020 8541 4949, **www.befrienders.org** (offers support to the distressed and suicidal).

Brook Advisory Centres, 421 Highgate Studios, 53–79 Highgate Road, London NW5 1TL, Tel: 020 7284 6040, Fax: 020 7284 6050, **www.brook.org.uk** (advice on sex and contraception for young people under 25).

National Association of Citizens' Advice Bureaux (NACAB), 115–123 Pentonville Road, London N1 9LZ, Tel: 020 7833 2181.

Relate: National Marriage Guidance, Herbert Gray College, Little Church Street, Rugby, Warwickshire CV31 3AP, Tel: 01788 573241, **www.relate.org.uk**.

Samaritans, The Upper Mill, Kingston Road, Ewell, Surrey KT17 2AF, Tel: 020 8394 8300, **www.samaritans.org.uk**.

CHILDREN AND YOUNG PEOPLE

One of the most popular areas in volunteering is working with children and young people. Not surprisingly, this covers a wide range of roles, suitable for both qualified people (teachers, social workers, special needs teachers and counsellors etc.) and the unqualified – although the latter will be mostly limited to administrative or part-time help positions.

Working in this sector is so far reaching it is impossible to summarise. Work can range from live-in positions in residential homes, where you will normally be expected to have some qualifications, to organising sports activities for children with learning difficulties. There are also opportunities for people to work on the telephone lines offering counselling to young people in need (through the organisation Childline), while some local authorities recruit mentors for young offenders. Some organisations require hands-on help, working directly with children, while others, such as Save the Children, recruit volunteers mostly for fundraising, admin and media work. Alternatively, you can contact nurseries and childcare centres to offer your assistance or contact local authorities for details of residential homes and local projects. Contact the National Children's Home, which offers residential care.

Here are some examples of the type of work available:

Giving talks at schools on issues such as sex or drugs abuse

Telephone counselling

Youth leader on community projects

Helping out at residential children's homes

Fundraising, publicity and media work

Teaching sports activities on youth projects

Administration

Running charity shops

Drama work with young people 'at risk'

Listening to children read at school

Mentoring young offenders

ORGANISATIONS

Hope UK, 25f Copperfield Street, London SE1 0EN, Tel: 020 7928 0848, **www.hopeuk.org** (encourages children and young people away from drugs and drink).

Life Education Centres, 1st Floor, 53–56 Great Sutton Street, London EC1V 0DE, Tel: 020 7490 3210, **www.lifeeducation.org.uk** (educates young people about drug abuse and AIDS).

ChildLine, 50 Studd Street, London N1 0QW, Tel: 020 7239 1000, **www.childline.org.uk**.

Action For Sick Children, 29–31 Euston Road, London NW1 2SD, **www.actionforsickchildren.org.uk**.

Barnado's, Tanners Lane, Barkingside, Ilford, Essex IG6 1QG, Tel: 020 8550 8822, **www.barnados.org.uk**.

Farms For City Children, Nethercott House, Iddesleigh, Winkleigh, Devon EX19 8BG, Tel: 01837 810573, **www.farmsforcitychildren.co.uk**.

Grandparents' Association, Moot House, The Stow, Harlow, Essex CM20 3AG, Tel: 01279 428040, Helpline: 01279 444964, **www.grandparents-federation.org.uk**.

NCH Action For Children, 85 Highbury Park, London N5 1UD, Tel: 020 7704 7000, **www.nch.org.uk**.

NSPCC, Weston House, 42 Curtain Road, London EC2A 3NH, Tel: 020 7825 2500, Fax: 020 7825 2525, **www.nspcc.org.uk**.

Save the Children Fund, 17 Grove Lane, London SE5 8RD, Tel: 020 7703 5400, **www.savethechildren.org.uk**.

Volunteer Reading Help, Charity House, 14–15 Perseverance Works, 38 Kingsland Road, London E2 8DD (the Readability Scheme brings together volunteers and children to develop reading skills).

VOLUNTEERS' STORIES

Actress Nicky Goodchild has volunteered for Scene and Heard for four years, mentoring disadvantaged children in the King's Cross area of London. In the eight-week courses, once a week, the children learn about creating stories and characters, culminating in a play-writing weekend where they write their own plays and have them performed by professional actors. Volunteers are all theatre professionals and as actors, 'dramaturges', directors, class volunteers or theatre technicians.

'It's the best fun we have all year,' Nicky says. 'The children are encouraged to write about non-human characters and the results are amazingly imaginative. In the last four years, I have played the Real Statue of Liberty from Birmingham, a piece of blue tack, an angel fish, a dirty worm and a bad ass American genie in a milk bottle.'

Nicky loves her work. 'It's a total joy – how many times are you going to get to play a piece of blue tack in your career? It also shakes away any cynicism, to see the pure imagination in children and see that there's such possibility in drama.'

The children benefit from the experience too, and often undergo remarkable changes. Nicky says, 'It's amazing to see what the children get out of it. They come to every performance and get to sit in the playwright's chair when their play is on, as well as taking a bow on their own at the end and with the actors. It can have an incredible effect on some of the children. At the end of the day, it's not just about play-writing – it's about giving children confidence, bringing them out and giving them one-on-one time with adults, which many of them otherwise don't have.' To find out more about Scene and Heard, visit **www.sceneandheard.org**.

ANIMALS

Given the British public's love for all soft and cuddly things, it's not surprising that caring for animals is one of the most popular areas for volunteers. Competition is therefore high, and many organisations need people more to help with the fundraising and administrative side than to work with the animals directly. That said, plenty of people manage to find unpaid work in animal centres and sanctuaries where they clean, feed, walk and play with the animals. Volunteers for the RSPCA can be engaged in a wide range of work including door-to-door collections, fundraising, helping with day-to-day care of animals in its centres and home checking before the animals are rehomed. Some centres may also require voluntary vets or veterinary nurses. I even know of one reiki healer friend who visited a cat sanctuary on a mission to find a pet, and ended up giving reiki to a traumatised cat that had been left abandoned in a dustbin.

Whatever you want to do, whether it's helping raise funds to protect endangered species or campaigning against vivisection, there are plenty of opportunities around.

Some ideas:

Organising publicity campaigns

Helping out at animal sanctuaries

Rescuing and re-homing abandoned animals

Cat-sitting while owners are on holiday

Street or door-to-door collections

ORGANISATIONS

Blue Cross, Shilton Road, Burford, Oxfordshire OX18 4PF, Tel: 01993 8255000, **www.bluecross.org.uk** (veterinary and welfare care for domestic animals).

Born Free Foundation (BFF), 3 Grove House, Foundry Lane, Horsham, West Sussex RH13 5PL, Tel: 01403 240 170, **www.bornfree.org.uk** (watchdog for animal treatment in zoos and promotes preservation of wildlife habitats).

British Union for the Abolition of Vivisection (BUAV), 16a Crane Grove, London N7 8LB, Tel: 020 7700 4888, **www.buav.org.uk**.

Cats Protection, 17 Kings Road, Horsham, West Sussex, RH13 5PN, Tel: 08702 099 099, Fax: 08707 708 265, **www.cats.org.uk**.

Compassion in World Farming, 5a Charles Street, Petersfield, Hampshire GU32 3EH, Tel: 01730 264208, **www.cwif.org.uk**.

International Fund for Animal Welfare, 87–90 Albert Embankment, London SE1 9UD, Tel: 020 7518 7600.

League Against Cruel Sports, Sparling House, 83–87 Union Street, London SE1 1SG, Tel: 020 7703 6155, **www.league.uk.com**.

Rare Breeds Survival Trust, National Agricultural Centre, Stoneleigh Park, Kenilworth, Warwickshire CV8 2LG, Tel: 02476 696551, **www.rbst.org.uk**.

Royal Society for the Prevention of Cruelty to Animals (RSPCA), the Causeway, Horsham, West Sussex RH12 1HG, Tel: 0870 010 1181, **www.rspca.org.uk**.

Royal Society for the Protection of Birds (RSPB), The Lodge, Sandy, Bedfordshire SG19 2DL, Tel: 01767 680551, **www.rspb.org.uk**.

Sea Watch Foundation – The Cetacean Monitoring Unit, 11 Jersey Road, Oxford OX4 4RT, Tel: 01865 717276, **www.seawatchfoundation.org.uk**.

Whale and Dolphin Conservation Society (WDCS), Brookfield House, 38 St Paul Street, Chippenham, Wiltshire SN15 1LY, Tel: 0870 870 0027.

WWF UK, Panda House, Weyside Park, Godalming, Surrey GU7 1XR, Tel: 01483 426444, **www.wwf.org.uk**.

ENVIRONMENT AND CONSERVATION

There are plenty of voluntary bodies and charities that work in conservation. Some of these, such as Greenpeace, focus on campaigning for a cleaner world and require people to help run campaigns, lobbying government and drawing media attention to environmental issues. Others, such as BTCV, take a more hands-on approach and organise conservation projects where volunteers work outside on tree maintenance, restoring waterways and protecting wildlife habitats etc. Qualifications needed depend on the type of work involved, but people with no previous experience can usually find work, although they will be expected to have a keen interest in conservation. BTCV run a loose, flexible scheme where volunteers can turn up whenever they want, even if it's only one day a year. Novice conservation volunteers can test the waters on one of the many short-term environmental/conservation residential projects available, where people can stay for a week on a camp in, say, the Lake District and try their hands at tasks such as dry-stone walling.

Working in conservation is extremely competitive, so paid work can be hard to find. However, after volunteering for a significant period, you may end up as project leader which can lead to a full-time position, and give you an excellent background to launch a career in environmental and conservation work. There are also opportunities for indoor work, from fundraising and admin to research and expertise from qualified engineers, surveyors and scientists.

COMMUNITY AND HERITAGE PROJECTS

Many volunteers in the UK are similarly based on community projects. These are organised in a local community, by an organisation such as CSV or through volunteer bureaux and the local authority. The work tends to have a specific aim in mind, such as clearing up a piece of wasteland frequently inhabited by drug users, restoring a village hall, creating a community centre, planting trees in an urban area or setting up a city farm. Most projects require a whole range of skills and expertise, including hands-on help in building, clearing, planting etc. and managing, budgeting, fundraising etc. As most community projects are organised on a local basis, there tends to be greater scope for trying your hand at new skills such as managing projects and team building than in the national charities and organisations.

Another possibility is working in heritage, most typically exemplified by English Heritage and the National Trust. Heritage projects are aimed at preservation work and include archaeological digs or restoring historic sites, and include excavating, restoration and running visitor attractions. To take part in an archaeological dig, you will normally need an archaeology degree. Other restoration projects may require builders, surveyors, historians and engineers. To find work try the Countryside Commission or the newspaper *The Conserver*. *Working with the Environment* by Tim Ryder and Elisabeth Roberts (Vacation Work) is also packed with organisations and useful information.

ORGANISATIONS

British Trust for Conservation Volunteers (BTCV), 36 St Mary's Street, Wallingford, Oxfordshire OX10 0EU, Tel: 01491 821600, **www.btcv.org**.

Commonwork Land Trust (CLT), Bore Place, Chiddingstone, Edenbridge, Kent TN8 7AR, Tel: 01732 463255, **www.commonwork.org**.

EarthKind, Enefco House, The Quay, Poole, Dorset BG15 1HG, Tel: 01202 682344.

Friends of the Earth (FOE), 26–28 Underwood Street, London N1 7JQ, Tel: 020 7490 1555, **www.foe.co.uk**.

Greenpeace, Canonbury Villas, London N1 2PN, Tel: 020 7865 8100, **www.greenpeace.org.uk**.

Groundwork, 85–87 Cornwall Street, Birmingham B3 3BY, Tel: 0121 236 8565, **www.groundwork.org.uk**.

Inland Waterways Association, PO Box 114, Rickmansworth, Hertfordshire WD3 1ZY, Tel: 01923 711114, **www.waterways.org.uk**.

Marine Conservation Society (MCS), 9 Gloucester Road, Ross-on-Wye, Hereford and Worcester HR9 5BU, Tel: 01989 566017.

National Trust, 33 Sheep Street, Cirencester, Gloucesterhire GL7 1RQ, Tel: 0870 609 5383.

WWOOF (Willing Workers on Organic Farms), PO Box 2675, Lewes, East Sussex BN7 1RB, Tel: 01273 476286.

RELIGIOUS CHARITIES

Many voluntary organisations are run by religious charities that provide a wide range of assistance both in the UK and throughout the world (see international section). Their work covers many areas which, rather than actively promoting the religion itself (as in traditional missionary work), put into action the principles of their beliefs. Typical causes include working towards peace and development, helping to alleviate poverty and providing medicine and health to the poor and dispossessed. Volunteers accepted on these projects are usually fully practising members of the affiliated religion, and will at the very least be able to demonstrate an active commitment to that particular faith. For more information, contact the church or organisation directly to see what opportunities they have. Here are some faith-based organisations: Christian Aid, The Church Army, Jewish Care, Quakers, Methodist Homes for the Aged and The Salvation Army.

PRESSURE GROUPS

Despite not having charity status, pressure groups and NGOs use huge amounts of volunteers to promote the causes they represent. This can include lobbying the government or organising media campaigns to grab the public's attention. Volunteers take up many roles from street collection to helping out at rallies. Many paid employers also start off as volunteers until eventually being offered contracts. Obviously it makes sense to have a particular passion for the cause you are representing. Some NGOs include Amnesty International, CND, Greenpeace and Global Witness. To find work write to the pressure group or NGO to enquire about voluntary opportunities. You can find lists of British NGOs (and charities) in the *Guardian Media Directory*. The website **ngonews.org** is a forum for information to be exchanged between NGOs around the world, and includes a massive directory of NGOs right across the globe.

BECOMING A TRUSTEE

Trustee work is a particular type of volunteering that involves giving advice in board meetings and making crucial decisions. All not-for-profits have a Management Committee or Board of Trustees to oversee the running of the organisation. Many trustees are brought on board by the organisation's director, maybe because they are a personal friend or business contact with a special interest in the cause the organisation is promoting, or because they are an expert in a relevant field. However, it is also possible to find a position as a trustee by contacting the organisation and offering your services. In this case highlight your interest in the cause you are representing, and what you have to offer. Voluntary experience with the relevant organisation, of course, will put you in a far stronger position.

Trustee involvement can be very satisfying if you want to have a say in the direct running of the organisation. Most trustees are not required for day-to-day work, but attend board meetings typically held four or five times a year.

INTERNATIONAL ORGANISATIONS

There are many organisations that run voluntary projects abroad or require volunteers to help with the work they do overseas. These typically include aid and disaster relief organisations, and those that work to relieve poverty or promote peace and development. The International Section covers these in more detail but for the moment it is worth saying that many of them require volunteers back at home to man phones, fundraise and do media/campaign work.

VIRTUAL VOLUNTEERING

One of the most exciting things to hit the voluntary sector in recent years is virtual or online volunteering. Perfect for those who like to laze in their pyjamas and save the world from the comfort of their own home, this style of volunteering has revolutionised the ways in which people give time. Popular in North America for some time, virtual volunteering is now catching on with many UK organisations who are recognising the benefits, such as drafting in a cross-section of people who otherwise might not have been interested in volunteering or don't have the time. So if you are time stretched through work or family obligations, have a disability or are housebound, or would simply prefer to work to your own pace, virtual volunteering could be the perfect option.

WHAT CAN YOU DO?

There are literally hundreds of ways you can give your time online, the only limit is your imagination. Here are some common ways in which people help:

Designing a charity's website
Constructing a database
Research and data analysis
Monitoring an online discussion group
Co-ordinating an online campaign
Clicking to donate money
Online mentoring
Translations
Writing case studies
Writing and editing articles

WHO CAN BE ONLINE VOLUNTEERS?

Virtual volunteering is suitable for all people who have regular, reliable access to a computer and the Internet. However, there are particular skills that are of value to a voluntary organisation. These include proven good writing ability, web design, programming knowledge, experience in project management, knowledge of another language and expertise in law or education. If you don't have any experience in these fields, however, there are still opportunities available to you, so, whatever your background, contact the organisation and tell them you are interested in offering online assistance. Make sure you have regular and reliable access to a computer and the Internet, and think carefully about whether you have the necessary qualities needed for this style of working. Online volunteering is very different from volunteering in a group, so ask yourself how comfortable you are working on your own. Are you self-motivated? Can you meet deadlines? A little self-reflection beforehand can avoid any unwelcome surprises later.

HOW TO FIND WORK

If you are interested in volunteering online, the first thing to do is check out Net Aid's website (**www.netaid.org**). This New York-based organisation connects volunteers to poverty-fighting organisations around the world via the Internet, and provides hundreds of opportunities to do volunteer research, writing, programming, networking and other activities without leaving home. The website is packed full of great information about how you can help online, as well as case studies, news and links to online campaigns and other organisations.

The American website Volunteer Match has hundreds of virtual volunteering opportunities. Go to **www.volunteermatch** and click on 'Virtual'.

The **do-it.org.uk** website contains some virtual opportunities.

You can also try Volunteers in Technical Assistance (VITA), which aims to empower those in developing countries through helping them with technological assistance. Visit **www.vita.org/**.

The UK project IT4 recruits IT experts to volunteer their skills for charities and community groups. Visit **www.it4communities.org.uk**.

YouthOrgUK is a virtual community for young people and professionals using the Internet for learning. The virtual community and website are entirely managed, developed and published by volunteers. Visit **www.youth.org.uk** for more details.

Time Bank may also be able to find you online opportunities. Go to its website **www.timebank.org.uk**.

The website Global Ideas Bank (**www.globalideasbank.org**) provides many links for other online opportunities, including details of online campaigns and charities where you can just click on the website to make a donation.

PART TWO: AWAY INTERNATIONAL VOLUNTEERING

6. INTERNATIONAL VOLUNTEERING

Whether it's trekking through the Brazilian rainforest, swimming with dolphins or teaching the poor and dispossessed in Nepal to read, the appeal of overseas volunteering is gaining in popularity. It's not hard to see why – what other 'holidays' combine the exoticism of travelling with the feel-good glow that comes from helping other people? Cue then the rise of the international volunteer – backpack at the ready, Tevas in place, always ready with a Messianic smile to muck in and do their bit. Add to this the ever-widening gap between the rich and the poor, and it looks as if volunteering and gap-year adventures can only be set to grow. Yet prospective volunteers are warned against making too many assumptions. Yes, much good is done in the name of volunteering, but it also has its shadow side and, as one experienced volunteer said to me, it's not for nothing that travelling is known as the new colonialism. All of this is to say: don't take yourself too seriously. Don't arrive expecting to dispense your platitudes of Western wisdom to eager locals who have no ideas to offer of their own. Don't patronise people. After all, you could be one of the many volunteers who return to say they learned far more from the locals than they could ever teach them.

WHAT ARE YOUR MOTIVES?

The first thing, then, if you are considering volunteering overseas is to analyse your motives. Gap years abroad have become a virtual rite of passage in recent years and, with the rise of eco-tourism, it's a trend that doesn't look set to go away. For the right kind of middle-class kid, eager to swap their tales of downtown slumming in Nepal through to trekking in the jungles of Thailand, overseas volunteering during the gap year is as much a stamp of identity as listening to the right music or wearing the right kind of trainers. But, beneath the sexy, glamorous image of international volunteering lies the gritty world of overseas aid and development.

As Alex Garland writes in *The Beach*: 'Collecting memories, or experiences, was my primary goal when I first started travelling . . . I wanted to witness extreme poverty. I saw it as a necessary experience for anyone who wanted to appear worldly and interesting.'

If sentiments such as these are close to your motives, you may want to rethink your plans. Why? Volunteering can be tough. Some projects run in developing countries where the basics we take for granted such as running water, electricity and a good level of healthcare might not exist. Some may even be operating in countries known to be international trouble spots. As Marco van Belle writes on the Irish website **www.backpacker.ie**: 'Solidarity work in a developing country is demanding. There are days when only a strong belief and conviction in why you are there will get you through.'

It is wise then, before signing up, to ask yourself some tough questions. Do you have a burning desire to help people? Do you want to do something impressive and exotic sounding to add clout to your CV? Or are you simply looking for a change of perspective? There's no need for self-judgement here – you don't have to be the next Ghandi on a mission to save the world, it's just wise to know exactly what you want to get out of it. For example, if you're primarily interested in having an exotic holiday or adding a bit of clout to your CV, you'd better steer clear of some of the more demanding development projects. There are plenty of short-term projects which you can pay to do instead.

Being clear about your motives isn't only recommended for your sake, but also for the sake of the people you are going over to 'help'. Most development projects need commitment – a reason why many NGOs are taking fewer overseas workers on board and focusing increasingly on professionals. Sending expatriate workers overseas is also expensive – not only is there the outlay in training and placing you, but there's the admin costs that go into all the million and one bits of paperwork that working overseas demands. So you do no one any good if you get bored after two weeks and want to return home. This may sound harsh, but every year a high proportion of volunteers on development projects return early, unable to cope with the political realities and conditions in which they have to live. No one likes to live with the sense that they've failed at something, so do yourself a favour and question your motives first. After all it's best to embark on such a journey with your eyes fully open. That way, everyone stands to benefit – including you.

One way to be sure about your motives is to cut your teeth volunteering at home first, something which many organisations recommend.

WHAT WILL YOU GET OUT OF IT?

For those who decide volunteering overseas is for them, you can be sure that you will gain plenty from the experience. International voluntary work isn't just about having an interesting holiday but can be just the ticket if you need a new lease of life. And it's not just for gappers: people young and old are now giving up their comfortable, cosy lives to venture out into the bewildering unknown of overseas volunteering, sometimes with life-changing consequences. There are plenty of stories of people who have volunteered abroad and come back to the UK to set up new careers, or start up their own charities. Volunteering abroad can also be a good option if you are living abroad as an expatriate spouse, and don't have the time or language/professional skills to commit to paid employment. Offering your help on a voluntary basis can be a stimulating way of integrating into the local community while your partner is out at work. It can also be a great way to learn valuable skills and practise a new language all at the same time. Germany, for example, has a variety of social projects where volunteers can work in 'social settings' such as hospitals or refugee centres and get a good grounding in social work. Then there are the other gap-year organisations that place people on newspapers overseas, offering good work experience for fledgling journalists who may be able to use the experience to break into a competitive career. In fact, if you think ahead and long term, your gap year or voluntary stint abroad could not only be a fascinating travel adventure but also a valuable launch pad for a new vocation.

VOLUNTEERS' STORIES

Katharine Dennison found her two-year VSO placement in South Africa helped her professionally. She started work in the marketing and communications office of a university and eventually set up her own HIV/Aids educational campaign. 'HIV/Aids is a big problem in all Southern African countries, so I felt I was meeting a need, that I could make a difference and make a long-term impact.'

Katharine was right – the campaign work she initiated – establishing a committee, starting sex education programmes and educational campaigns, and working in a HIV-Aids hospice – is all continuing today and, as a result, the committee has introduced voluntary counselling and testing facilities.

Katharine says her volunteering work opened doors for her professionally. 'There were far more possibilities open to me than in the UK. Skills and experience are really valued there and I was organising things from major conference management to developing policies on car pools.' Katharine now has a paid position in the voluntary sector, overseeing volunteers schemes at Staffordshire University.

CULTURAL INSIGHT

So what else will you get out of it? How about the chance to experience up close and personal the bizarrities and paradoxes of another nation's culture? Ruth Asher sees volunteering as an essential part of any trip. 'I always try to do a volunteer work camp as part of my travels as it adds a different dimension to my trip. I think it's the only way you can fully experience authentic life there.'

SO WHAT OPPORTUNITIES EXIST?

Whatever you decide, you can be sure that there are plenty of opportunities for volunteering overseas. Most of the work is residential and set up through an NGO or volunteer agency. Work can involve a myriad things, including eco work, conservation, renovation, health work, teaching, special needs or archaeology. Many voluntary programmes run on the basis of work camps, where participants live in the same place, often a large tent, and work is focused on completing a specific task – such as renovating a fifteenth-century church, planting trees or clearing land to make a park for children.

Generally speaking, if you want to volunteer overseas, your best bet is to fix up work through an organisation first, either a sending agency or a charity/NGO at home or in the country you intend to visit. Although it is possible to just turn up and find volunteer projects, most people who do this stumble across the work while travelling in the country.

FIXING UP WORK THERE

Of course, there are exceptions to every rule. Some rare, adventurous souls make a point of picking up work as they arrive, travelling around from conservation work to charity work, and there will be some space given to talk about what resources can help in this area. However, at the very least these people tend to be experienced volunteers, not to mention experienced travellers. And you can bet that they will have networks in the country and have done their research first.

Generally, specific information on finding local voluntary work opportunities on the spot is hard to find. This is largely because, while many countries have a strong tradition of unpaid community support, it is not necessarily known as 'volunteering'. Often such work is built into the whole social experience and is not even classed as work. Such countries will not have a voluntary work infrastructure in place and will not have contacts and official brokerages or organisations.

Another thing to say is, no matter how much good you intend, never ever turn up in a war zone and expect to provide help. You may think you are acting out of everyone's best interests, but aid agencies around the world insist that people who do this are more hindrance than help. The best way people can help, they say, is by donating money at home. Not only will you be putting yourself in extreme danger, but you will also be placing an extra burden on the organisation you have come to help. The last thing a disaster setting needs is well-meaning but non-skilled people wandering around. That said, of course, there is a huge need for the right skilled people but these should apply through the agency first.

VOLUNTEER ORGANISATIONS

Broadly speaking, most voluntary projects fall into two categories – long-term assignments working for the large NGOs, and medium- or short-term work for smaller NGOs or dedicated sending agencies (such as gap-year organisations) where you often pay for the privilege. The big difference between them is that the large NGOs are increasingly looking for professionals with solid vocational skills and experience, while the smaller NGOs and agencies expect little in the way of previous experience.

INDIGENOUS PROGRAMMES

Most countries, of course, will have their own indigenous programmes, or you can apply to charities and NGOs and ask them if they need help. In order to take part in indigenous volunteer schemes, you will often need to find a hosting organisation in your home country to take care of the administration involved in placing you. Some indigenous organisations, however, will organise the placement themselves and not require a hosting organisation. If you are trying to find a hosting organisation in your country, contact the volunteer bureaux or any large sending agency such as CIEE and Concordia (who say they can provide details of hosts for most nationalities).

VOLUNTEERING IN DEVELOPING COUNTRIES

Many opportunities in volunteering overseas lie in developing countries. Some of these are heavily reliant on aid work, which is often provided by religious organisations. These agencies look for a variety of skills. These include:

Medical

Nursing

Technical, such as engineering

Teaching

Practical, such as building

Business skills

Working in these countries may involve a certain degree of discomfort. Basics such as running water, electricity and a certain standard of healthcare may not exist.

LARGE NGOS

In recent years the large NGOs, such as the Red Cross, Concern and Oxfam, have become increasingly professionalised, to the extent that some positions are now paid and even come with perks such as houses. Many NGOs require a wide range of professions including teachers, nurses, journalists, lawyers, business managers, engineers and doctors. Most placements last for around two years and often require overseas experience.

DEDICATED SENDING AGENCIES

Those looking for more short-term work can try one of the many dedicated sending agencies that offer short-term volunteer assignments. Many of these require nothing more than the ability to speak English, although they may ask for graduates or undergraduates. In most cases, you will have to pay a fixed fee, which may include travel, insurance and orientation costs. Placements can last anything from three weeks to a few months and support a huge range of 'causes', from building schools in Eastern Europe to conservation work in South America. The rewards can be immense but some have been criticised for being nothing more than 'glorified travel agents'. If you are opting for one of these organisations to work in developing countries, then be prepared to do your research and ask some tough questions first.

WHAT QUALIFICATIONS WILL YOU NEED?

Working for one of the large NGOs on long-term assignments will require the necessary vocational qualifications that your profession demands, and some years' experience. Most organisations, however, are looking for specific skills and are not so interested in formal qualifications. Some of the sending agencies may demand nothing more than that you can speak good English. That said, some placements might require a university degree, four or five GCSEs, including Maths and English, or an appropriate vocational qualification (such as nursing).

HOW MUCH WILL IT COST?

If you are taking part in a project set up through a sending agency or gap-year organisation, you will most likely have to pay for the experience. Some organisations, like Concordia for example, require only a registration fee of around £80 and perhaps a small amount of money for a food kitty. Other more elaborate programmes, such as eco programmes in Africa, can cost around £1,000–2,000, which might not include flights but will include free board and food, training and equipment. Payment for work is obviously minimal, but some placements may include a small amount of pocket money per week. Make sure you know exactly what the fee covers before you commit to taking part in a project.

FINDING THE RIGHT PROJECT FOR YOU

Once you have scrutinised your motives, sit down and make a list of all you have to offer – what type of skills do you have, where do you want to go, and what do you feel particularly attracted to? What do you want to gain from the experience? How long do you want to go for? If you're looking to pay for the assignment, what is your budget? Then it's time to start scouring the web. Rest assured that there are plenty of opportunities out there – whether you want to take part in urban inner-city schemes in Italy or work the fields like Jean de Florette. Once you have come up with a list of possible projects, it's now time to put them under the microscope. Many of these projects sound fascinating on paper – so fascinating, in fact, that the temptation may be to rush in and sign up straight away. Don't. Take it slowly. There are a great many volunteer/gap-year agencies now and the quality can vary enormously. Don't be afraid to spend a long time on this process. International volunteering is a world in itself, and it's far better to take the time to think things through carefully before committing to something you're not one hundred per cent sure about.

QUESTIONS TO ASK YOUR VOLUNTEER ORGANISATION

If there is a fee, what does this cover exactly?

Do you have to arrange for your own travel?

How much support do you receive once you are on your project?

What are the development philosophies behind the organisation?

What are its short- and long-term goals?

ORIENTATION COURSE

One of the first things to check is whether they provide an orientation course. If you are taking part in a development project, this is an absolute must. The best organisations will provide you with orientation before you go, and a day or so once you arrive. This should include a brief introduction to the history and political background of the country, and a basic grounding in the language.

WORKING IN EMERGENCY SETTINGS

Faced with the horrifying images of war from the insular comfort of our far-off Western homes, is it any wonder that some people may feel moved to do something to help? The reality, of course, is a long way from the ground. Working in disaster zones is usually reserved for specialist staff sent from aid and relief agencies. Relief workers are highly qualified specialists in their professional fields and have overseas experience.

If you are a doctor, nurse, water and sanitation engineer or logistician and have overseas experience, you may be able to register with relief agencies on Rosters or Registers. A selection of agencies that hold emergency registers include Save the Children, Christian Aid, Oxfam, Tearfund, World Health Organisation or the International Health Exchange. Before contacting them, make sure you have the necessary skills and can fly out at short notice. These agencies are notoriously overstretched and have only the time to deal with genuinely relevant enquiries.

According to the World Service Enquiry, the following skills are often required in relief/ emergency work:

Finance/Administration

Health care/Nutrition

Civil/Construction/Building

Community mobilisation

Electrical sources and supply

Environmental management

Information/PR/Media

Information Technology

Institutional development

Logistics and Distribution

Mechanical engineering

Mine clearance

Needs and impact assessment

Personnel management

Programme management

Project management

Radio telecommunications

Roads and bridges

Sanitation

Security

Technical supervision

Training and development

Vehicle and mechanical plant

Water sources

Water supply and distribution

STARTING A CAREER IN INTERNATIONAL AID AND DEVELOPMENT

If you are seriously considering a career in international aid and development, the first thing to do is check out the World Service Enquiry. This organisation has a huge range of resources, including an email course, one-to-one advice sessions, a specialist vacancy magazine, *Opportunities Abroad*, and the *2004 Guide*. For more details, contact World Service Enquiry, 233 Bon Marché Centre, 241–251 Ferndale Road, London SW9 8BJ, Tel: 0870 770 3274, Fax: 0870 770 7991, **www.wse.org.uk**.

For further advice and support, you can join Aid Workers Net (**www.aidworkers.net**), a forum for aid workers to exchange information and offer guidance.

THE JOB SEARCH

FINDING WORK BEFORE YOU LEAVE

There are so many volunteer projects throughout the world that there are hundreds of ways to start your search. Here are a few ideas:

THE INTERNET

Just a few hours surfing the Internet should give you a good idea of the staggering range of opportunities out there. By far the most useful, of course, are those websites especially dedicated to international volunteering opportunities. These will also carry links to many NGOs and volunteer agencies' websites.

The European Commission-funded Euro-Volunteers Information Pool lists voluntary projects in France, Germany, Greece, Luxembourg and the Netherlands. The website also includes a searchable database for voluntary initiatives in each country and hopes to expand to include many other EU countries, so it's worth keeping an eye on. Go to **www.euro-volunteers.org** for more information.

Do It (**www.do-it.org.uk**) carries listings for overseas opportunities, although it is primarily geared towards UK volunteering.

The Worldwide Volunteering website **www.worldwidevolunteering.org.uk** has 900 volunteering organisations and 250,000 placements in 215 countries including the UK.

Action Without Borders (**www.idealist.org**) lists numerous volunteer opportunities in around 23,000 non-profit and community organisations around the world.

The World Volunteer website (**www.worldvolunteerweb.org**) provides volunteer news and information from all over the world.

The NetAid Online Volunteering service (**www.netaid.org/ov**) is managed by UN Volunteers and has numerous virtual voluntary opportunities to suit a wide range of people including homemakers, retired people, students and professionals.

Voluntary Work Information Service (**www.workingabroad.com**) is an international networking service for volunteers, workers and travellers on volunteer projects in over 150 countries worldwide. The website lists a diverse range of voluntary projects all over the world for all nationalities including thousands of local grassroots organisations in Asia, Africa, Latin America, Europe and North America. It also includes a personalised search where you can key in your details and see what organisations fit your requirements.

Energize links volunteer opportunities worldwide, as well as links to other volunteer opportunity websites. Go to **www.energizeinc.com**.

Evolunteer is a searchable database of volunteer opportunities as well as other volunteer resources. Go to **www.evolunteer.co.uk**.

Oneworld.net lists volunteer opportunities worldwide. Go to **www.oneworld.net/article/frontpage/10/3**.

The website **www.backpackers.com** has a notice board for volunteer work.

For conservation voluntary opportunities around the world, go to the Green Volunteers website: **www.greenvol.com/**.

The US Study Abroad website, **www.studyabroad.com**, runs details of internships and volunteer programmes and has listings for different countries around the world.

OTHER WEBSITES WORTH LOOKING AT ARE:
www.volunteermatch.org (US-based website)
www.ecovolunteer.org (worldwide eco-conservation projects)
www.responsibletravel.com (adventure holidays)
www.gapwork.com (gap-year information and listings)
www.volunteersolutions.org (American website for voluntary opportunities)

NEWSPAPERS
Some national and local newspapers carry vacancies for voluntary work. The most well known is the *Guardian* (Wednesdays) which carries vacancies

for overseas voluntary work. It is also worth keeping an eye open in the travel supplements (the *Guardian*, Saturdays; the *Observer*, Sundays).

A good port of call is also *Overseas Jobs Express*, a fortnightly newspaper with advice, reports and advertised vacancies and available by subscription or in newsagents: PO BOX 22, Brighton, Sussex BN1 6HT, Tel: 01273 699 777.

Home and Away is a monthly expat magazine that runs job vacancies and may carry volunteer opportunities. Write to Expats House, 29 Lacon Road, London SE22 9HE, Tel: 020 8299 4987.

You can also place a Situations Wanted advert in newspapers in the country you are visiting. You can sometimes do this from the UK over the phone or fax, and pay by credit card. Alternatively, you can get an advertising agent to do it for you. Look in the Yellow Pages for agents. *Loot* has an International Jobs Offered/Wanted section and some volunteers find projects by placing adverts in the *Lady*.

EMPLOYMENT AGENCIES

You may be able to find out about overseas volunteer opportunities by contacting the Overseas Placing Unit at your local job centre. These tend to consist of unfilled vacancies on projects run by overseas European Union governments and are often looking for professional people who can speak a foreign language. If there are no suitable vacancies, you should be able to fill in a form ES13 which will keep your details on file until a suitable vacancy arises, when you will be contacted.

You can also check out the the European Employment Services (EURES) website which has details of vacancies throughout the EU and available to all EU/EEA members (**www.europa.eu.int/jobs/eures**). Again, this network is usually more suited to professionals with sought-after skills, and the jobs advertised often require fluency in the language of the country you are targeting.

TRADE PRESS

Keep an eye open in the relevant trade magazine to see if there are any volunteer opportunities in your particular profession. Names and addresses can be found in Benn's Media Directory and Benn's Media Directory International (both of which are usually available at main libraries) or contact the relevant professional bodies or trade unions. Other magazines to check are the *Conserver*, church magazines such as the *Friend* (run by Quakers), and the charity press (see chapter three).

Voluntary Sector, published by NCVO Publications, contains news and information on those working for voluntary agencies. Contact NCVO Publications, Regent's Wharf, 8 All Saints Street, London N1 9RL, Tel: 020 7713 6161.

FUNDRAISING EVENTS

Also keep an eye open for fundraising and sponsorship events advertised in the national media. Many large NGOs are now turning their attention to organising high-profile sponsored treks/marathons and bike rides in a bid to raise money, and some of these include stints doing voluntary work.

CONTACT THE ORGANISATIONS DIRECTLY

Once you have done your research, you can also contact the organisation directly, approaching either the sending agencies or, if you feel you are suitably qualified, one of the large charities. Several of the large NGOs such as Red Cross, Oxfam, Tearfund, Médecins Sans Frontières and Greenpeace have national bodies all over the world and frequently place volunteers. (See the Directory for contact details of all these kinds of organisations.) Many volunteers also find work through contacting charities and NGOs in the country they are hoping to visit. In this case, follow the advice given under 'Indigenous Programmes' about finding a hosting organisation.

VOLUNTEER SCHEMES

Young people aged between 18 and 25 can fix up voluntary work through the European Voluntary Service (EVS), a programme set up by the European Commission to take part in work as a volunteer for six to twelve months for not-for-profit projects abroad. The aim of the EVS is to allow everyone to volunteer without any extra cost, so you don't need to commit any financial resources towards a project. You need to apply through a local sending agency which you can find out about through the EVS website at **www.soforevs.org/introUK.htm**.

The European Commission also organises the YOUTH programme, open to 15- to 25-year-olds in thirty European countries. The scheme offers the possibility for both group exchange and individual voluntary work. In addition it runs schemes for other nationalities including Latin America, South Eastern Europe, Russia and the Ukraine, Mediterranean and Middle East countries. Go to **www.europa.eu.int/comm/youth** for more information or write to 7582748, Bundesverwaltungsamt, 50728 Koln, Germany (for postal enquiries).

The Association of Voluntary Service Organisations (AVSO) is the European platform for not-for-profit organisations active in the field of long- term voluntary work. Although it does not organise voluntary placements itself, it represents more than eighty organisations, most of which recruit volunteers. You can search for projects on its website **www.avso.org**.

The British Council runs a variety of exchange programmes. Its Connect Youth scheme promotes non-formal exchanges of young people between the United Kingdom and other countries. These programmes range from group exchanges to individual voluntary service. Opportunities include European and Bilateral Youth Exchanges, English Language Summer Camps and Language and Culture courses for Youth Workers, as well as placing English language assistants abroad. For more information go to www.britishcouncil.org or write to Connect Youth, British Council, 10 Spring Gardens, London SW1A 2BN, Tel: 020 7389 4030, Fax: 020 7389 4033. For information on developing exchanges with Commonwealth countries, contact Commonwealth Youth Exchange Council, 7 Lion Yard, Tremadoc Road, London SW4 7NF, Tel: 020 7498 6151, Fax: 020 7720 5403.

The European Diaconal Year Network organise Diaconal Year programmes in Austria, Belgium, Denmark, France, Germany, the Netherlands, Sweden and the United Kingdom. About 3,000 young people volunteer for ten to twelve months of service each year. Their placements are in children's homes, centres for persons with physical and learning disabilities, hospitals, social projects (drugs, homeless, refugees) and parish work. For more information go to www.timeforgod.org/edyn.htm.

VOLUNTEER DIRECTORIES

With the growth in interest in volunteering, it's not surprising that there are plenty of good publications listing volunteering opportunities. The following publications are particularly useful:

The Green Travel Guide: Greg Neale and Trish Nicholson (Earthscan Publications).

Working with the Environment (2nd Edition): Tim Ryder and Elisabeth Roberts (Vacation Work Publications).

International Voluntary Work (2003, 8th edition): Victoria Pybuss (Vacation Work).

Worldwide Volunteering for Young People (3rd edition): Roger Potter (How To Books).

World Volunteers: The World Guide to Humanitarian and Development Volunteering (Green Volunteers Publications).

The WSE have published a 2004 Guide containing advice about volunteering and working overseas for development. It also lists relevant agencies to contact if you are seeking a gap-year or short-term voluntary placement in the UK or overseas. Contact the World Service Enquiry, 233 Bon Marché Centre, 241–251 Ferndale Road, London SW9 8BJ, Tel: 0870 770 3274, Fax: 0870 770 7991.

FINDING WORK THERE

As always, the key to finding volunteer projects abroad is to speak to people and keep a watchful eye open for opportunities. Although it can be tricky travelling without the support of a reputable organisation, some experienced volunteers say that, with a little effort, you can find voluntary opportunities more easily than you think. Twenty-year-old Clare Lewis has volunteered extensively in Romania, India and Peru, both through organisations and independently. Her advice is to volunteer through a reputable organisation first but, after that, try venturing out alone. She says, 'Your first time volunteering can be very scary so it's nice to have the backup of a good organisation, especially if things go wrong. After that, however, you can fix it up on your own. It's easier to find voluntary work than you think – a lot of it is about asking the locals and just getting out there and doing it. You don't realise but there are loads to do – when I was teaching in India it was easy to go into schools and ask if they wanted help. We did it one day in a remote rural village, just talking to the children and playing games with them. In Peru, one school offered to give me free Spanish lessons if I taught some classes.'

Another thing to bear in mind is that volunteering on one project may well lead to another. Iain Hook taught maths, biology and sports in a secondary school in Kingston, Jamaica. Although he originally fixed up work through the voluntary organisation Global Action, after the year was complete, he stayed for another two years in a post the school had specifically created for him.

The most important thing is to give things the chance to happen by cultivating the right attitude. Like how?

- **Do your research.** Check out the volunteer situation thoroughly before you arrive. Have a good idea of what volunteer infrastructure exists and take a list of all the relevant brokerages and organisations. Also check out the weather, geography and transport situation.

- **Make sure you speak some of the language.** This is essential if you are turning up on spec hoping to find voluntary work. Why? Chances are the information isn't going to fall into your lap easily. You will need to read the local literature, listen to the radio, keep your wits about you and, most importantly, speak to people.

- **Make contacts in your target country before you leave.** Friends overseas can be a lifeline when you are travelling. Not only can they take you to the right bars, the right libraries and introduce you to the right people, but they can also help translate anything you don't understand and use their networks to hunt out local information.

- **Tell everyone you know about your plans before you leave.** You never know, your colleague or neighbour could know someone in Sweden who could have exactly the right kind of information you want.

THE JOB SEARCH

CONTACT THE ORGANISATIONS DIRECTLY
One of the easiest ways to find projects overseas is to take a list of volunteer agencies to contact once you are there. In some cases it can work in your favour to meet the organisation in person first. Make sure you have a copy of your CV, references and some well-prepared answers about what you think you have to offer the scheme. You will obviously be in a much stronger position if you are easy to get hold of, so take a mobile phone or a hostel address where you can be contacted should a vacancy arise.

NEWSPAPERS

Keep an eye open in the local and national press, where vacancies may be advertised. Many libraries stock a range of foreign newspapers, while many UK embassies and consulates have reading rooms where you can read a selection of papers.

WORD OF MOUTH

Speak to everyone you meet and make a point of asking around for community projects. This is the fastest way to find out what is going on in your local area. Staying in hostels is obviously going to increase your chances of meeting people who can put you in touch with other people who can point you in the right direction.

EMPLOYMENT AGENCIES

Some state employment agencies may carry details of volunteer projects. However, most vacancies that exist will be suitable only for people who speak the national language and may require professional experience and qualifications.

LEG WORK

In some circumstances it pays to simply turn up in person and ask whether there are any opportunities for volunteers. This is often the way to offer help in orphanages in Romania or India, for example. Make sure you take your passport to show, a copy of your CV and any references. In circumstances where you will be working with children, the authorities will have to check for a criminal record before offering you work.

TOURIST OFFICES

Some volunteers spot adverts placed in tourist offices. Other good places to head for include libraries, university notice boards, English-speaking bars and bookshops.

VOLUNTEER BROKERAGES

Most European countries, the US, Canada and Australia have a well-established network of volunteer brokerages that match people to voluntary schemes. While they may not organise projects of their own, they may well put you in touch with voluntary organisations that are looking for help. You can find the addresses for these voluntary service bureaux from the embassies, although many are listed in this guide. As always, you are more likely to strike lucky if you can speak at least some of the language of the country you are visiting.

VOLUNTEERS' STORIES

Charlotte Duck writes about her six weeks in the remote Alaskan wilderness.
'This year I decided to swap the luxury of a sun-sea-sand holiday for six weeks
in the White Mountains wilderness, 120 miles north of Fairbanks, Alaska. I was
taking part in scientific projects for the American Bureau of Land Management
(through BSES Expeditions), undertaking limestone cave surveys and fish
inventories. However the trip threw up more adventures than we could ever have
possibly imagined.

'After several nauseating journeys on buses, we finally arrived at base camp,
where we had scientific inductions as well as learning wilderness survival
techniques, including how to prevent bear attacks. For the next two weeks we
spent our time rafting and then walking back to base camp over the remote
White Mountains. Every morning we got up, had breakfast and then psyched
ourselves up for wading into the freezing cold water in our sandals to get to our
rafts. The rafting was difficult upstream as the creek sometimes flowed very
swiftly, and sporadically threw out a series of rapids for us to conquer. During
the rafting adventure I was able to appreciate the staggering scenery. Conifers
and mountains, all completely undisturbed by human influence, surrounded the
creek and, as we continued downstream, the scenery became more spectacular
with craggy ridges shadowing us. It was amazing to think that we shared our
lives with all the other animals in that area, in particular the beavers who were
our bathing companions when we were brave enough to wash in the icy cold
water.

'We had a few days' break from rafting to explore the limestone caves at
Limestone Gulch. We camped on a ridge, which gave us the most tremendous
view that served to remind me of how small I am in the grand plan of things.
This particular area was great for supplementing my food rations as it provided
blueberries and cloudberries. This food supplement was much welcomed, as
you can imagine, due to our normal diet consisting of porridge for breakfast, dry
crackers with Spam (yuck!) for lunch and dehydrated meals for dinner. Each
week, we have seven days' food rations issued to us and inevitably a swapping
frenzy ensues. Food, and in particular sweets, had replaced currency for us out
here, and a definite snack hierarchy resulted, with Twix the most valuable and
granola bars the least.

'On our penultimate day of rafting we saw a bear. On the horizon it appeared as a
dark spot and every now and again he would come towards us, before backing
off again and eventually disappearing behind some trees. The sky at night in
Alaska was something that I will never forget. It was so clear due the fact that
we were far away from civilisation and there was no light pollution. We saw
hundreds of stars including the Big and Little Dipper, as well as shooting stars.
The sunrises and sunsets were also among the most beautiful I have ever seen –
blood red with pinky clouds.

'A week later I found myself back in my bedroom, with the novelty of normal life
wearing off, and dreaming of the Alaskan wilderness. I wake up and my first
thoughts are of confusion as I wonder where my tent companions are. It takes a
few moments for me to realise that I am alone in my bed at home with even less
time to start thinking about going again!'

7. PREPARING TO GO

So, you've decided what to do and now you're ready for the adventure of a lifetime. Before you jump in, however, take time to do a little preliminary preparation. Here's everything you need to know:

VISAS AND WORK PERMITS

One of the first things you will have to check is whether you need a visa/work permit. Unfortunately, finding this information isn't easy. By far the most straightforward route is to undertake voluntary work through an organisation that nine times out of ten will organise the work permit/visa situation for you. For those of you who are attempting to find work as you go, be prepared for a long slog in trying to make yourself understood. In the course of researching this book, I have sent and replied to countless emails explaining as patiently as I can that, yes, I know the law regarding visas for paid work, but not for working voluntarily. The situation seems to be made doubly complicated by the fact that some countries don't call unpaid work 'volunteering'. Despite having a long-standing tradition of altruistic community work that would put many of us Westerners to shame, it seems working voluntarily in many countries doesn't come with a label. Therefore, finding out the exact visa requirements can be a complicated, laborious process. All of this isn't to put you off – the fact is that plenty of people do volunteer overseas every year and manage to find their way through the labyrinth of visa regulations.

Besides, the general rule is that the same rules that apply to paid employment apply for voluntary work. Basically, if you need a work permit/residence permit to work legally in a country, you will need the same documentation and conditions to undertake voluntary work. This isn't always the case – the UK, for example, has separate regulations regarding unpaid volunteering – but it's a useful assumption to make to save yourself from landing in any uncomfortable situations. As always, make sure you do your research. Visa regulations have a habit of quickly changing so make sure you get the most up-to-date information before flying out. If your particular country demands that you obtain your permit before entering the country, apply for your permit well in advance as some applications can take up to six weeks to process. At the risk of stating the obvious, bear in mind that visa rules vary widely from country to country. Some countries may require you to have fixed up work before you arrive and require a long raft of documentation. Many will require evidence of sufficient funds (often £2,000) and proof you intend to leave in the form of a return ticket.

Cunning travellers, of course, have long been known to practise a little resourcefulness and imagination. Need to show proof of funds? Ask a friend to deposit a couple of grand in your bank account, photocopy the proof and pay him back later. Need a job before you arrive, although you want to work voluntarily? If you have contacts in your target country, ask them to help you fix up work before you arrive so you can find an initial entry into a tightly regulated country. Once you're there, you may be able to drop the work and fix something else up instead.

Given the unofficial nature of volunteering, it is, of course, quite easy to undertake voluntary work on a tourist visa. This sounds harmless enough – and in many countries it is – but do be aware that in some countries working without the necessary permit can carry some harsh penalties. In America, for example, it can lead to hefty fines and even deportation.

FINDING VISA INFORMATION

The good news is that many embassies and consulates now have websites where you can download documents and find the necessary information. The Embassy World website, **www.embassyworld.com**, has a database of worldwide embassy contacts. You can also try the country's government's websites, some of which carry useful information.

The World Travel Guide website (**www.travel-guides.com**) carries country-by-country information including visa requirements.

The website for the UK's Foreign Office (**www.fco.gov.uk/travel**) lists visa requirements for many countries, as does the private visa agency Thames Consular (**www.thamesconsular.com**).

There are also many online agencies that, for a price, offer to arrange your visa for you. However, going through the consulate might still be the best (and cheapest) option. Try **www.visaservice.co.uk**, a commercial site that can obtain visas for companies or individual travellers. For work permits in the UK, USA and some European countries, try **www.visa-free.com**.

INSURANCE

Swept away by the excitement of planning your overseas escapade, the last thing you want to do is sit down and talk insurance. I don't blame you, but the fact is that with the best will in the world accidents can happen. You may fall ill; you may get mugged; your passport or bags or travellers' cheques may be stolen. According to the Foreign Office, out of the 53 million overseas trips British nationals make each year, as many as one in seven of them fail to take out adequate travel insurance. Many live to regret it. Make sure you don't.

Of course, accidents are more likely to happen if you are living three hundred miles from the nearest hospital, living in communal tents in the Australian rainforest, drinking out of drums filled with rain water, building villages in a malaria/cholera endemic area or travelling through a high-risk country. All of this isn't to scare you – all the large NGOs and the smaller responsible ones will have strict guidelines in place to protect you from accidents and will have evacuation procedures in place if things turn nasty. They should also provide medical insurance and training, and you'd be well advised to check this thoroughly before committing yourself to any organisation. However, regardless of whether you are volunteering in a group or travelling solo, you should still take out your own travel medical insurance. Why? Volunteering of all kinds could introduce you to some pretty testing situations which carry more risks than normal 'travelling'.

VOLUNTEERS' STORIES

Ellie Sandercock had to be repatriated back to the UK after she was injured in a car crash in Nigeria. On the flight back, the nurse told her that, had she not been insured, the journey would have cost her between £30,000 and £50,000. Ellie was working as a VSO volunteer at the time. 'I was travelling in a bush taxi three hours from the capital of Nigeria, when the car skidded off the road after the tyre blew out. There were no seat belts so I was thrown through the window and fractured three of my vertebrae.

'It took 24 hours to get to a hospital with X-ray facilities. The local hospital had no equipment and, as there weren't any phones working in the town, we had to send a handwritten note via a driver to the capital city, Abuja, where the VSO office was based. They then came and picked me up and, the next morning, took me to the national hospital.'

Although the next hospital had a higher standard of equipment, Ellie still had to wait hours to get an X-ray. 'In Nigeria the patients' families are expected to take care of food, clothes and washing as the hospital don't provide it. I was very relieved that VSO took it on themselves to become my surrogate family for the week.'

Seven days later, Ellie was flown back to the UK on a stretcher, on a standard BA flight. It was six months before she had fully recovered. She says: 'Anyone who goes travelling without proper insurance needs their head examined.'

THE E111 FORM

For EU members travelling in Europe, the first thing to do is get hold of the E111 form. This certificate entitles EEA members to urgent medical treatment in the European Economic Area (EEA) and can be obtained from the post office, where it has to be stamped in order to be valid, or from the Department of Health. The free booklet 'Health Advice for Travellers' contains an E111 form. Call 0800 555 777 or look on **www.doh.gov.uk**.

Keep it safe, preferably with your passport and carry it with you while travelling in the EEA area. Bear in mind that, even with the correct E111 form, you still have to pay for the treatments and then claim back the costs later. Remember, too, that E111 form does not include repatriation.

There are a number of other countries that have reciprocal healthcare arrangements with the UK, which are not dependent on possession of an E111. These are Anguilla, Australia, Barbados, British Virgin Islands, Bulgaria, Channel Islands, Czech Republic, Falkland Islands, Hungary, Isle of Man, Malta, Montserrat, New Zealand, Poland, Romania, Russia,

Slovakia, St Helena, Turks and Caicos Islands, NIS (except Latvia, Lithuania and Estonia) and Yugoslavia.

There are one hundred other countries, including popular travel destinations such as the US and Canada, that have no healthcare agreements with the UK. It is therefore vital that you have adequate medical insurance cover.

THE E111 AND WORKING ABROAD

The most important thing to bear in mind is that the E11 form does not cover you if you are living permanently in a foreign country, or taking up work there. However, if you are working temporarily abroad and it has been confirmed by the Inland Revenue National Insurance Contributions Office that you (and your employer) continue to pay UK national insurance contributions, you are entitled to Form 128.

Students working abroad as part of their UK studies may be entitled to Form 128 – contact the Inland Revenue for details.

GETTING THE BEST INSURANCE DEAL

Whatever your circumstances, it's best not to rely on the E111 form, if only because it doesn't include the cost of repatriation. The first thing, then, is to get some comprehensive insurance cover, which should include the following things:

Personal liability, for injury or damage to others and their property

Cancellation, if you have to cancel or abandon your trip, to start as soon as you book your trip

24-hour emergency service and assistance

Possessions cover, including money and documents to a specified amount

It can also cover personal accident (money paid on death or permanent disability) and legal expenses (to help you pursue compensation for damages following personal injury)

Shop around. There are hundreds of travel insurance policies out there so take it slowly and make sure you have thought carefully about the cover you need. Bear in mind that the cheaper policy isn't always the best option as it might not offer the cover you need. Don't feel you have to buy insurance from a travel agent when you buy a flight ticket, no matter how much they pressure you, as you may well be able to get a better deal elsewhere. There are also certain companies that specialise in offering policies to cover working abroad and many backpacker policies specifically cover casual work. The government's Insurance & Assistance Partners Page (**www.fco.gov.uk/servlet/Front**) has links to insurers while there are also websites that will search to find you the best deal. Try **www.easycover.com** and **www.1stoptravelinsurance.co.uk**.

Make sure you have good medical cover. A good standard of medical cover should include any medical bills and repatriation, which means an air ambulance service to fly you home. Repatriation cover is crucial as being flown home can cost thousands of pounds, ranging from £300 for a scheduled flight from the Mediterranean to £35,000 for an air ambulance out of North America.

Check you know what your policy covers. Make sure you get a deal that covers everything you want to do. Some policies exclude 'dangerous activities', for example, so if you have a passion for extreme sports then make sure it's covered in your policy. It is also crucial to check you are covered for the whole period you are away and the countries you are going to. If you are not sure how long you intend to stay away, find a policy that allows you to extend it to cover the additional time you are away. If you are away for a full year, there are certain companies who specialise in annual travel insurance.

Be honest in your application. Most insurance application forms require information on any pre-existing medical conditions. If this applies to you, be honest about your health, otherwise it might invalidate a medical claim.

Read the small print. Be alert for any extenuating clauses and conditions. Some policies may guarantee free cover which may not prove adequate if you run into any difficulties. Others may have clauses which exclude certain countries and activities. Some policies may exclude manual work and/or refuse to give out money if you were working at the time when the accident happened.

Take the right documentation. Wherever you go, make sure you take your policy and the 24-hour emergency phone number. If anything does go wrong, keep as much paperwork as possible, such as police report, tickets, receipts and medical bills etc., to help prove that what you're claiming for actually happened. Even then, you may not be entitled to as much as you think, as insurers rarely give out anything like full compensation.

FLIGHTS

Once you've obtained the appropriate visa, it's time to put your money where your mouth is – and book a flight. Buying a ticket is usually the first tangible proof that your trip is going to happen so you may be tempted to rush right in and buy the first exotic-sounding ticket you find. Don't. There's a huge range of choice out there, so take it slowly and make sure you shop around.

WHICH TYPE OF FLIGHT IS RIGHT FOR YOU?
The first thing you will have to decide is what kind of ticket you want, depending on your particular circumstances. If you're volunteering through an organisation, chances are that they may arrange a flight for you,

although many deals now come with flights excluded from the overall price. Otherwise you will have to buy the flight yourself, which, given all the choice, can be a bewildering experience. Here are some points to bear in mind:

- **If you are heading for one destination for a set period and know when you are due to leave, you may want to book a return flight. Open returns are a particularly favourite as they guarantee a fully paid-up return but give you the flexibility of choosing when you leave.**

- **Split tickets, which go via another destination, and often with two airlines, are also a good deal and can be cheaper than booking a straight direct flight.**

- **Single flights are only a good idea if you are certain you can fix up paid work when you arrive, and even then can be a risky option.**

- **If you're intending to incorporate your volunteering project into a wider globetrotting stint, as many people do, round-the-world tickets offer the luxury of stopping off at a number of destinations for the price of around £700 to £1,500. They can also serve as proof in obtaining a visa that you are planning to leave the country and give you the impetus to take in a number of countries while you are there. Some airlines also operate free loyalty schemes whereby round-the-world trips can earn enough points or air miles to grant you another free ticket.**

FINDING THE BEST FLIGHTS

Luckily, in this age of the global traveller, there are plenty of resources to help travellers make the best, most informed decision. Many guidebooks, newspaper travel sections and tourist-board websites will include practical advice on the best way of getting there, but don't neglect your trusty travel agent. Approached at the right time – say, at the least busy time of the day, such as early morning or late afternoon – and buttered up with a polite and friendly phone call, some travel agents may be in a more relaxed frame of mind and willing to divulge the insider knowledge they don't otherwise volunteer. They may also be in a position to haggle with the airline company. If you can't get the price you want, consider changing your departure date or time – sometimes leaving on an earlier or later flight can save you some pennies. Also, be aware that flying on a weekday is often cheaper than travelling at the weekend.

Once you have some quotes, make a note of them and then phone around other agents to compare. Once you've found the best flight, don't be afraid to pounce, but do make sure that the travel agent is registered with the Association of British Travel Agents (**www.abta.com**).

TIPS ON GETTING THE BEST DEALS

Do your research. Once you have decided on your budget and destination, do your homework in the guidebooks, newspaper travel sections and tourist-board websites to find the best way of getting there

Take time to shop around. Bear in mind that, on any one flight, the chances are that the passengers will have paid a variety of prices.

Use the Internet. The web is teeming with good resources for the cost-conscious traveller, from travel newsgroups where you can find out about the best deals to the numerous fare-comparison websites (**www.expedia.co.uk** or **www.travelocity.co.uk**). The website **www.priceline.co.uk** allows you to offer your own price for flights to airlines. If you are buying over the web, make sure the flight is covered by Air Travel Organisers' Licensing (Atol) (**www.atol.org.uk**).

Try contacting the airlines directly. Cutting out the travel agent can sometimes save you money and introduce you to deals you might otherwise not hear about. The travel section of the *Guardian* website also has a useful section where you can find out which airlines fly to which destinations – visit **www.guardian.co.uk/travel/cheapflights**.

Book your flight well in advance of your departure date. Airlines sell only a limited number of seats at the lowest fares so, when those sell out, the price goes up. Many discount fares require that you make a reservation 7, 14 or 21 days before your trip depending on the fare, with some even requiring a reservation 30 days in advance.

Be flexible about flight times. You can dramatically alter the price of your flight by choosing a cheaper time to go. Avoid flying out at the weekend, and instead go for mid-week. If you can't find the price you want, ask your travel agent if flying on an early or later time will make a significant saving.

Consider couriering. If you're really strapped for cash, couriering items for businesses can cover the cost of a flight, or at least some of it. Check out the International Association of Air Travel (0800 074 6481, **www.aircourier.co.uk**) and Air Courier Association (00 1 303 279 3600, **www.aircourier.org**) for more information.

DISCOUNT FLIGHT AGENCIES

Thanks to the rise of the low-cost flight, there's never been a better time to swap your hard-earned pennies for a really good deal. If you're travelling long haul, it's worth going to a specialist. Here is just a small selection:

Cheap Flights (**www.cheapflights.co.uk**) is an online service that lists the day's cheapest flights available from subscribing UK flight agents.

North South Travel, Moulsham Mill, Parkway, Chelmsford, Essex CM2 7PX (Tel: 01245 608 291) is a small travel agency which offers discount fares worldwide and uses all available profit to support projects in the developing world.

Flightbookers, 177–178 Tottenham Court Road, London W1 (Tel: 020 7757 2444) or Gatwick Airport, South Terminal (Tel: 0870 8888881 – 01293

568300, **www.flightbookers.co.uk**) offers low fares on a good selection of scheduled flights.

STA Travel are worldwide specialists in low-cost flights for students and under-26s (but other customers are welcome) and has branches in London, Leeds, Bristol, Newcastle, Manchester, Liverpool, Oxford, Edinburgh, Glasgow and Aberdeen and on many university campuses. It also has two hundred offices abroad. Check out **www.statravel.co.uk** for more details.

Trailfinders, 194 Kensington High Street, London W8, Tel: 020 7938 3939; 48 Earl's Court Road, London W8, Tel: 020 7938 3366; 1 Threadneedle Street, London EC2, Tel: 020 7628 7628; 58 Deansgate, Manchester, Tel: 0161 839 6969; 254–284 Sauciehall Street, Glasgow, Tel: 0141 353 2224; 22–24 The Priory Queensway, Birmingham, Tel: 0121 236 1234; 48 Corn Street, Bristol, Tel: 0117 929 9000; 4–5 Dawson Street, Dublin 2, Tel: 01 677 7888, **www.trailfinders.co.uk**.

Bridge the World, 47 Chalk Farm Road, London NW1, Tel: 020 7911 0900, **www.bridgetheworld.com**.

FINANCES

All this volunteering can be an expensive business. For one thing there's the fact that you will (mostly) be working for free, and then there's also the chance that you will have to pay for the experience. This is particularly true for voluntary projects that cross over into adventure holidays. Some of these can cost around two thousand pounds excluding flights. Other projects, such as European workcamps, are a significantly cheaper option but may still require an outlay of a few hundred pounds.

The other consideration is that, depending on how long you go away for, you may have to give up your job and prepare for a period of unemployment before and after your trip. This is true for medium-term volunteering where you will be away for three to six months and may have to give up your job, which can put extra financial pressure on you. By far the most radical step, however, is long-term volunteering, where you may be away for a minimum of two years. This type of volunteering is a total lifestyle change, although VSO does provide a basic allowance and grants, including a lump sum once you return (depending on how long you have volunteered with them).

HOW MUCH MONEY WILL YOU NEED?

All of this is to say that volunteering overseas may require some pretty shrewd financial management. The amount of money you will need, of course, depends on where you are going, how long for and the structure of the particular type of project you are volunteering with. Some organisations include board, accommodation, travel costs including flights, with even spending money thrown in. Some may even pay out a basic subsistence allowance every week, while others may ask you to contribute to a kitty. Then there are the other examples: the smaller, indigenous NGOs which require only that you save up enough money to get over there and fund all costs yourself.

Basically, if you are landing in a foreign country with no work lined up and intending to work for free, you are going to need a comfortable sum to tide you over. The bottom line is that volunteering requires some really strategic financial planning. Whatever you hope to do, and wherever you hope to go, the fact is you will have to drum up a little money first. Most travelling advice recommends people allow around £20 a day, but this can vary widely from country to country. Volunteering in Scandinavia, for example, is obviously going to require a hugely different budget than working in Thailand. It also doesn't take into account the different perks that come with various projects, such as free board and food. It is also highly recommended that you take some emergency funds to fall back on in a crisis. This can often take the form of credit cards, although a bit of extra loose currency is also a good safety precaution.

Here are some budgeting considerations to take into account:

- **How flexible do you want to be? Are you going solely for the duration of the project, or do you intend to use the opportunity to see some of the country? How much travelling do you intend to do? If you do intend to move around, do you know the costs of travel and accommodation?**

- **How do you intend to travel to the project? Is the cost of this included in the overall sending-agency fee?**

- **If you intend to find paid work abroad to partly finance your trip, do you have a good idea of how easy or difficult it will be in the country you are visiting? Have you thoroughly researched the employment situation?**

- **What costs does the voluntary project include? Will you need extra money for food and board? Will you have to sort out your own accommodation? If so, will you need to put down a deposit on an apartment? How much on average are hotels/hostels?**

FUNDING

Some entrepreneurial volunteers manage to fund their trips by their own fundraising activities. The website for Gap Activity Projects (**www.gap.org.uk**) has some great examples of people who have raised money this way. You could also just opt for the hard slog. Alison Neighbour from Chepstow says raising the funds to go on her volunteering trip to Massachusetts was perhaps the hardest part. 'But,' she says, 'I was determined to do it all by myself with no help from my parents. I worked full-time in a shop for six months, doing sixty-hour weeks in the busy Christmas period, and also wrote a weekly column for a local newspaper. In total I managed to raise nearly £5,000, and I even have a little bit left for university!'

SAVING MONEY

The golden rule to saving money is to think a little, often. Bear in mind that £1,000 is only 50 lots of £20, which sounds much more manageable. Of course, like anything in life, you might have to make adjustments in order to reach your target. Like what? Like cutting back on those extravagant nights out, doing without the latest clothes and forgoing any trips down Bond Street.

Here are some strategies that could help:

- **Could you take a sabbatical? Could you persuade your employers that it is in their interests to give you time to do this project? Could you arrange fundraising events or organise sponsorship?**

- **Do you own property? If so, could you borrow money against your mortgage? Or remortgage your property at a higher level and then use the money to fund your volunteering trip? Borrowing £5,000, for example, could only work out as an extra £30 per month on a 25-year mortgage. Does your mortgage allow you to take payment holidays? If not, could you swap it for a more flexible arrangement? Maybe you could rent out your property for the period you are away? Do you have any friends who could do some house-sitting? You could offer them reduced rent if necessary.**

- **Is it possible to move back home with your parents? Even if you still have to pay money towards your keep, the amount you save in bills and council tax could make a serious difference to the amount you could save every month.**

- **If you are renting, could you share a double room with a partner? Could you move to a cheaper area?**

EXPENSE SHEET

Flight tickets

Travel and medical insurance

Visa

Vaccinations

Living costs

Special clothes

Equipment

Transport

Emergency money

WHAT KIND OF MONEY SHOULD I TAKE?

Many volunteering projects take place in remote areas where banks and money exchanges may be hard to find. It makes sense, then, to give some serious thought to what form of money to take. As always, there is no one right way. Travellers' cheques, for example, are much safer than hard currency as they come with a guarantee and require a signature (i.e. yours) to change in the first place. They are also a handy option if you are travelling to countries such as China where the movement of currencies between countries is restricted. (You can find out which ones by asking at banks.) In these situations you can only change your money into the local currency once you have landed.

That's all very well, you say, but what if you're stuck in the most northerly far-flung reaches of Greenland where banks where banks and money exchanges are a little thin on the ground? Quite. Which is why it takes some thinking about. The other point about travellers' cheques is that, each time you cash them, the banks tend to take upwards of one per cent commission which can take a sizeable lump out of your budget. If you do take them, make sure you keep the carbon copy separate from the serial numbers in case they get stolen, and leave someone trusted back at home a copy of the serial numbers.

EMERGENCY MONEY

One of the kindest things you can do for yourself is allow yourself the option of dipping into emergency funds. Extra money can make all the difference in times of crisis, which, yes, do happen sometimes and, even if you don't use it, having the money available can be worth it just for the extra peace of mind. One of the easiest ways to cushion yourself is to take a credit card with a sizeable limit. Many cards also come with travel and personal accident insurance cover and 24-hour emergency assistance.

Another option is to keep some emergency funds in a bank account at home and leave a trusted friend written permission to draw on the account, should you require. Make sure you notify the bank before you leave. Then, should an emergency arise, your friend can draw out some funds and send it you by transfer. Transferring money is easy to do in most major towns and cities, providing you have ID. Look out for Western Union and Money Gram agents or you can ask at your local bank, where you may have to pay a charge.

WHAT TO TAKE WITH YOU

Many voluntary organisations will issue you with a list of essential items to take. What this will include will, of course, depend on where you are going, how long for, what the climate is like and what work you will be doing. Make sure you know exactly what kind of work you will be doing and if there are any special tools you need to bring yourself. If you are doing conservation work in a hot climate you might need sun hat, sun screen, gloves, ointment for cuts and work boots, for example.

For those adventurous souls who intend to find voluntary work when you arrive, it can be useful to be prepared for anything. In these situations backpacking equipment, such as a tent, sleeping bag, torch and first aid kit, will mean you are ready to take advantage of any opportunities that arise. That said, don't think you have to take everything you need all in one go, particularly if you are intending to travel to a variety of places. If, for example, you are moving from a cold to a hot location, you can always have your clothes sent ahead of you to a *poste restante*. You can also mail clothes back home after you've finished, if you don't think you will need them again. Special equipment such as diving and camping gear can be rented out, instead of lugged along.

CLOTHES

This shouldn't need to be said, but do take time to think carefully about the climate you will be living in. I know a few people who arrive in their chosen country only to find the weather is completely different from what they expected and they have to buy a whole new wardrobe. Remember, too, that there can be huge regional variations in temperatures and climates, so make sure that you look up the weather in guide books or on the Internet for the exact region you will be visiting. Bear in mind that the same place can have vastly different climates from winter to summer.

DO TAKE

T-shirts and tops. Worn in layers these provide the same warmth as a sweater but take up much less room and are very versatile if you are moving from a hot to a cold climate.

Thick warm socks – warm, snug and good for hiking and sore feet. The sartorial equivalent of comfort food.

Fleece jackets – both warm and light, and make comfortable pillows.

Loose, baggy clothing in light colours and lightweight fabrics is cooling in warm climates and good for protecting yourself from mosquitoes. Cotton and linen clothes allow the skin to breathe and don't irritate the skin like artificial fabrics such as nylon and Lycra.

Long-sleeved tops, long trousers and skirts – to cover the whole body when entering temples etc. in Muslim countries.

Waterproofs – transparent macs or ponchos can be folded away into small packs so they hardly take up room.

Comfortable, practical shoes. Think carefully about the work you will be doing and what kind of shoes it will require. Remember, too, that you could be wearing these shoes for a very long time so make sure they are comfortable. Sandals (particularly Tevas) are the favourite shoes for backpacking. Trainers are good but can get very smelly, while flip-flops are ideal for beach living and hot climates. Take a few pairs, but bear in mind that shoes can be very heavy and take up vital room.

A sarong – good for covering you up in Muslim countries and handy for the beach.

AVOID
Expensive designer clothes. Not only could they be mislaid in transit by airlines, but they are also more likely to deteriorate in a sweaty rucksack.

New shoes that are likely to cause you discomfort and pain. Whatever shoes you take, make sure they have been broken in first.

Skimpy clothes in Muslim countries – remember that dressing like Demi Moore is likely to offend in some countries, as is topless sunbathing (both sexes included).

RUCKSACKS
If you are backpacking around, one of the best things you can do is kit yourself out with a good rucksack. Priced from £50 to £150, a good rucksack should last you for years and be like a trusty, old friend – comfortable, supportive and *very* enduring. For the best sacks, opt for the quality brands, such as Karrimor, Berghaus, Lowe Alpine, Kathmandu and the New Zealand brand Mac Pac. Most backpacks come in two basic models: the hiking pack, which loads from the top, sits well on the back and is the standard fare of most backpackers; but far the handiest model is the second option, the travel bag or sack, which is perfect if you are moving from an urban to a rural area. By zipping the back system away and thus removing all straps and dangly bits, you can transform your lumpy, unwieldy backpack to a smart, cosmopolitan suitcase, which is ideal if you are living in a variety of locations.

Here are some other points to bear in mind when choosing a rucksack.

- **Make sure the rucksack is a manageable size. Yes, you want it to be roomy, but not so bulky it is too cumbersome to carry. Generally, there are two schools of thought about size: the first favours a large rucksack, half-filled, to give you plenty of room to fill it with items when you return. The other system plumps for the leaner, more manageable versions. By buying small, they reason, you are forced to travel light.**

- **Make sure it has an adjustable back system so you can change the position of the shoulder straps to suit your frame.**

- **If you intend to carry heavy loads, the hip belt should be thickly padded. This will take the strain off your shoulders and back and channel most of the weight down to your hips and legs. The waistband should also be hard and stiff.**

- **The backpack should have strong stitching and be made from heavy-duty waterproof material, such as ripstop, to prevent rips developing into holes.**

- **Don't automatically go for the cheapest model. The more expensive brands come with hardwearing features such as fully adjustable** straps and made from hardwearing material and are more likely to last for a long time.

- Pack your rucksack so the weight is evenly distributed and doesn't pull too much on your back and weigh you down.

- Place toiletries and lotions in waterproof sealable bags to guard against spillages. Do the same for important documents.

- Make sure your pack is extra waterproof by buying a special rucksack liner or use a dustbin liner.

- Secure your rucksack by attaching small padlocks to double zips on the pockets and lid. They can also be used to secure to luggage racks on overnight trains and buses.

- Attach a tag to your rucksack with your name on it. You can also stick an address label inside a side pocket.

DOCUMENTS

Taking the right documentation can make all the difference between extending your stay in a country and being booted out the moment you arrive. That may sound extreme but, believe me, it happens. Having the necessary paperwork is also important if you are unlucky enough to fall victim to crime, such as having your travellers' cheques stolen, and you need to make an insurance claim. Make sure then that you take all the necessary documents with you, and understand the bureaucracy rules so you can provide whatever proof they demand. Other documents to take include international driver's licence, student card and international youth hostel card (if applicable) and eight passport-sized photos for visas, residence permits and travel passes.

- Take a day bag and money belt or bum bag. A money belt is one of the most essential things you can buy and will keep all your important documents together. Wear it under clothes, strapped around your waist, and try not to use it to store petty cash or anything that you will need to access every five minutes. Use it to keep important documents such as passport, airline tickets, travellers' cheques, credit card and insurance policy.

- Make two photocopies of each document. Leave one set of photocopies at home with friends or relatives, who can fax/email them on to you in case of emergency. Take the other photocopies with you but keep in a separate place from the originals.

- Make a record of information such as credit card numbers, travellers' cheques serial numbers and passport details and email to your email address. If you need to access this information, you can always pick it up at any cyber café in the world. You can even scan in your documents and email them to yourself, or use the Lonely Planet's ekno service (www.lonelyplanet.com), which allows you to store important information online.

ESSENTIALS CHECK LIST

DOCUMENTS
Passport

Air and rail tickets

Visas

Travellers' cheques

Sterling or dollars

Foreign currency

Insurance certificate

ID cards

IYHA membership card

Spare passport photographs

Photocopies of all your important documents

International driver's licence

Details of accommodation and voluntary project's addresses

Contact details for agency in the country/manager/emergency contact

Maps

Vaccination certificates

TOILETRIES
Shaving oil and razors

Tampons and sanitary towels – make sure you're stocked up so aren't caught out short in remote areas. In developing countries they can be very expensive

Glasses or contact lens gear

Towels

Toothpaste and toothbrush

Sarong

Lip salve

Moisturiser

HEALTH
Anti-diarrhoea medicine and other relevant pills, e.g. anti-malaria and bilharzia pills depending on where you are going (see Health section)

Rehydration sachets to restore your body after a bout of diarrhoea

Sun cream – protection and after sun

Calamine lotion

Iodine – to make water safe to drink and sterilise wounds

Sting relief cream

Sterilised needle kit

DEET-based insect repellent

Mosquito net

Existing medication

Small scissors

Painkillers

Bandages

Plasters

Antiseptic cream

E45 cream

Safety pins, gauze and bandage tape

Condoms

Other contraception – if you are on the pill, make sure you have enough pills to last for the period you're away

USEFUL ITEMS

Batteries

Padlock and chain

Knife and fork

Sewing kit

Swiss Army knife

Plastic bags – small, big, sealable

Plenty of tissues and wipes – keep in a dry waterproof bag

Travel alarm clock with time zones if you intend to do a lot of travelling around

Travel wash and peg-free washing line

Sunglasses

Phrase books

Torch

Gifts/souvenirs to hand around to fellow volunteers or locals you may work with

Comfort food – or one luxury item

OPTIONAL BITS AND BOBS YOU MAY OR MAY NOT NEED
Earplugs – useful in noisy hostels and hotels, or for sleeping on trains

Travel plugs – for all your electrical appliances, such as a hairdryer or laptop. The Help for World Travellers website **www.kropla.com** has a list of the different sockets, voltage and phone plugs used around the world

Personal stereo and music, with radio function if you want to take in the local sounds

Travel iron – bulky, but could be useful if you have to trawl round to interviews and make yourself look reasonably presentable

Sleeping bag – bear in mind that in popular trekking centres in Asia you can rent bags very cheaply

Camping gear

Cigarette lighter – to light campfires, candles, mosquito coils etc.

Notepad and pen/journal

Camera and film

Mobile phone and adaptor – key in useful telephone numbers such as embassies and consulates, and emergency numbers of the agency you are working for

Copies of your CV – in a waterproof folder, several copies and a copy on hard disk

Copies of important certifications – again, make photocopies and keep in a waterproof folder

WHO TO GO WITH?

TRAVELLING COMPANIONS

Everyone has their favourite travel bust-up story: the hilarious time when they poured beer over a friend, left them stranded on a remote island or didn't speak for four whole days. The only thing is it wasn't so amusing at the time. You might blank it out now but those stories were born out of hot weather, dehydration, delayed planes, cancelled trains and just plain old-fashioned irritation. Of course travelling at the best of times puts friends under stress and triggers unexpected grievances. But working on a voluntary project? Doing unfamiliar work? Integrating into a community of new people? Pitted against fresh challenges?

All of this isn't to put you off, but it is to say that deciding who to go with is very important. Why? Choosing the right travelling companion can make or break the trip. On the good side, travelling with a friend can add to the adventure of a lifetime, having a soul mate there to console you, support you, make you laugh and help you in a hundred practical ways. It can also drag you down, hold you back and prevent you from mixing with people. So, if you do decide to go with a friend, here are some things to bear in mind:

Do you have the same sense of humour?

Does your companion bear grudges?

Are they sociable people – will they make an effort to integrate with the group, or will they cling to you and inhibit you from meeting new people?

Does this person have any habits that annoy you? An irritating laugh? A frustrating way of never admitting they're wrong? It may not seem a big deal now, but remember that you are going to be with this person every day, and those irritating habits may loom and grow and *really* start to annoy you.

ADVERTISING FOR A TRAVEL COMPANION

The other alternative is to advertise for a travelling companion. This can be done through most magazines and newspapers with a classified section, or target the travelling magazine. The magazine *Wanderlust* runs a section called 'Connections' where you can advertise for a travelling companion.

TRAVELLING WITH A PARTNER

For the romantically inclined, volunteering overseas with the love of your life may sound like the ultimate bonding adventure. There's something about meditating in exotic climes and helping to right the injustices of the world that can elicit a starry-eyed response in certain kinds of people. Two words: get real. Living in a mixed community, in testing circumstances, working for no pay, trying your hand at skills you may never have done before, struggling with a foreign language in an alien climate, dealing with mosquitoes, culture shock and extremes of weather? Well, it hardly makes for a walk in the park. At the very least, it's bound to uncover a side of yourself you may never have seen before. Or, for that matter, seen in your partner. So do yourself a favour and give some serious thought to whether your relationship is up to it or not.

Of course, volunteering with your partner can and does work. Time and time again, people leave for overseas projects and come back fully bonded and ready to pledge their lives to each other. When things get tough, having someone you can turn to for consolation and comfort can be a massive support. But it can cut both ways. You may also argue or split up and see previously hidden unattractive sides of each other. How strong is your relationship? How well do you know each other? How well do you think you will adapt to having other people around, living at close quarters? Is your partner the jealous kind? Do they need a lot of attention? Will they hold you back and stop you making friends? Above all, don't use volunteering as an exercise in bonding – if you have relationship issues, try a tantric sex workshop or see a Relate counsellor instead.

TRAVELLING ALONE

For those brave enough to do it, volunteering solo could be the best decision you ever make. On your own you are more likely to meet more people, open up to new experiences and have nothing short of a total transformation. Why? Thrown back on your own company, you not only will become your own best friend but are also more inclined to fully embrace the new adventure. Of course, travelling solo still comes with drawbacks. Like what? Like how about loneliness, inconvenience, not having the support of someone you know and increased vulnerability to crime. But, if you follow the safety guidelines, travelling solo doesn't have to be a gamble. If you're living in a group, it's invariably the feisty singletons who integrate the most easily. So, if you're on the path for nothing less than self-reinvention, don't be afraid – go it alone.

8. HEALTH AND SAFETY

In all the excitement of planning your trip, make sure you don't neglect taking the best health and safety precautions. With thirty million trips abroad made every day, it is easy to grow complacent about the risks you may be encountering. Bear in mind that travelling to some countries can expose us to dangers that we may not be used to. Volunteering in particular can place us in testing conditions, wherever we're working on international aid projects, work camps or ecological projects in the rainforest.

KEEPING HEALTHY

The first thing then is to make sure you are covered with good health insurance and have all the necessary vaccinations. If you travelling through an organisation, they should inform you of all the latest requirements, but it will do no harm to do your own research to make sure the information is up to date. Most voluntary organisations will arrange insurance cover for you, with some even including vaccination costs. The best will provide you with a list of health precautions and items to take. Of course, how in-depth this is will depend on where you are travelling. Working on camps in Europe is obviously not going to carry the same dangers as taking part in ecological work in the jungle and, if the latter applies to you, you'd be well advised to make sure your organisation is offering adequate support. If not, it might be worthwhile seeking out a more informed organisation. Working in refugee camps in disaster-relief settings is going to carry heightened risks so make sure you are adequately protected. In these cases, the usual travel-health advice may not be enough, so make sure you seek guidance from a reputable travel-health expert.

GETTING THE RIGHT INFORMATION

Travel medicine is constantly changing so getting the most up-to-date information is paramount. When it comes to travel health, it's best not to rely on your GP. Yes, they can give you good general advice but for the best, most up-to-date advice you can't beat the services of a really good travel-health expert. Luckily there are plenty around. The Internet also has many good sites. Here are some resources:

The Department of Health in the UK publishes a free booklet on health risks and vaccines for each country. Call 0800 555 777 or look on **www.doh.gov.uk**. This also includes an E111 form and gives details on medical insurance and getting help in different countries.

The Nomad Pharmacy runs an advice line on 09068 633 414 (calls cost 60p per minute) or you can visit their Travellers' Store at 3 Wellington Terrace, Turnpike Lane, London N8 0PX and 40 Bernard St, London WC1N 1LJ.

The Centres for Disease Control (CDC) (**www.cdc.gov/travel/bluesheet.htm**) and the World Health Organisation (WHO) (**www.who.int/en**) have set up guidelines and health information for the international traveller.

MASTA Travel Health Centre (52 Margaret Street, London W1, Tel: 020 7291 9333, website: **www.masta.org**) has up-to-date information on travellers' diseases. It also runs a travel-health advice line, Tel: 09068 224 100 (calls cost 60p a minute).

The website **www.tripprep.com** is dedicated to travellers' health and has plenty of up-to-date information about tropical diseases and health risks.

For pre-travel information on any destination, and advice when you are away, visit **e-med.co.uk**. The online support service was created by Dr Jules Eden especially for travellers who find themselves a long way from a doctor, although you will have to pay for the advice. He also answers queries about travel health in the Travel section of the *Guardian* every Saturday.

TRAVEL CLINICS

British Airways Travel Clinic provides vaccinations, up-to-date advice and travel-healthcare products and has 28 regional clinics in the UK. Call 01276 685040 for the one nearest to you.

The Hospital for Tropical Diseases has a travel clinic and recorded message service which lists appropriate immunisations, Tel: 020 7388 9600 (calls cost 50p a minute).

There is also a 24-hour Malaria helpline running recorded messages, Tel: 0891 600 350 (calls cost 60p a minute).

Trailfinders also runs a no-appointment-necessary immunisation clinic at 194 Kensington High Street, London, Tel: 020 7938 3999.

Fleet Street Clinic (29 Fleet Street, London EC4Y 1AA, Tel: 020 7353 5678) provides vaccinations and up-to-the-minute advice.

GETTING THE RIGHT VACCINATIONS

Top of the list in healthcare is to make sure you get the right vaccinations. This cannot be emphasised enough, as in recent years travel experts have been warning of a worrying trend for overconfident travellers to forgo the necessary immunisations. Not only that but, with the number of infectious diseases around the world rising, the risks only look set to grow.

Why is it so important? Here in the West many contagious diseases have been eliminated and we enjoy a level of healthcare other countries can only dream about. But this comfort and shelter comes at a price. Exposed to some conditions in developing countries to which we have never developed a resistance, our bodies simply cannot cope. Having a vaccination injects your body with a harmless version of the disease and allows your body to develop immunity.

Of course shelling out £60–100 on a full vaccination (which is what it typically costs) may seem like a lot on top of the other outgoings, such as backpacks, insurance, flight tickets etc., but it can be worth it for the extra peace of mind. Besides, if you do a lot of travelling, the costs can be spread over many trips. Some injections are available on the NHS – see your GP for more details – while some organisations include the cost of vaccinations in the fee for the entire trip.

WHICH VACCINES SHOULD YOU HAVE?

Under current law the only vaccine that is compulsory for any country is Yellow Fever, but there are hundreds of other diseases that are worth immunising yourself against. The following is a general guide to which vaccines are recommended for different global areas. To get more specific information, contact a travel medical expert or visit one of the numerous excellent websites that carry highly detailed information.

- **Typhoid and hepatitis A vaccines are both recommended for most parts of the world, including parts of Europe.**

- **Malaria pills are essential for most places in parts of South America, Asia, Africa and the Caribbean.**

- **Meningitis A and C vaccines are recommended for sub-Saharan Africa, but also Brazil, India and Nepal. (According to Nomad Travel Clinic over 200 people died from meningococcal Meningitis serotype C in Rwanda in June 2002.)**

- **Japanese encephalitis vaccines are recommended for rural and extremely wet parts of Asia.**

- **Watch out for rabies, especially in parts of South America, Asia and Africa.**

- **Update your protection against tetanus, polio and in some cases diphtheria, especially if it's more than ten years since you were last vaccinated.**

Make sure you allow plenty of time for the vaccinations to take effect. According to the World Health Organisation, travellers should start their arrangements four to six weeks in advance. The immunisation process may take a few weeks, so it is important to allow your body time to adjust before you travel. Typically, a single vaccine takes two weeks to have the full effect. However, see your doctor even if you are going at short notice as some protection is usually better than none.

DISEASES YOU CAN'T IMMUNISE AGAINST

There are also plenty of tropical diseases out there that it isn't possible to immunise yourself against. Here are some of them:

DENGUE FEVER

Dengue Fever is a mosquito-borne disease that has recently seen a massive outbreak in Rio, Brazil, Ecuador and the Galapagos. Primarily a disease of the tropics, the risk of transmission is generally higher in urban areas, particularly during and shortly after the rainy season.

Symptoms: Symptoms include a sudden onset of high fever, severe headaches, joint and muscle pain, nausea/vomiting and a rash. The rash may appear three to four days after the onset of fever. It can occasionally produce shock and haemorrhage, leading to death. The illness may last up to ten days, but complete recovery can take two to four weeks. Infection is diagnosed by a blood test that detects the presence of the virus or antibodies.

Treatment: Alert your doctor if you have any fever illness occurring within three weeks after leaving an endemic area. Treatment tends to focus on alleviating the symptoms, such as bed rest, fluids and medications to reduce fever, such as acetaminophen.

Prevention: There is no vaccine for dengue fever, so the best precaution is to avoid mosquito bites by remaining in well-screened or air-conditioned areas.

Risk areas: Dengue Fever tends to be most prevalent in urban areas. It poses a health hazard to travellers in Africa, South East Asia and China, Indian sub-Continent, Caribbean Islands and South and Central America. There is also a small risk in the Middle East and there have been periodic epidemics in Queensland and the Torres Strait Islands of Australia as well as most of the South and Central Pacific Islands.

CHOLERA

Cholera is an acute diarrhoeal illness caused by drinking water or eating food contaminated with faeces. Although the infection is often mild or without symptoms, it can sometimes be severe. Cholera outbreaks are rare and arise only in extremely dirty conditions. However, the disease can spread rapidly in areas with inadequate treatment of sewage and drinking water.

Symptoms: It is estimated that one in twenty infected persons experience profuse watery diarrhoea, vomiting and leg cramps leading to dehydration and shock which, without treatment, can be fatal. People who develop severe diarrhoea and vomiting in countries where cholera occurs should seek medical attention.

Treatment: Cholera can be simply and successfully treated by taking an oral rehydration solution, a prepackaged mixture of sugar and salts to be mixed with water and drunk in large amounts. This should be taken as soon as possible to replace the fluid and salts lost through diarrhoea. Antibiotics can also help.

Prevention: Follow the rules for food and water hygiene (see next section). There is no vaccine available for cholera in the UK or the US. There are oral vaccines for cholera licensed outside the UK but these are generally not recommended for travellers. However, if you are visiting a country that has a massive active cholera outbreak or you are working in a refugee camp in a disaster setting, getting hold of such a vaccine may be advisable. Ask the voluntary organisation you are travelling with and seek the advice of a travel-health expert.

Risk areas: Cholera outbreaks are rare, and spring up only in extremely dirty conditions, but there have been very recent cases in the Ivory Coast and Burundi, Africa.

MALARIA

Malaria is a potentially fatal disease, passed on through bites from a mosquito infected with a parasite known as Plasmodium. With 500 million new cases a year, malaria is a leading cause of death and disease in the world and constitutes a huge global health problem. In the UK alone there were twelve malaria deaths last year, and 2,000 people returned to the UK with the disease. Taking anti-malaria medication, then, has never been more important, but in recent years the press has been so bad about some malaria pills, it's a wonder anyone takes them at all. Some malaria pills such as Larium have been found to cause depression, mood swings and hallucinations. Meanwhile, in other malaria regions, there are cases where mosquitoes are developing resistance to the pills. Given such bad press, it's easy to opt not to take the pills at all. If you do decide this, make sure you are rigorously attentive to protecting yourself against mosquito bites. However, malaria is a potentially fatal disease and it's worth saying that travel-health experts strongly advise that travellers take some form of anti-malaria medication.

Symptoms: Symptoms include feverish attacks, influenza-like symptoms, diarrhoea, tiredness and a whole range of symptoms, including coma, which can flare up within a year of returning from an infected area.

Treatment: It is essential that malaria is treated as soon as possible to guard against the possibility of death. If you exhibit any of the symptoms within a year of travelling to a malaria endemic area, make sure you seek medical help. If you are travelling to a malaria area where it will be difficult to get speedy medical attention, it's a good idea to take a 'standby treatment kit'.

Prevention: The first rule of thumb is to seek the advice of a travel-health expert, as guidelines for anti-malaria medication are constantly changing. There are regions where mosquitoes are developing resistance to certain drugs, so you need to find out which prophylactic is appropriate for the area you are visiting. No malaria pill is one hundred per cent effective so whether you do decide to take a prophylactic or not, make sure you follow the advice for bite avoidance.

Anti-malaria medication: Traditionally the most popular prophylactic is Chloroquine. However, resistance to Chloroquine is increasingly spreading and now exists throughout sub-Saharan Africa, South East Asia, the Indian sub-continent and large portions of South America. There are also some areas that are resistant to proguanil, another prophylactic.

Larium: Top of the list in the Rogues' Gallery of anti-malaria medication is the mefloquine brand Larium. Larium's big selling point is that it only has to be taken monthly, unlike other medication that requires daily pills. Unfortunately, the selling points stop there. In recent years, Larium has been found to trigger 'neuro-psychiatric problems', including depression, nightmares, suicidal tendencies, dizziness, disorientation and mood swings. Stories abound of travellers developing long-term depression after taking the drug, and it was even blamed recently for a gap-year student's suicide. Such is the scare that Roche, the company that makes Larium, has recently added the risk of suicide to its list of the drug's warnings. However, according to experts, these side effects do not affect everyone and if you have already taken it and suffered no side effects so far, it is highly unlikely that you will start to develop symptoms now. Larium cannot be prescribed to someone with a history of mental health problems.

Larium alternatives: If you are unhappy about taking Larium, there are other alternatives. Doxycycline can be taken in malaria-resistant areas but, unlike Larium, it should be taken every day and shouldn't be taken if you are pregnant. One of the best alternatives to Larium is Malarone (one tablet taken daily), which, like Larium, can be used in many Chloroquine-resistant areas. One of the big advantages of Malarone is that, instead of having to take it four weeks after you have left the malaria area, you only need to take it for seven days. However, it is more expensive than other prophylactics, and the medical press has recently reported the first cases of Malarone resistance. There are also homeopathic prophylactics available, although there is no conclusive evidence to show that they work.

Risk areas: The risk is particularly high in sub-Saharan Africa and Solomon Islands. Other areas are South America, the Indian sub-continent and the Far East.

VOLUNTEERS' STORIES

Maria Gold contracted malaria when she was volunteering in Nigeria, despite the fact she had been taking Larium and sleeping under a mosquito net. She says, 'Every volunteer I knew in Nigeria had had malaria at some stage mainly because of the problem of drug resistance. It was only a mild case – I just felt like I had flu, and after a week I felt fine. But if I hadn't been taking Larium I could have been a lot more ill, so it's not worth taking any chances.'

Luckily she had her own malaria treatment kit, containing the drugs Fansidar and quinine. Maria says, 'It's a good idea to take a medical kit if you are going somewhere where medical advice is hard to find. But it should only be used in an emergency. These are serious drugs and shouldn't be used lightly.'

She also recommends taking a good, up-to-date travel-health book. 'In West Africa there are many counterfeit drugs on the market and some doctors can try to prescribe every drug under the sun. Good medical advice can be hard to find.'

BITE AVOIDANCE

Of course, since malaria is an insect-borne disease, the best defence is not to get bitten in the first place. Protecting yourself against insect bites can significantly reduce the risk of contracting other tropical diseases such as Japanese B encephalitis.

- **Cover up the skin and use good insect repellent. DEET-based is best but lemon eucalyptus derivatives have been shown to be as effective.**

- **Use a good mosquito net. Make sure it is tear-free and impregnated with insecticide.**

- **Make sure you are well covered by wearing loose, baggy, long-sleeved shirts, trousers and socks.**

- **Some travellers swear by using essential oils such as citronella in their room and lavender on their body to keep mosquitoes and other insects away.**

- **Vitamin B12 and garlic capsules are said to encourage your body to secrete an insect-repelling odour.**

Jason Gibbs from the Nomad Travel Clinic has the following tips:

- **Use a 50 per cent DEET (diethyltoluamide)-based product to spray on exposed skin**

- **Citriodiol-based products instead are good for young children, or if you are pregnant or have sensitive skin**

- **The best bed nets should be box-shaped as they allow you room to move around underneath**

- **Spraying clothes and bed nets with permethrin crystals will glue and burn mosquitoes instead of repelling them**

- **In high-risk wet areas, canoeing down the Amazon or trekking through the jungle, get the maximum protection by spraying your clothes with permethrin, using a 100 per cent Deet-based solution on the extremities of your clothes (such as collars, cuffs, socks, ankles and hat) and the 50 per cent Deet-based repellent sprayed on the skin.**

- **Burning coils, knock-down sprays, plug-ins (where there is a reliable electricity supply) and head nets are useful for cooking or fishing outdoors, particularly in the early evening**

FOOD, WATER AND HYGIENE
Many other diseases can be easily avoided by following food and water precautions. The golden rule is 'peel it, boil it, cook it or forget it'.

FOOD PRECAUTIONS FOR TRAVEL TO HOT COUNTRIES
The following information on food and hygiene has been compiled by Richard Dawood, physician at the Fleet Street Clinic and author of *Travellers' Health: How to Stay Healthy Abroad*, 4th edition, OUP.

Intestinal infections – especially travellers' diarrhoea – are very common in travellers to hot countries and the chances of being affected range from 40 to 80 per cent. The main reasons are:

Rapid growth of bacteria and viruses at warm temperatures

A generally increased risk from eating many meals in public hotels and restaurants

Poor hygiene and an increased risk of contamination in poor countries

A contaminated drinking-water supply

Almost all cases can be prevented by careful attention to food hygiene. Here's a quick guide to the kinds of foods that are most likely to be safe, and the foods that are best avoided:

USUALLY SAFE
Freshly, thoroughly cooked food, served hot (i.e. heat sterilised)

Fruit easily peeled or sliced open without contamination (bananas, papayas)

Freshly baked bread

Packaged or canned food (take emergency supplies)

Bottled drinks opened in your presence – safest carbonated

Coconuts (usually contain 1pt sweet water)

Boiled water, tea

If there's nothing safe on the menu, ask for chips, omelettes or any dish that must be cooked to order

USUALLY RISKY
Shellfish/seafood (need eight minutes' vigorous boiling to be made safe)

Salad vegetables, unless thoroughly washed in clean water

Rare meat, raw fish

Buffets, food left out in warm temperatures

Food on which flies have settled

Food stored and reheated after cooking

Food requiring much handling – canapés

Spicy sauces, salsa, mayonnaise, left out on the table

Unpeelable fruit (berries, grapes)

Fruit peeled by others (fruit buffets)

Food handled with dirty fingers

Milk products, ice cream

Fruit juices from street vendors

Ice (in your drinks, but also in your butter dish, etc.)

Tap water – even for brushing teeth

Utensils are often contaminated: in Asia, disposable bamboo chop-sticks are cheap, easily available and ideal for travel

Hospitality: if food is not safe, refuse it

TREATMENT OF TRAVELLERS' DIARRHOEA
Not all cases need treatment: most cases of travellers' diarrhoea improve on their own within 48 hours.

TREATMENT OPTIONS
The following treatments are available:

Oral rehydration Replacing lost fluid is one of the most important aspects of treatment, especially when fluid losses are made worse by a hot climate or exertion, and especially in children or elderly people. The best approach is to drink plenty of oral-rehydration solution (e.g. Electrolade, Dioralyte).

Anti-diarrhoeal medication The most effective and fast-acting drug is loperamide (Imodium, Arret); this does not treat the underlying infection, which usually clears up on its own. It should not be used for children; it is otherwise widely considered to be a safe drug; studies have shown that this drug does not prolong infection. The dosage is two capsules initially, followed by one with each loose stool.

Antibiotic treatment The most suitable choice should be discussed with your doctor, and there are advantages and disadvantages that need to be carefully considered, but ciprofloxacin is one possible option. The doctor who prescribes it should give detailed information about side effects and situations in which it should not be taken.

DECIDING WHICH TREATMENT TO USE
The following simple scheme is sometimes helpful:

Mild symptoms Unformed stools, increased frequency: no specific action necessary, consider loperamide (Imodium) if symptoms interfere with your travel plans and daily activities.

Moderate symptoms Watery stool, not causing undue distress: drink plenty, consider taking oral-rehydration solution; consider taking loperamide (Imodium) to control symptoms, and consider taking a single dose of ciprofloxacin.

Severe symptoms Copious watery stools, with or without cramps: commence oral rehydration; consider a three-day course of ciprofloxacin.

A more detailed scheme to follow (including treatment of different types of dysentery) can be found in *Travellers' Health: How to Stay Healthy Abroad.*

WHEN TO SEEK MEDICAL ATTENTION

- high fever (above 40°C)

- significant fever lasting longer than 48 hours

- diarrhoea lasting longer than four days

- severe diarrhoea with or without vomiting, with difficulty keeping up with fluid and salt replacement

- diarrhoea with blood

All of these are symptoms that justify getting skilled advice and follow-up; laboratory tests may also be necessary.

BEFORE YOU LEAVE MAKE SURE YOU:

- Research your country by looking at the relevant websites.

- Get hold of a copy of The Department of Health's free booklet *Health Advice for Travellers* (if you are a UK citizen).

- Find out your blood group.

- Visit your dentist well in advance. Dental treatment can be extremely expensive overseas, not to mention difficult to find, so make sure you book an appointment well before you leave and have all fillings, loose teeth, etc. treated.

- See your GP for a check-up and tell him/her about your travel plans.

- Have all the necessary vaccinations well in advance. The World Health Organisation recommends that you do this at least six weeks before you leave to allow plenty of time for vaccinations to take effect. Immunisation against Hepatitis B, for example, can take six months to give full protection. Other vaccinations cannot be given at the same time. However, see your doctor even if you are going at short notice – some protection may be better than none.

- Have all the necessary medication and equipment.

- If you want to take any sort of medicine with you – either prescribed or bought from a pharmacist – find out if there are any restrictions on taking it in and out of the UK or the country you are visiting. Ask the relevant Embassy or High Commission or the Home Office Drugs Branch (Tel: 020 7273 3806). Make sure you know the brand name and chemical name of the drugs you are using, and check the availability in the country you are visiting. Remember, some medicines available over the counter in the UK may be controlled in other countries, and vice versa.

WHAT TO DO IF YOU BECOME ILL

Before you sign up for a voluntary project, check to make sure that you are adequately protected should you fall ill. If you have travelled through a reliable organisation, they should have a good system in place.

- Do they have good first aid facilities such as an emergency medical kit?

- Will they endeavour to get you medical attention immediately? If you have to travel to the nearest hospital – in some cases crossing borders – is this covered in the cost? Does the programme include health and medical insurance?

- If so, what does this include – does it include repatriation, for example?

- Is there someone close who has had medical/first aid training?

- If you are not working in a group but outside in the general community (such as in some of the gap projects teaching in a school or working on a newspaper), is there someone in the country/town who can help you in a crisis? Do you have their contact number or address?

- Is there 24-hour emergency support?

Make sure you tell your project manager as soon as you feel ill, or seek medical attention as soon as possible. Bear in mind that seemingly harmless infections may spread quickly and become more serious in dirty conditions and certain climates too. Don't feel that you have to struggle on heroically, or are losing pride by seeking medical help. Living in a foreign climate is exposing your body to all kinds of risks it isn't necessarily used to.

Unfortunately, many countries don't have the kind of health service we are used to in the UK and other Western countries. In some African countries you may have to cross borders before you can get the medical services you need. Be aware, then, that it may take a long time to see a doctor and you may experience delays and complications. It also may be expensive – cue another lecture on taking out adequate medical insurance. To make the process as painless as possible, make sure you have all the necessary documentation (such as passport, vaccination certificates, etc.) close at hand, and know exactly what your insurance cover includes.

WHAT TO TAKE

FIRST AID KIT
Taking a good first aid kit and emergency medical kit can go a long way in helping you out in a crisis. A first aid kit should include: a packet of adhesive dressings, some insect repellent and antiseptic cream. Water-sterilisation tablets will take up little space and could be useful. If you are staying somewhere where there is a risk of serious diarrhoea, rehydration sachets are also useful. You should also take anti-malaria and bilharzia pills depending on where you are going.

EMERGENCY MEDICAL KIT
If you're outside Western Europe, North America and Australia/New Zealand, carry your own set of sterile equipment, which you can buy from

most travel-health clinics or pharmacists. These contain a variety of sterilised and sealed items of equipment, such as syringes, needles and suture materials, and are essential in developing countries or those with a high risk of AIDS. The Department of Health's website (**www.dog.gov.uk**) tells you exactly what the kit should contain, as well as other excellent advice – make sure you take a look.

SEXUAL HEALTH

According to the World Health Organisation (WHO), there are approximately 333 million cases of STDs (excluding AIDS) worldwide each year, most affecting the 15- to 30-year-old age group. South and South East Asia, and sub-Saharan Africa are the most affected areas with the highest rates of syphilis, gonorrhoea and chlamydia in the world, but, wherever you are going, it's still worth taking precautions. Marie Stopes International (**www.mairestopes.org.uk**) has plenty of good information on sexual health including the availability of contraception and abortion across the world.

Symptoms of having an STD are:

Discomfort or pain on passing urine
Unusual penile or vaginal discharge
Slight tingling at the tip of the penis
Genital sores, ulcers or warts
Genital and/or testicular pain
Unusual vaginal bleeding
Swollen lymph glands
Itching and/or rash on the body
Wart-like lumps around the anus
Fever
Pain during sex

SEXUAL HEALTH TIPS

- If you suspect you have an STD, don't try to treat it yourself but see a doctor immediately
- Make sure you take enough contraceptive pills to last you for the whole trip
- Take responsibility for using condoms yourself and don't rely on your partner to bring it up
- When buying condoms, check the sell-by date. Bear in mind that in hot climates the extreme heat may rot the rubber, so buy them from air-conditioned shops and keep them in the fridge or the coolest part of your backpack
- If you are a woman travelling in a traditional Muslim country and don't feel comfortable asking for condoms, bring a large stock from home

AIDS

Volunteering in many developing countries may well offer you firsthand experience of living and working with HIV-infected people. According to the WHO, there were an estimated 2.8 million HIV/AIDS-related deaths in 1999 alone, and it is estimated to be growing all the time. With no vaccination against HIV, taking precautions has never been more important. Obviously, the risk of contracting HIV is much more prevalent if you are working in the developing world – South Africa, Botswana, Namibia, Zimbabwe, Zambia and Malawi have the highest incidence of HIV in the world, with an estimated minimum of fifteen per cent of 15- to 49-year-olds being infected. But, wherever you are, it is still wise to exercise vigilance and follow the following precautions.

Don't

> **Share a needle or syringe (including dentistry, tattooing, body piercing and acupuncture)**
>
> **Have unprotected sex with a new partner**

Do

> **Avoid contact with blood products**
>
> **Use condoms**
>
> **Carry your own sterile needle set if you are travelling in high-risk areas**
>
> **Exercise discrimination in who you have sex with (remember that condoms are still not one 100 per cent protection against contracting HIV)**

SAFETY OVERSEAS

- Educate yourself about the health risks in the country you are visiting.

- Immunise yourself against the diseases found in that country.

- Allow plenty of time for the vaccine to take effect. The World Health Organisation advises that travellers start their arrangements four to six weeks before they leave.

- Avoid tap water – boil it or use bottled water from a sealed container for drinking, brushing teeth or washing food. Don't take ice in drinks.

- Eat mainly cooked food. Check that food has been thoroughly heated through.

- Guard against insect bites. Use a 50 per cent Deet-based mosquito repellent to spray on exposed skin (or a citriodiol-based product if you have sensitive skin or are pregnant). The best mosquito nets should be box-shaped and impregnated with permethrin. Make sure they are well tucked in and have no tears.

- Even if you intend to stay in the big cities and live in the lap of luxury, don't assume that you are not at risk of contracting a tropical disease in an endemic country.

- Keep it in perspective. Take care, but try not to worry so much you forget to enjoy your trip.

KEEPING SAFE

Volunteering can put you in touch with the most dangerous of conditions in the most extreme of places. You may find yourself working in countries torn apart by civil war or working in a refugee setting or helping out in villages ravaged by AIDS. All of this can seem exciting from afar, but the reality on the ground can be very different. If you are opting to do voluntary work in remote areas in developing countries, do make sure that there is a suitable infrastructure to help you out in a crisis. I know of one woman who volunteered in the Sudan and complained that she received little support. Many of the big voluntary organisations have a 24-hour emergency service, but the local or smaller companies may not be able to offer the same level of protection. Make sure you know what system they have in place first.

- **Before you go, research your country and check to see how safe it is. Don't just rely on what you read in the newspapers and books, but go to the best sources of up-to-date information.**

- **The Foreign and Commonwealth's Office's website www.fco.gov.uk (click on Travel) carries comprehensive advice on which countries to avoid. It also has a travel advice number you can ring on 020 7008 0232.**

- **Americans can contact the US State Department Travel Advisory Service on 00 1 202 647 5225 or go to www.travel.state.gov for more information.**

- **Most other governments have websites that carry advice on travelling and international trouble spots. Travellers' websites and chat rooms can also be a good source of information. Wherever you go, make sure you have left contacts and details of your itinerary with your relatives and friends.**

THE RISK OF TERRORISM

Of course, one of the crucial issues in recent months has been the increased likelihood of terrorist attacks. It's important to not make too much of this – after all, intimidating us and disrupting normal life is exactly what terrorists want. Besides, the chances of being caught in a terrorist attack are still extremely rare. That said, terrorist attacks on Western targets are definitely on the rise, so it's only sensible to take a few wise precautions. As always, check the background of the country you are visiting before you leave. Keep abreast of events in the newspapers and check the government's website for countries it advises not to travel to. Once you are there, monitor the media and be sensitive to the culture. Look out for anything suspicious such as an unattended bag at an airport or a group of people acting suspiciously around an obviously 'Western' institution. If something does catch your attention, report it to the local police – according to the FCO, many terrorist attacks have been foiled by the vigilance of ordinary people.

CRIME

Hands up – how many of us have landed in a foreign country feeling and looking lost and a little worse for wear? Maybe it's too many gin and tonics on the plane or maybe it's general disorientation from jet lag and hours of travelling, but is it any wonder even the most streetwise among us is more likely to fall victim to crime? Of course, you don't want to be so cautious that you spoil your trip, but it's wise to take a few precautions.

KEEPING SAFE

- Take your own safety locks/padlocks. If you are staying on a camp or in a village where you can't lock the doors at night, use your own locks to secure your rucksack or your bedroom door. You can also use them to fasten baggage to the rack on overnight trains.

- Keep photocopies of important documents in a separate place from the original documents.

- Carry money and important documents in a money belt under your clothes.

- Never fight someone if you are being mugged. Your rucksack, travellers' cheques, wallet, etc. may be important to you, but they're definitely not worth sacrificing your life.

- Carry a decoy wallet with a small amount in, say $10, enough to be credible. In the event of being mugged, hand over this wallet instead.

- Observe the ways of the natives and try to blend in. The less you look like a tourist, the less your chances of being mugged/harassed/followed, etc.

- Never leave important documents and valuables in hotels or hostels.

- Keep a small amount of money separate from your everyday money in case of robbery, so you have cash to use in an emergency.

- Avoid wearing or carrying expensive-looking clothes or items such as jewellery, watches or cameras, etc.

- Be wary of accepting food and drink from strangers, especially on trains. It's not unknown for thieves to drug food and drink and, once you are asleep, make off with your things.

WOMEN TRAVELING ALONE

If you are a female solo traveller, travelling outside the Western world, you may want to take extra precautions. In some countries, it is wise to be very aware of the kind of messages you give out. Avoid making direct eye contact, which can be misinterpreted as a come-on by some, and make sure you are dressed appropriately. Some women find extra comfort in wearing fake wedding rings, with some even producing photos of 'hubby' on occasion. Try not to let your caution spoil your trip, but following a few precautions can reduce the chances of getting into any awkward situations.

- Carry enough cash on you at all times so you can take a taxi if you feel someone is bothering you.

- If you arrive late at night, either book a pre-paid taxi or make sure the taxi is licensed by the airport.

- Observe the way local women dress and, if it's appropriate, cover yourself up. In Muslim countries, you should cover your shoulders and head. You'll feel less conspicuous and won't draw unwanted attention to yourself.

- Take a sarong – they're easy to pack and you can adapt them for any occasion.

- Wear a fake wedding ring to ward off unwanted attention. You can even take a picture of 'hubby' (real or imagined) if you think it might add credibility.

- Plan your routes in advance – that way you don't have to rely on asking directions or drawing unnecessary attention to yourself.

- Walk tall and try not to appear vulnerable. Even if you are lost, try to look as if you know where you are going.

- Always lock the hotel/hostel doors and windows at night. Make things doubly secure by taking your own padlock.

- If you are travelling on public transport at night, try to sit near the driver.

- Join up with other women travellers, if you want, but don't feel that, just because you're on your own, you have to surround yourself with other people.

- Keep your folks back home up to date with your whereabouts. Phone/email regularly and leave a contact address and details of where you are staying.

WHAT HAPPENS IF YOU HAVE TROUBLE?

If you run into trouble, the first thing to do is tell the voluntary organisation and contact your relatives and friends at home. You may also want to use the Consulate, which is a part of the Embassy or High Commission in most countries and is there to help you if you need emergency help overseas. Most towns and cities have smaller Consulate Offices in cities and towns, which should be able to assist, should an emergency arise: before you travel, compile a list of consular addresses in the country you are visiting.

If you are British and there is no British Consulate where you are, you can use the consulate or embassy of any other EU member state. Remember, too, that under UK law British Consulates charge for their services. The Foreign and Commonwealth Office's website has more information on fees.

Here is a list of what a UK Consulate can and cannot do for you. Most other consulates will offer the same support, but make sure you check before travelling.

A British Consulate can:

Issue emergency passports

Contact relatives and friends and ask them to help with money and tickets

Advise on how to transfer funds

At most posts (in an emergency) advance money against a sterling cheque for £50 supported by a banker's card

As a last resort, provided strict criteria are met, make a repayable loan for repatriation to the UK

Provide a list of local lawyers, interpreters and doctors

Arrange for a next of kin to be informed of a death or accident and advice on procedures

Contact British nationals who are arrested or in prison, and in certain circumstances arrange for messages to be given to relatives or friends

Give guidance on organisations experienced in tracing missing persons

A British Consulate cannot:

Pay your hotel, medical or other bills

Pay for your travel tickets except in very special circumstances

Undertake work usually done by travel representatives, airlines, bank or motoring organisations

Get better treatment for you in hospital or prison than is provided for local nationals

Give legal advice, instigate court proceedings on your behalf or interfere in local court procedures to get you out of prison

Investigate a crime

Formally assist dual nationals in a country of their second nationality

Obtain a work permit for you

DANGEROUS ANIMALS

Volunteering on some projects can put you at an increased risk of encountering dangerous animals. If this is a natural part of your work, your voluntary body should definitely have given you guidelines – make sure you feel adequately equipped before you leave. Wherever you are, make sure you follow the rules to the letter and heed the advice of local trekkers who will have had years of experience. Typical advice includes:

Never run from a tiger. Instead stand and wave your arms and make lots of noise.

If you are sleeping in the jungle, make sure your tent is zipped up and light fires and lanterns at night.

Never walk without your shoes in Asia, Africa and South America where poisonous snakes can bite your bare feet.

If you do meet a snake, don't try to attack it – you'll only succeed in inciting its rage.

If you do get bitten, keep your limbs still so the poison will take longer to spread through your body, and send for help immediately.

9. CULTURE SHOCK

Whether you are monitoring bio-diversity in Greenland or Shamanic dancing in the Ecuadorian jungle, chances are it might take a bit of getting used to. Culture shock can hit even the most experienced of travellers, so it's best to follow a few wise words to make sure you are prepared. Of course, half the reason we do these things is for the kick up the ass it brings. For adrenalin junkies, there's nothing like breaking through comfort zones to get that pleasing jolt that comes from seeing new places and meeting new people in the most outlandish of circumstances. Let's face it, if you wanted ordinary, you wouldn't be opting to volunteer in the first place. So a certain amount of culture shock is to be expected, of course.

That said, there are times, such as your first night, when making the transition smoothly has a lot to recommend it. Landing in a foreign country for the first time can be a bewildering experience. Add to that the pressure of jet lag, struggling with a new currency and understanding an unfamiliar language, and it's not surprising that things can go wrong. This is particularly true if you are travelling to the more remote areas where a Western face carries certain political connotations. So do yourself a favour and make sure you're prepared.

If you don't believe me, try freeze-framing the picture at the moment you first arrive. Imagine stepping out into a foreign airport. You're surrounded by signs in a language you barely understand. People stand and stare, enthralled by your Western clothes. Touts circle you, offering you a bed for the first night. Disorientated, you step outside: you have no idea where you are going, and no idea how to get there. The heat is stifling and people around you jostle you for change. Suddenly, unexpectedly, a total feeling of disorientation sweeps over you. You are alone in a foreign country and you feel very, very strange.

Even the most experienced travellers can have moments like these. So it's no wonder that most of the biggest hiccups happen on the first night. Without your wits totally about you, you're at an increased risk of falling prey to crime. Without wishing to scare you, there are common stories of taxi drivers and airport officials deliberately setting up scams designed to catch foreign travellers at their most vulnerable. There's something about travelling long distances that switches even the most carefully attuned radar off for the night. So what can you do first?

Book a bed for the first night in a hostel.

Pre-book a taxi through the airport if you are arriving late at night or in the early hours of the morning.

Try to make sure the hostel is in an area where there are plenty of others nearby. Then, if things do go wrong, you should be able to find a room somewhere else.

Phone up to confirm the booking a few days before you leave, so you don't have any nasty surprises when you arrive.

Make sure you have all the necessary documentation in a safe place that is easy to access. Keep passports, travellers' cheques and airlines tickets in your money belt.

Keep some loose change in your pocket for trains, buses, etc. so you don't have to keep taking out big notes.

Try to get to grips with the currency before you arrive.

Look up transport timetables on the web in advance.

Get a map of the city before you arrive.

Buy a good up-to-date guide book.

If you know someone who lives nearby, ask to stay for the first couple of nights or, at the very least, meet up with them for a basic orientation course.

DEALING WITH CULTURE SHOCK

It happens to all of us. You've waited ten months to get here, saved up hundreds of pounds and talked to your friends in vivid detail about every aspect of your trip. Maybe you've given up a job, walked out of a relationship or even sold your home. And then you arrive, and it hits you like a slap in the face. Culture shock. It's not what you expected. You don't feel elated or curious – you just feel depressed and lost, and strangely alone.

If this happens, don't be too alarmed. Adjusting to a foreign culture can take time for the best of us, and it's nothing to feel bad about. It's not unusual to miss your culture more than you expected – even the most cosmopolitan of us can find ourselves moaning for a 'decent' cup of tea and wondering what we're missing in *EastEnders*. Culture shock is part of the inevitable transition when one changes from a visitor to a part of the culture. The best thing to do, then, is to turn to your network of friends and know that it will pass. After all, living in an international community in a foreign culture is bound to bring up a certain amount of disorientation.

EASING THE TRANSITION
Culture shock can be triggered by many things. Maybe your experiences don't fit with the exotic pictures you imagined. Maybe the language barriers are too great or the change in climate is too overwhelming. All of this is a natural part of the process of adapting to a different culture, so don't be too hard on yourself if feelings like this arise. It's worth it, however, to think in advance about what could make the transition easier. So take a moment to think about the things that rock your world. Chocolate, music, yoga, a good book, essential oils, a photo of your children, a recording of your favourite comedy show … When depression bites, what are the things you turn to to get you smiling? Whatever it is, do yourself a favour and include this on your

list of essential items. Don't go overboard – you don't want to load yourself down with your entire library of self-help manuals or favourite CDs – but the odd chosen item could go a long way in soothing you in a crisis. From comfort food to a leather-bound journal, a little luxury is no wasted extravagance when you're shacked up in a tent two thousand miles from home.

STAYING IN TOUCH

For most of us, however, there's nothing like travelling for achieving that exhilarating sense of completely getting away from things. Freed from the usual routines, old lives can melt away and seem like a distant, blurred dream. That's all well and good, but do take time to remember that there will be people back at home thinking about you. Fed through the sensationalist eye of the media, national emergencies can quickly become distorted and encourage your loved ones to jump to all kinds of conclusions about how safe you are. It's a good idea, then, to work out some guidelines about staying in touch before you leave. This way, should a real emergency arise, at least you know you'll have people back at home ready to bale you out, should the occasion demand.

Do

> Negotiate a realistic agreement with your loved ones about how often you'll be in touch. Avoid the temptation to make promises you can't keep. You'll only worry them if you don't keep to the agreement, so, if you say you'll phone every two weeks, make sure you know that you'll keep your word.

> Give your partners and family a copy of your itinerary before you leave. This way they'll have a basic idea of your whereabouts. Include flight details (times, airports, carrier and flight numbers) and if possible fax numbers for work and hotels.

> If you are working for an organisation, leave them contact details and names.

> If trouble flares up, make a point of phoning your loved ones to let them know you're safe. Remember that safety issues have a way of being distorted through the media, so try to look at the situation from the perspective back at home. You might know that you were miles away from a terrorist attack, but all your loved ones will know is that you are living in the same country. Phone your folks/friends back home to reassure them all the same.

WAYS TO STAY IN TOUCH

Many voluntary projects take place in remote settings, out in the wild where shops and money exchanges may be hard to find – not to mention telephones. It's wise then to think carefully about ways to stay in touch as you never know when an emergency may arise.

TELEPHONE

As marvellous as the wonders of science are, there are still times when you can't beat hearing a well-loved familiar voice on the end of a line. Unfortunately, using a public telephone overseas can be a stressful business. Luckily, there are plenty of telephone tools to keep you one step ahead. Here are some of the most convenient:

Telephone cards. One of the handiest things for travellers is telephone charge cards. These enable you to bill the cost of a call to a pre-existing telephone number (your home number or parents, for example), thus saving you the hassle of fumbling with loose change in an unfamiliar currency. They are also easy to obtain and available through most telephone companies. Prices do vary, however, so make sure you shop around.

Another option is the International pre-paid phone cards, although these don't work in every country so check beforehand. After paying up-front for credit, of say £20, you are then given a PIN or access number to dial every time you make a call. Generally cheaper than making a normal international call, rates for these cards vary from country to country so make sure you know the costs for your particular country beforehand. International pre-paid phone cards are available from many companies – try One-Tel, Planet Talk and Alpha Telecom.

Taking your mobile. It's not for nothing mobiles are one of the top-five most popular travelling items taken overseas: having your own mobile will not only reassure your loved ones back at home, but it will make you feel a lot safer and lot more in control. It will also assist you greatly if you are hoping to find voluntary work as you travel around. You can also pre-programme into your mobile the telephone number of the nearest British Embassy, High Commission or Consulate in the country you are visiting as well as other convenient phone numbers. Check the service thoroughly before travelling. Most networks will contain everything you need to know on its website or literature. Oftel, the Office of Telecommunications, has plenty of good advice on cost saving and using your mobile abroad on its website **www.oftel.gov.uk/publications/mobile**. Make sure you check it out.

Using your mobile phone abroad

Check with your existing mobile network to see if they allow 'international roaming' so you can use your mobile abroad. This can take up to fourteen days to install so do it well in advance of departure date.

Check that your existing handset will work in the country you are visiting.

Check the costs of calls and texts in the country you are visiting.

If you are using a pre-paid mobile international-roaming service, make sure you know how to use your credit card to top up your calling credit before you leave, or take extra vouchers, as they may be hard to obtain abroad.

SIM cards (the small cards that let the phone work on a particular mobile network) can easily be swapped round to get you a cheaper deal. You can buy SIM cards for foreign networks at most international airports and holiday destinations, including UK retailers in some European countries.

Keep a note of your mobile's serial number, your mobile telephone number and the telephone number of your operator's customer services (including UK dialling code) in a safe place, separate from your mobile phone. Contact your network service provider if it is stolen.

Bear in mind that you are required to register your mobile telephone if you enter Russian Federation countries.

Voice mail. Voice mail is an extremely handy service for travellers as it allows you to pick up and leave messages on your own personal answer service, from any telephone in the world. Bear in mind that you usually have to pay to pick up your messages as well as leaving them (the answerphone you call is usually based in your home country) so ask people to only leave messages in an emergency. You may also have to buy a keypad before you leave (around £10) in case you can't find a touch-tone phone.

Other telephone points to bear in mind

Some public telephones accept credit cards although the instructions may not be in English.

Telephones in post offices and telephone offices tend to have less background noise and can be easier to use with instructions sometimes in English.

Many telephone offices allow you to make reverse-charged calls or have a Home Country Direct Facility, where you can call the operator in your home country and then use a credit card or reverse charge call.

FAX

Faxes are another fantastically handy way of staying in touch: cheap, easy and simple to use. Before you leave, supply your folks/partner/loved ones with the fax number of hostels, hotels and work.

POSTE RESTANTE

Never mind the wonders of science, there are still times when you can't beat a long, handwritten letter from home – or, even better, a food parcel stacked with all your favourite goodies. If you have no fixed address and expect to be travelling around, one of the best ways to stay in touch is to set up a poste restante address. This allows people to send you a letter via the main General Post Office in the city you are staying, which you can collect by turning up and showing your passport. The mail will be kept for anything from one to six months, although different post offices operate according to different systems and some may throw away uncollected mail after only one month. In most cases, uncollected mail will be returned to sender.

If possible, it's best to get the address of your main post office from a phone book or guide book. If not, mail should be addressed to your name, followed by Poste Restante, General Post Office and the name of the city. The mail will normally be filed away alphabetically. To avoid any problems, ask people to address mail to an agreed name (minus Mr, Mrs, Ms) so you know what you are looking for. Bear in mind that, to the people filing it, your name is a foreign language so discourage friends from addressing the envelope to your Christian or nickname. The last name should be underlined and all words written in capitals.

EMAIL

Thanks to the power of technology, the Internet has revolutionised the way travellers, well, travel and communicate with people back home. No matter where you are, in just a few clicks you can send your great travelogue across the virtual waves to be read minutes later by your loved ones. You can also send circulars, digital photographs and even fix up a time to be spotted on webcamera. You can set up free email accounts courtesy of yahoo and hotmail, which can be accessed from any computer system.

Thankfully, in these enlightened days of technology, cyber cafés can be found in most cities and towns. (You can find out addresses of cyber cafés on **www.cybercafes.com**.) Many of them allow you to feed in digital images so you can create your own virtual postcard.

MAKING THE MOST OF YOUR TRIP

Whatever you decide to do, you can bet that it will be a momentous experience. It's a good idea, then, to think ahead as to how you will save this experience. Why? This project could be one of the most exciting things that has ever happened to you. It also may be life changing. So look forward to it. Savour the experience.

Here are a few ways you can really make the most out of it.

KEEP A JOURNAL

Even if you don't consider yourself a budding writer, there's something about recording your thoughts in writing that can really capture the moment. I once did a workcamp in France and, years later, I still have the notebook I wrote, teeming with descriptions, to prove it. Reading those impressions now floods light on a chapter of my life that might otherwise be almost forgotten. The smell of the rain in the mornings. The sound of twenty different accents singing Pink Floyd songs around a campfire. The village cat, the local hazelnut wine – all of this springs back into life every time I re-read those sentences. I've also found journals from my sister's trip to Russia, and letters sent from a friend travelling in Australia, and what strikes you at once is the immediacy and vivid detail: it's not that they were trying to write an opus, but somehow just the act of recording what they felt, saw and thought had the effect of capturing another world. Living in any foreign culture is a fascinating experience, so make a note of it. Get it down.

As Marco Van Belle writes on the website **Netbackpacker.com**: 'Volunteering and travelling are two completely different experiences. I've come home to find myself feeling as if I never really left in the first place. I stepped out of time when I landed in Nepal, and the subtlest of changes at home seem odd without the passage of time to explain them. My memories too feel like fantasies, dreams of a parallel world visited only in my imagination. But when I look through my journal I know. I did feel the fury of that earthquake. I did bounce around the back of that pick-up truck. I did dance on a roof top drenched to the skin and not caring. And 59 kids learned how to punctuate. I boarded the bus to leave feeling as if I had gotten a lot more out of it than they did.'

PHOTOGRAPHY

If you fancy a future on the *National Geographic*, you can't do worse than investing in a really good digital camera or taking up a course in travel photography first. Check with your local college to see if they run photography classes.

WORKING IN AN INTERNATIONAL COMMUNITY

Whether you are working on a newspaper in the Ukraine or building schools in Mozambique, one thing you can be certain of is that you will be working in an international community. As exciting as this may sound, it's still worth noting that working in a group in Darkest Peru can bring up exactly the kind of tensions that slaving away nine to five in a London office can bring. In short, people are people, wherever you go – mostly nice, occasionally nasty, and all weathering the bumpy ride that working with other people can bring. Living and working as part of a community aimed towards a common goal is going to take a certain amount of tolerance and adaptation. It's wise, then, to go prepared – expect to be stretched, challenged and blasted out of your comfort zones.

- **Don't make assumptions, least of all based on somebody's nationality. National stereotypes carry a dreary predictability and are hardly the best way of creating positive, personal relationships.**

- **Don't boast about the so-called superiority of your nation, and never attack anyone else's nation or politics. In my workcamp in France, I remember having to justify the UK's politics to some people from Czechoslovakia and it was a little irritating to say the least. I was clearly viewed as a rampant capitalist just by virtue of the fact that I came from the UK, despite the fact that I'm not right-wing at all. That said, if people do criticise your nation, try to keep it in perspective and keep an open mind. Removed from the insular cocoon of our native culture, it can be a rude awakening to see your home country through** the critical eyes of another nationality. Given recent world events, this has particular resonance now, so, if people do launch an attack on your country's politics, try not to take it too personally and, above all, don't turn it into argument.

- Respect religious and cultural differences and don't ram your own morality down other people's throats.

- Practise a little humility. You may feel as if you're going over offering the biggest favour of your life, but many volunteers return saying they learned more from the locals than they ever taught them.

- Take gifts from your home country to offer people – these can include local food, magazines, souvenirs and photos and postcards of your home town. Bear in mind that what may seem mundane to you can be wildly exotic to other people. When I was teaching English to Japanese people, I developed a thing about Japanese packaging and would gratefully accept food boxes and sweet wrappers as if I'd been handed priceless gems. In return my Japanese friends would pounce on packets of English tea as if they had been offered the Holy Grail.

LANGUAGE

Obviously one of the most important ways to embrace the culture you are visiting is to learn a little of the language before you go. Many voluntary projects include a wide range of nationalities and English, as the international language, will be the most widely spoken. That said, by their very nature, volunteer projects are meant to engage with the local community, so speaking the local lingo is by far the best scenario. It can also be good to make sure you are well grounded in another European language such as Spanish or French, which other volunteers may speak well. Most voluntary organisations operating outside Europe will run some kind of orientation course which should ideally include a crash course in the native language. On the other hand, you can't beat taking a language course yourself – look up schools and classes on the Internet or in the Yellow Pages, or head for the local library or university notice board. If money isn't a problem, there are plenty of language courses on cassettes, videos and CDs that can give you a thorough introduction.

An even cheaper option is to advertise in the local paper/shop windows/libraries/local English schools to give one-to-one conversational English classes in exchange for private tuition in your chosen language from a native speaker. This works particularly well if you live in an area where there is high concentration of tourists or language students. You can also do this when you are abroad – it's a great way of meeting locals and getting involved with the community. Look out for adverts in English-language cafés and bars, or on university and hostel notice boards.

COMING HOME

For other people culture shock can kick in most once we've returned home. This is particularly true if you've been signed up for a one-year/two-year programme in a developing country with a culture that is remarkably different from our own. Some of the large NGOs have returned-volunteer programmes and, if you are signing up for the long haul, you might want to ask what support is offered when you return home. VSO, for example, runs a debriefing weekend for returned volunteers. One former VSO volunteer says, 'VSO is very supportive about helping you to reintegrate into UK society and find work. In fact, when we were in South Africa we had regular newsletters about paid opportunities in the UK voluntary sector that we could apply for from abroad.'

Of course, making the transition at home can be a shock even if you have only been away for a few months. Seeing your home culture through fresh eyes can offer new insights, not all of them welcome. I know of people who, after a stint in India, come home to repeatedly bemoan the crass materialism of their own Western culture. They may be right, but they're certainly not doing themselves any favours by repeatedly telling their friends. Faced with the same negative diatribe, is it any wonder people get a glazed look and start to seek the company of other friends? It might seem unfair, but do remember that there are plenty of things that other nations would be proud to have – like democracy, freedom of speech, human rights and a good level of healthcare.

The more positive aspect of this, of course, is that you can use your newfound knowledge to stimulate a change here. Instead of moaning and dwelling on the negatives, you can petition your government to back development programmes, start a support group, donate to a charity or volunteer at home.

VOLUNTEERS' STORIES

Katharine Dennison spent two years in South Africa with VSO, and found returning to the UK just as much of a culture shock as starting her placement. She says, 'For one thing I'd forgotten how cold it was – it was 38° when we left South Africa and when we got off the plane it was –8°. I was also startled at how few non-white people there were – I had been living in rural South Africa where there were only a handful of white people in a black community, so that took some getting used to. I also couldn't get over how much choice there was – in South Africa, you could go into a local shop and find there wouldn't be any fruit or veg for a week, whereas, here, you can walk down a supermarket aisle and find yourself surrounded by a huge variety of goods flown in from all over the world. For the first few months, I couldn't choose. I spent hours in shops not being able to make up my mind.'

Katharine's experience also made her realise the good things about the UK. 'It's definitely made me appreciate what we have here. I will never slate the public transport, NHS, post offices or banks here because, when you don't have them in place, it makes life so much harder. In rural South African communities you have to pay for your own health, and I knew neighbours who couldn't afford the treatment they needed. The public transport is also not safe and we weren't encouraged to use it. There were lots of road deaths and accidents.'

VOLUNTEERING IN DEVELOPING COUNTRIES

You would have to be living on Mars not to be aware of the terrible injustices that exist in this world. The poor are getting poorer while the rich reap all the benefits that living in the wealthiest countries brings. Much talk has been made of wiping out the Third World debt and every day in the newspapers rows rage on about the relative benefits and drawbacks of trade laws. Whatever your views, volunteering in many cases is going to put you slap bang in the middle of directly experiencing these inequalities. How you cope with this is obviously going to depend on your personality and politics. But don't underestimate how it might affect you. Your outlook may change. It may even depress you. So, before you commit, take some time to reflect on how you might react to witnessing certain situations. Like what? Like seeing babies colour-coded to signal their parents died from AIDS. Like teaching school children and finding candle wax on their homework because they can't afford the luxury of electricity. Like seeing women spat on because they're not adequately covered. Or being propositioned for sex every time you walk out of the door. Or living in countries torn apart by civil war. Meeting girls in orphanages who have been sold into prostitution by their fathers. Finding yourself in the middle of anti-Western riots. These may sound extreme but, in the course of interviewing travellers, I have heard stories about all these and countless other things.

KNOW YOUR RIGHTS

Volunteering in some countries can be potentially dangerous. The danger is also becoming more widespread and, with the rise in interest in international volunteering, it is worth noting that there are a small number of NGOs or agencies operating in troubled countries that might not have such stringent procedures in place. In the course of researching this book, I have interviewed volunteers who were thrown into countries known as international trouble spots and given little support or training. It is vital then to make sure you know your rights, and check what guidelines are in place, should there be trouble. The large NGOs automatically have an evacuation procedure and subscribe to the People in Aid code (to see the full code go to **www.peopleinaid.org.uk**). If you are volunteering through a smaller NGO or agency, follow this advice:

- **Choose a trusted organisation.**

- **Check that you will be evacuated in case of trouble.**

- **Have good medical insurance including repatriation.**

- **Register with the Foreign Office as soon as you arrive. In the event of an emergency situation, they will be able to contact you and help you if necessary. In some countries where there is a large proportion of British residents, such as Kenya, there are area wardens who will contact you to check you are OK if there is trouble.**

AID WORK

Working in emergency and disaster settings is a dangerous occupation. It can introduce you to all kinds of threats, from health risks to violent crime to political coups, and get you tangled up in all kinds of trouble that may well be beyond the reach of international diplomacy. According to the UN, at least 27 aid workers were killed by violence in 2001, with at least 48 killed the year before. If you are interested in starting a career in aid work, then be aware that you are facing serious risks, so taking care is imperative. Make sure your sending NGO follows the People in Aid code, and that before you start you receive adequate training. For further advice and support, you can join Aid Workers Net (**www.aidworkers.net**), a forum for aid workers to exchange information and guidance.

PART THREE: WHERE TO GO

EUROPE

10. AUSTRIA AND SWITZERLAND

AUSTRIA

Volunteering is a popular activity in Austria, with more than a quarter of the population active in the voluntary sector on a regular basis. Many of the Austrian essential services are run by volunteers, including all libraries (except in the largest cities). Roughly a fifth of all Austrians hold responsible official functions within the voluntary sector. In fact, according to a government report, without this voluntary commitment, many aid organisations in the social, health and humanitarian sphere would not exist.

VISAS AND REGULATIONS

As Austria is a member of the EU, all EU nationals have the right to live and work in Austria without a visa for no longer than three months. EU citizens who intend to stay longer than three months should register with the Aliens Adminstration Office within three days of arrival. They do not, however, require a work permit.

NON-EU NATIONALS

Non-EU/EEA nationals who want to live and work in Austria or the Schengen Area should apply for a work and residence permit, normally outside Austria. Work permits can be hard to obtain unless you work for an international organisation or have essential skills that Austrians and EU citizens can't provide. Log on to **www.austria.org.uk**, Link: Aufenthalt, for visa information and applications or, for information on work permits, **www.help.gv.at**, Link: Aufenthaltserlaubnis.

FINDING WORK ON THE SPOT

With such a strong tradition of volunteering, projects should be easy to come by through word of mouth. However, despite the increasing importance of English, a good level of Austrian German is certainly more likely to open doors for you.

Head for the local *Arbeitsmarkt* (job centre) as it sometimes carries details of voluntary work and have a good reputation for assisting foreigners. It also has an online job search on its website (**www.ams.or.at/**), which is in German.

Also check out The Austrian Volunteer service website **www.freiwilligenweb.at/**, which lists news on volunteering and voluntary opportunities, also in German.

The local and national newspapers, such as *Die Presse* (**www.DiePresse.at**), *Kurier* (**www.kurier.at**) and *Der Standard* (**www.derStandard.at**), contain supplements on job vacancies in their weekend editions.

The Association of Voluntary Service Organisations (AVSO) is the European platform for not-for-profit organisations active in the field of longer-term voluntary work. Although it does not organise voluntary placements itself, it represents more than eighty organisations, most of which recruit volunteers. You can search for projects across Austria on its website: **www.avso.org**.

FINDING WORK BEFORE YOU ARRIVE

Voluntary organisations that run schemes and workcamps in Austria are Across Trust, Camphill Village Trust, Global Outreach Mission UK, International Voluntary Service, Intercultural Youth Exchange, Prince's Trust, Travel Active and Christians Abroad.

Inter Cultural Youth Exchange offers one-year placements in Germany or Austria under the European Voluntary Scheme to 18- to 25-year-old European nationals on a pocket money, board and lodging basis. See **www.icye.co.uk** for details.

WWOOF Austria can arrange working vacations on organic farms in Austria. For Euro 20/US $25 and two IRC (International Reply Coupons), you receive the illustrated farm list with more than 130 farms representing the whole range of organic farming interests (including bio-dynamics, permaculture and other systems, vineyards, eco-tourism, farm shops and co-operatives). Send a letter with two International Reply Coupons, briefly introducing yourself. However, experience has shown that some farmers do not respond and expect you to call by telephone when in Austria. If so, you are advised to make an appointment, otherwise the farmer may turn you away. For more information go to the website **www.members.telering.at/wwoof.welcome** or write to Willing Workers on Organic Farms, Hildegard Gottlieb, Langegg 155, A 8511 St. Stefan ob Stainz, Tel/Fax: 00 43-3463-82270.

Euro Practice (**www.euro-practice.com**) organises work-experience placements for European students in Austria and has offices in France, England, Germany and Spain.

Village Camps (**www.villagecamps.com**) arranges work for the summer in multi-activity language children's camps in Austria and Switzerland. Contact Village Camps, rue de la Morache, 1260 Nyon, Tel: 00 41 22-990-9405, Fax: 00 41 22-990-9494.

USEFUL ADDRESSES

The Overseas Placement Unit (part of the UK Employment Service) produces a leaflet, *Working in Austria*. It is available from Job Centres and Euroadvisers in the UK or by writing to: Overseas Placing Unit, Rockingham House, 123 West Street, Sheffield S1 4ER.

SWITZERLAND

Despite the fact that Switzerland is a prosperous country, voluntary activities play an important role. One in four people carry out some form of voluntary work, with a similar number involved in informal unpaid activities such as helping neighbours or looking after other people's children. Like many European countries, Switzerland has committed more resources to its voluntary infrastructure in recent years. There has even been new legislation designed to further volunteers' interests. Not only are all volunteer-using institutions soon supposed to issue a social service certificate listing the work done and skills acquired in carrying out voluntary work, but there has also been recent talk of allowing volunteers tax relief or better access to training courses.

However, getting around the notorious Swiss red tape is a challenge. In the past, Switzerland has had a reputation for not exactly opening their arms to non-nationals, but this situation is gradually changing (see Visas and Regulations). However, the country is notorious for its complicated bureaucracy, so make sure you have as much of the documentation required as possible before arriving in Switzerland. Speaking Swiss German is usually required, and sometimes French or Italian – remember that Switzerland is divided into three language zones (German (Swiss German), French and Italian) and the dominant spoken language will depend on which region you find work in. Switzerland is also a tightly regulated country and has a high cost of living.

Sports and cultural associations are the most popular institutions to give time to, but Switzerland also has a strong green movement and there are opportunities to be found in welfare work, education, religion and politics. There are also many voluntary agencies and organisations in Switzerland which send volunteers overseas.

VISAS AND REGULATIONS

In order to work in Switzerland, be it in paid or voluntary employment, you will require a work permit. This law is about to change in June 2004 for EU nationals, however, so check the situation first on the website **www.foreigners.ch**, which carries extensive consular information.

Switzerland has always had a tough reputation when it comes to immigration, but the situation is gradually improving. Despite not being a member of the EU, Switzerland has recently signed a bilateral treaty on free movements with the European Union, granting EU nationals the right to live and work in Switzerland provided that they satisfy certain requirements. This basically means that EU nationals may now enter Switzerland for job-hunting purposes. No permit is required for a period of up to three months. If they have not found a job after this time, a short-term residence permit (L permit) will be granted for another three months' job-hunting. This permit must also be obtained if you do find work, and is valid for a period of three months to less than a year.

If you wish to stay for longer than this, you should apply for a residence permit (B permit), which is valid for five years. This primarily concerns salaried employees who are in possession of an employment contract lasting for more than one year. However, people who are not 'gainfully employed' can also obtain this permit, provided that they possess sufficient financial resources and hold health and accident insurance policies which cover all the risks.

At the time of writing (2003), obtaining a work/residence permit is subject to the priority of Swiss employees, a check on compliance with professional and locally customary wage and working conditions, and special quotas for European nationals (115,500 short-term residence permits and 15,000 five-year residence permits will be available every year). However, these requirements will gradually be lifted as the twelve-year transitional period develops.

NON-EU NATIONALS

Non-EU nationals are still subject to the same stringent immigration rules and will find working legally in Switzerland difficult, even in a voluntary capacity. The best strategy to adopt is to find an exchange programme between Switzerland and your country. Canadians can take advantage of The Canada–Switzerland Young Workers Exchange Program, which gives Canadians the opportunity to work in Switzerland for a period of four to eighteen months. Contact International Youth Experience, The Canada–Switzerland Young Workers' Exchange Program, 12, rue Laval, Aylmer, Quebec, Canada, Tel: 00 1 (819) 684-9212, Fax: 00 1 (819) 684-5630 for more details.

FINDING WORK ON THE SPOT

There are several good volunteer bureaux in Switzerland, although non-nationals may find themselves hampered by the fact that the information is often presented in the official language of the region (French, German or Italian). Given the difficulty in obtaining work permits for non-EU nationals, those wishing to do short term voluntary work may find it more appropriate to work on a tourist permit. According to the Swiss branch of WWOOF many of their volunteers work this way. However it is advised that you check the work permit situation thoroughly, as illegal labour may result in heavy penalties for both the employers and illegal labourers. In fact, the advice given from WWOOF can be well applied to many voluntary-work situations: in particular, it advises Eastern European students and those from Third World countries not to send any money for membership without first securing a valid document allowing entry into Switzerland, since a visa can take a long time to process or be hard to obtain. It also says that, if you need help in order to get a visa, or are planning only a short WWOOF stay, then it is not likely that you will find a host who will make the effort of applying for a work permit for you.

FINDING WORK BEFORE YOU ARRIVE

The best way to find voluntary work in Switzerland is to arrange it before you arrive. Some of the main voluntary organisations organise schemes and workcamps here, including Concordia, Camphill Village Trusts, International Voluntary Service, Prince's Trust and Travel Active. Americans can try Volunteers for Peace Service Civil International and International Volunteer Projects.

UK voluntary organisation Concordia can fix up work as farmer assistants through the non-profit-making organisation Landdienst-Zentralstelle (Postfach 728, CH-8025 Zurich, Switzerland, Tel: 00 41 1-261 44-88, Fax: 00 41 1-261-44-32, Email: admin@landdienst.ch, website: **www.landdienst.ch**). Wages are around £190 per month plus free board and lodging. Send an SAE to Concordia, Heversham House, 20/22 Boundary Road, Hove, East Sussex BN3 4ET.

Education for Development's (EFD) committee needs volunteers to help at its Swiss branch. The committee organises fundraising activities to raise community awareness about disadvantaged children in Vietnam and to raise funds for EFD. Tasks include fundraising, administration and organising campaigns to raise public awareness. To find out more go to **www.educationfordevelopment.org**.

The Swiss-based organisation Pan Eco organises voluntary work in nature reserves in Switzerland, as well as placing volunteers all over the world on development projects. Contact Foundation PanEco, Chileweg 5, CH-8415 Berg am Irchel, Switzerland, Tel: 00 41 52 318 23 23, Fax: 00 41 52 318 19 06, website: **www.paneco.ch**.

The NGO IC Volunteers connects volunteers and organisers of non-profit-making projects, in particular social, humanitarian, environmental and scientific conferences. Volunteers are welcome from all over the world to assist at its Geneva office. It also trains and places volunteers to work with not-for-profit organisations, and recruits trains and co-ordinates volunteer interpreters for Raising the Voices, a training programme for survivors of landmines. In 2002, languages required included English, French, Spanish and Portuguese, and recently there have been calls for Afghan, Khmer and Tamil speakers. Contact IC Volunteers, PO Box 755, 1211 Geneva 4, Switzerland, Tel: 00 41 (0) 22 800 14 36, Fax: 00 41 (0) 22 800 14 37 or 321 53 27, website: **www.icvolunteers.org**.

VOLUNTEER BUREAUX

Bourse du Bénévolat was formed by the Conseil des Anciens In Geneva as a forum to link volunteers with voluntary organisations and opportunities. You can search for volunteer opportunities once you have registered on its website **www.benevoles-ge.ch/**. Contact Bourse du Bénévolat, c/o Conseil des Anciens, 48, rue de Montchoisy, Case postale 6212, 1211 Geneva 6, Tel: 00 41 22 735 79 35.

Action Benevole, Association pour l'Étude et la Promotion de l'Action Bénévole, Maupas 49, CH-1004 Lausanne, Tel: 00 41 21 646 21 96, Fax: 00 41 21 646 18 97, Email: info@benevolat.ch.

Fachstelle für Freiwilligenarbeit im Kanton Thurgau, Frauenfelderstrasse 37, 8570 Weinfelden, Tel: 00 41 71 626 58 42, Fax: 00 41 71 626 58 49, website: **www.sozialzeit.org/**.

Benevol Schweiz, Verein Fach – und Vermittlungsstellen für Freiwilligenarbeit, Schwarztorstrasse 20, 3007 Bern, Tel: 00 41 031 398 40 85, Fax 00 41 031 398 40 86, website: **www.benevol.ch**.

WWOOF-Switzerland: For around US$15 or 15 Euro you can obtain a WWOOF-Switzerland farm list of about 45 farms all over Switzerland, where, in return for your help, you receive meals, a place to sleep and a practical insight into organic growing methods. Write to WWOOF Switzerland, Postfach 59, CH-8124 Maur, Switzerland.

USEFUL ADDRESSES

Austrian Embassy, 18 Belgrave Mews West, London SW1X 8HU, Tel: 020 7235 373, website: **www.austria.org.uk** or 3524 International Court, NW, Washington, DC 20008, USA, Tel: 00 1 202 895 6700, website: **www.austria-emb.org**.

Swiss Embassy, 16–18 Montague Place, London W1H 2BQ, Tel: 020 7616 6000, Fax 020 7724 7001, Email: swissembassy@Lon.rep.admin.ch, website: **www.swissembassy.org.uk** or 2900 Cathedral Avenue, NW, Washington, DC 20008, USA, Tel: 00 1 202 745 7900, website: **www.swissemb.org**.

11. BELGIUM AND THE NETHERLANDS

BELGIUM

Volunteering in Belgium has much to recommend it. The first advantage is its thriving expat scene. Almost a third of the population is made up of foreigners, which makes integrating into this country a less daunting prospect than in other countries. Belgium is also the centre for the European Union, and accordingly has plenty to offer English-speakers, with a high standard of English throughout. Outside Brussels, however, you will fare better in your work search if you speak one of its three official languages – Dutch in Flanders, French in Wallonia and German in the Eastern cantons.

Like the Netherlands, Belgium is a high-volunteering country, where about 25 per cent of the population regularly give their time for free. Civic and community development is the most popular form of unpaid work, particularly campaigning work within local voluntary or statutory organisations. There is also a strong element of visiting and befriending. Unlike most other places in Europe, people in Belgium show a firm moral responsibility to volunteer, and believe it improves social status.

VISAS AND REGULATIONS

EU nationals are free to live and work in Belgium, but if you intend to stay for over three months you should register within eight days at the local town hall. Here you will be issued with a temporary *certificate d'immatriculation*, valid for three months, or a *certificate d'inscription au registre des etrangers*, lasting for one year. You should also be able to get hold of a copy of its magazine *Newcomer*. Although this is mainly aimed at the professional or managerial people relocating to Belgium, it has some useful information for anyone wishing to live there.

NON-EU NATIONALS

Non-EU nationals must first find work and get hold of a work permit and residence entry visa before arriving in Belgium. According to Belgian law, your prospective employer must first prove that there is no local source of labour or skills in the Belgian labour force to fill the job and, in most cases, the same rules usually to voluntary work. If you are in any doubt, contact your Belgian Embassy or the nearest Belgian Consulate for details.

FINDING WORK ON THE SPOT

Belgium can be a good option for the travelling volunteer who wants to turn up and find work, and has good volunteer centres, particularly the headquarters for European Volunteer Centre (CEV) (**www.cev.be**). Non-nationals can also try the state employment agency (VDAB, FOREM or ONEM depending on the region).

FINDING WORK BEFORE YOU ARRIVE

Across Trust, Concordia, Christians Abroad, Global Outreach Mission UK, International Voluntary Service, Intercultural Youth Exchange, Institute of Cultural Affairs, Prince's Trust, Quaker Voluntary Action and European Voluntary Service all organise voluntary schemes in Belgium, while Americans can try Volunteers for Peace, Sierra Club and CIEE.

To work on city farms, contact the National Federation of City Farms in the UK (Tel: 0117 923 1800) who can give you contact details for the European Federation of City Farms which supports 880 farms in nine countries including Belgium.

Année Diaconale is the Belgian branch of the European Diaconal Year Network, which places volunteers on Christian-based schemes. Contact Année Diaconale, SPJ, Rude du Champs de mars 5, 1050 Bruxelles, Belgium, Tel: 00 32 2 513 24 01, Fax: 00 32 2 511 28 90.

The Association of Voluntary Service Organisations (AVSO) is the European platform for not-for-profit organisations active in the field of longer-term voluntary work. Although it does not organise voluntary placements itself, it represents more than eighty organisations, most of which recruit volunteers. You can search for projects across Holland and Belgium on its website **www.avso.org**.

For Mother Earth/Voor Moeder Aarde are always in need of volunteers to help in the office, reception, kitchen and restaurant. Go to **www.motherearth.org** for more information, or contact Maria-Hendrikaplein 5–6 (opposite Gent Sint-Pieters Station), 9000 Gent, Belgium, Tel: 00 32 9 242 87 52, Fax: 00 32 9 242 87 51.

Natuur 2000 (Bervoetstraat 33, B-2000 Antwerpen, Belgium, Tel: 00 32 3 231 26 04, Fax: 00 32 3 233 64 99) uses volunteers to assist with its nature conservation activities in Belgium for young people, as well as an environmental information centre. Volunteers should be aged between 16 and 23 and have experience in field biology or environmental conservation.

Education for Development's (EFD) committee needs volunteers to help at its Belgian branch. The committee organises fundraising activities to raise community awareness about disadvantaged children in Vietnam and to raise funds for EFD. Tasks include fundraising, administration and organising campaigns to raise public awareness. To find out more go to **www.educationfordevelopment.org**.

VOLUNTEER BUREAUX

The 'Vlaams Steunpunt Vrijwilligerswerk vzw' (formerly known as the 'Platform voor Voluntariaat') is the Flemish Centre for voluntary work. The organisation is open to all volunteer organisations and forms a bridge between voluntary workers and organisations employing volunteers. Its website **www.vrijwilligerswerk.be** has a database in Dutch with available volunteer vacancies. There is also a network of 'Provinciale Steunpunten' regional offices in each of the Flemish provinces.

You can also try:

Association pour le Volontariat, Rue Royale 11, 1000 Bruxelles, Belgium, Tel: 00 32 2 219 5370/5396, Fax: 00 32 2 219 3248, Email: volontariat@swing.be, website: **ww.volontariat.be**.

Het Punt Brussels Volunteer Centre, Treurenberg 24, 1000 Brussels, Belgium, Tel: 00 32 2 218 5516, Fax: 00 32 2 218 7166, Email: hetpunt@busmail.net, website: **http://hetpunt.vgc.be**.

Also keep an eye open in *The Bulletin*, which is an English-language newspaper with a Situations Vacant column.

THE NETHERLANDS

Finding voluntary work is a good option in the Netherlands, which has a high rate of volunteering and a very well-developed volunteering infrastructure. Organisations are well funded and organised, and Dutch volunteers are said to enjoy their work very much, with some workers being offered expenses. Sporting and recreational volunteering is particularly popular, as is serving on committees and carrying out fundraising. According to research from the National Centre of Volunteering, volunteering is seen as being strongly linked to playing an active role in a democratic society and there is less of a perception that volunteers are filling statutory areas of responsibility.

VISAS AND REGULATIONS

The same rule as with all EU member states applies: EU nationals are free to enter Holland to look for work for up to three months. However, you may be asked to prove that you have adequate means for the duration of your stay and that the cost of your return journey is secured. Once you are there, EU/EEA citizens must register with their local Foreign Police registration office (*Vreemdelingenpolitie*) within eight days of arrival. If you are intending to look for work (and are without a work contract) you will be asked to show your passport at the Foreign Police Registration Office to get a police permit.

If you wish to work for more than three months, you must apply for a residence permit (*Verblijfsvergunning*) from the Town Hall or community office – *Stadhuis* or *Gemeente*. You will need to present your passport, police permit, SOFI number, two photographs, a full version of your birth certificate and, in some cities (e.g. Amsterdam), proof from your landlord that you have a permanent address.

NON-EU NATIONALS

Visitors from Australia, Canada, Japan, New Zealand and the US don't need a visa to enter the Netherlands for stays of up to ninety days. They are also allowed to work for less than three months but must report to the Aliens Police within three days of arrival. Their employer must also obtain an employment permit for them (*tewerkstellingsvergunning*), although this is rarely issued for casual work.

If you wish to stay for more than three months you must first obtain a work permit before entering the country. Work permits can be difficult to get hold of for non-EU nationals and you may have to show proof of return fare and sufficient funds to support yourself.

FINDING WORK ON THE SPOT

Turning up to find voluntary work is a real possibility in the Netherlands, thanks to its excellent job-finding network. You can try one of the many job sites geared especially to voluntary work (see Volunteer Bureaux) or visit the state employment service which is said to be helpful towards foreigners. Another option is to try the private employment agencies called *Uitzendbureaux*, which carry details of casual and sometimes voluntary work. The newspapers also run vacancies.

FINDING WORK BEFORE YOU ARRIVE

Many of the main voluntary organisations organise schemes in the Netherlands, including Concordia, Quaker Voluntary Action, Camphill Village Trust, Prince's Trust, Earthwatch, Global Outreach Mission UK, International Voluntary Service and Travel Active.

Americans can take part in projects organised by Volunteers For Peace which has thirty short-term international workcamps in the Netherlands. The Christian-based Brethren Volunteer Service has programmes in various cities in the Netherlands, while the CIEE runs international volunteer programmes in various countries including the Netherlands. Contact CIEE, 7 Custom House Street, 3rd Floor, Portland, ME 04101, United States, Tel: 00 1-800 407 8839, Fax: 00 1 207 553 7699.

Humanitas is a national member-based organisation for social services and community development and places around 10,000 volunteers in around eighty local branches. Volunteers work in a range of roles, helping the elderly, organising social contacts for people who suffer from loneliness, setting up programmes for children from dysfunctional families, helping people sort out financial problems and counselling transsexuals and their relatives. Humanitas also employs professionals in training, counselling, housing, learning difficulties, caring and social work. Contact Humanitas, Nederlandse Vereniging voor Maatschappelijke Dienstverlening en Samenlevingsopbouw, PO Box 71, NL-1000 AB Amsterdam, Tel: 00 31 (0)20 - 523 1100, Fax: 00 31 (0)20 - 622 7367, website: **www.humanitas.nl**.

The Dutch Youth Association for History (NJBG) organises archaeological and restoration camps in Holland, and other countries. Visit its website www.njbg.nl/ or contact Bureau NJBG, Prins Willem Alexanderhof 5, 2595 BE Den Haag, Tel: 00 31 70 - 347 6598, Fax: 00 31 70 - 335 2536.

VOLUNTEER BUREAUX

Vrijwilligers Centrale is the main voluntary agency in Amsterdam and is based at Hartenstraat 16 (Tel: 00 31 (0)20 530 12 20). If you understand Dutch, you can also try its website: **www.vrijwilligerscentrale.nl/**.

You can also try SIW, the Dutch youth exchange organisation (Vrijwilligersprojeckten, Willemstraat 7, Utrecht, Tel: 00 31 30-231 7721), which organises about twenty projects in the Netherlands, as well as overseas workcamps for Dutch people. Projects are organised through partner organisations in other countries. For more information, go to **www.siw.nl/index**.

The Dutch jobcentres, *Arbeidsbureau* (AB), are available to EU nationals after completing the entry formalities listed above. For addresses look in the Yellow Pages (*Gouden Gids*) or contact Central Bureau voor de Arbeidsvoorziening, Boerhaavelaan 7, Postbus 883, Nl-2700 Aw Zoetermeer, Tel: 00 31 79 - 371 2000, Fax: 00 31 79 - 371 2099.

USEFUL ADDRESSES

The Belgian Embassy, 103 Eaton Square London SW1W 9AB, Tel: 020 7470 3700, or 3330 Garfield Street, NW, Washington, DC 20008, USA, Tel: 00 1 202 333 6900, website: **www.belgium-emb.org**.

The Ministère de l'Emploi et du Travail can supply you with information and application forms for work permits. Contact Ministère de l'Emploi et du Travail, 51, rue Belliard, 1040 Brussels, Tel: 00 32 (02) 233 41 11, Fax: 00 32 (02) 233 44 8851.

Royal Netherlands Embassy, 38 Hyde Park Gate, London SW7 5DP, Tel: 020 7584 5040, or 4200 Linnean Avenue, NW, Washington, DC 20008, USA, Tel: 00 1 202 244 5300, website: **www.netherlands-embassy.org**.

You can get the free booklets *Working in the Netherlands* and *Working in Belgium* from Employment Service, Overseas Placing Unit, Rockingham House, 123 West Street, Sheffield S1 4ER.

OTHER USEFUL RESOURCES

The website Free Flex (**www.freeflex.nl/**) lists volunteer opportunities in the Netherlands searchable by sector (in Dutch).

Vrijwilligersnet (**http://vrijwilligers.intranets.com**) is aimed at Dutch volunteers, at those who do voluntary work in the Netherlands and at those who work as volunteers for Dutch organisations.

The website for Dutch Company Pages has a volunteer page listing voluntary opportunities: **www.dmo.com/dyp/147,12,0.html**.

Also try **www.vrijwilligersplein.nl/** (in Dutch). The website for Nederlandse Organisaties Vrijwilligerswerk or Dutch Organisations Volunteer Work

(NOV) has useful links to other related sites. Visit **www.nov.nl/links/index.html**.

The Dutch section of the European Employment Services of the European Union (**www.hesp.nl/eures**) has links to the government employment agencies, private employment agencies and other job sites.

To search for NGOs in Netherlands in The Hague, go to **www.thehaguelegalcapital.nl/lc/organizations/ngos**.

Holland is one of the five countries featured on the European Commission-funded website The Euro-Volunteers Information Pool, which includes a searchable database of voluntary initiatives in Holland, as well as France, Greece, Luxembourg and Germany. Go to **www.euro-volunteers.org**.

The press and word of mouth are very important mediums for job-hunting in Holland. Most Dutch national and regional newspapers such as *De Telegraaf*, *Het Algemeen Dagblad* and *De Volkskrant* carry job advertisements, especially on Saturdays. There is also *Intermediair*, a weekly paper for graduates. Check the classified advertisements under *Personeel Gevraagd* (Personnel Wanted).

12. EASTERN EUROPE AND RUSSIA

EASTERN EUROPE

Most Eastern European countries are well served for voluntary opportunities, with many of the major organisations arranging placements here. Opportunities range from two- to four-week workcamps focusing around a specific community-centred task, such as renovating an old church or building a well, to teaching English in Bulgaria, working in a Romanian orphanage or work experience on a Hungarian newspaper. Gap-year travellers can rest assured they are well served in this respect. Turning up and finding work on indigenous programmes, however, is tricky, as the number of Eastern European voluntary organisations is very limited. If you don't want to go through a Western organisation, the best bet is to contact one of the volunteer bureaux in the particular country you are interested in before you arrive and ask them if they know of any local opportunities.

The voluntary situation varies depending on where you go. According to the Czech Republic's national volunteer centre, Hestia, for example, the Czechs have a deeply engrained distrust of voluntary work, while other countries such as Lithuania are finding that the voluntary sector can ease the pressure on the state by providing much-needed services.

The point to remember about Eastern and Central European countries is that many are in a fragile and volatile condition. Many countries are still adapting after years of enforced communism; poverty levels can be high and conditions may be shocking in the eyes of affluent Westerners. Volunteering in the Former Yugoslavia, for example (Croatia, Serbia, Bosnia and Slovenia) may be particularly demanding, and some workcamps require only experienced or professionally skilled volunteers. In many cases, prospective volunteers are advised to take part in an international workcamp in western Europe first. Wherever you wish to go, and for whatever causes, make sure you think carefully about how you may cope with working in such cultures.

With EU membership looming for eight countries, however, it looks as if the situation is set to change further. People interested in volunteering in these countries are advised to keep a watchful eye on the situation.

EU MEMBERSHIP
On 1 May 2004, the following ten countries will be joining the European Union (EU): Cyprus, the Czech Republic, Estonia, Hungary, Latvia, Lithuania, Malta, Poland, the Slovak Republic and Slovenia. The following visa and regulations are correct at the time of writing, but will change when the countries are EU members to accord with EU regulations. Clearly, this has numerous benefits for EU nationals who wish to turn up and find work without having the obligation to obtain a work permit.

International Volunteers for Peace (IVP), the Australian branch of Service Civil International (SCI) organises camps in Eastern Europe. Contact IVP, 499 Elizabeth Street, Surry Hills, NSW 2010 Australia, Tel: 00 61 2 9699 1129, Fax: 00 61 2 9699 9182, website: **www.ivp.org.au/**.

THE CZECH REPUBLIC AND SLOVAKIA

At the moment, in order to undertake voluntary work in the Czech Republic, you will have to obtain a visa. This can be a complicated procedure and basically requires you to fix up work before you arrive, which rules out the possibility of turning up and finding projects as you travel around. Many of the main volunteer-sending agencies operate workcamps in the Czech Republic, including Earthwatch, Concordia, Quaker Voluntary Action, Youth Action for Peace, Christians Abroad, UNA Exchange, while Americans can try Service Civil International.

Although grassroots programmes are generally hard to find, the Czech Republic's national volunteer centre, Hestia, in Prague should be able to notify you of any opportunities. Its website is an excellent introduction to volunteering in the Czech Republic, and includes lists of voluntary organisations and centres throughout the country. It also has details of local voluntary positions open to young people from all over the world, such as summer workcamps at Ledovec helping to finish basic reconstruction of a therapeutic centre for people with mental handicap and/or psychiatric disease. Go to **http://volunteer.cz** for more information.

Prague is well served for English-language newspapers such as the expat newspaper the *Prague Post*, where you can keep an eye open for advertisements for volunteers. The Czech newspaper *Annonce*, which specialises in classifieds, is worth checking out. You can also try the notice boards in the English-language bookshops and libraries, and put up an advertisement yourself.

The Czech Republic has a strong environmental movement which can be seen in its wide range of eco-NGOs, including Rainbow movement Děti Země (Children of the Earth), Tereza, Greenpeace, Ecocentres and the Czech Union of Conservationists. There is also a strong human rights movement, mainly because of the fall of the previous regime.

To find out about volunteer opportunities in Slovakia, contact Slovak Humanitarian Council, Slovenska Humanitaria Rada, Ruzova Dolina 27, SK 82109 Bratislava, Slovakia, Tel: 00 421 7534 13970, Fax: 00 421 7534 13970.

Brontosaurus Movement, Brontosaurus Council, CR, Bubenska 6, Praha 7, Czech Republic 170 00 (Tel: 00 42-2-667-102 45), needs volunteers for its environmental summer workcamps. Write to the International Co-ordinator enclosing an International Reply Coupon for a copy of the list of summer camps open to non-nationals.

VISAS AND REGULATIONS

The regulations for obtaining visas for the Czech Republic are complicated and mired in red tape. British citizens holding British passports do not require a visa to enter the Czech Republic for tourist stays of up to six months and for short business trips. The passport has to be valid for a period of at least 270 days. Most other European nationals and US nationals do not require a visa for tourist stays of up to three months.

For any other purposes, voluntary work included, at the moment you will need a visa. There are two categories of visas: 1) visa up to ninety days; 2) visa over ninety days. For both you have to apply at the Czech Embassy, preferably in the country of your residence. You will have to prove the purpose of your stay in the Czech Republic by a document confirming your engagement in voluntary work there, i.e. in the case of volunteering for a charity/educational facility/government project – an original confirmation of the organisation; in the case of volunteering for a company – confirmation of the Labour Office that the activity is not considered work and therefore there is no need to apply for a work permit.

For further assistance, UK citizens should call 020 7243 7988 for information on a visa over ninety days, and 020 7243 1115 for information on a visa up to ninety days.

The website for the Czech Embassy in London has plenty of information. Go to **www.czechembassy.org.uk**.

After 1 May 2004 the Czech Republic will be a member of the EU and EU nationals will be able to live and work there without a work permit.

HUNGARY

Like the Czech Republic, the best way to find voluntary work in Hungary is to fix up a place on a workcamp/project before you leave. Some organisations requiring volunteers for programmes in Hungary are Earthwatch, Christians Abroad, Gap Activity Projects, International Voluntary Service, Prince's Trust, Quaker Voluntary Action, VSO, World Exchange and Youth Action for Peace. BTCV run summer projects.

To obtain a farm list for WWOOF-Hungary, contact WWOOF, H-2105 Godollo, GATE Kollegium, Ungarn Hungary or Biokultura/WWOOF: Hungarian Association of Organic Growers, Biokultura Egyesulet, 1023 Budapest, Toruk u. 7 em 1, Hungary. Biokultura requires volunteers to work on placements on organic farms and gardens in Hungary.

Like Prague, Budapest has several English-language newspapers that have good classifieds sections listing all types of work, such as *Budapest Week*, *Budapest Sun* and the *Budapest Business Journal*. There are also two popular Hungarian newspapers that are well known for their free classifieds – the *Expressz* and *Hirdetes*. Try putting an advert in here, or head for the notice boards in the English-language bookshops and libraries.

VISAS AND REGULATIONS

All foreign nationals intending to stay longer than ninety days in Hungary must obtain a visa beforehand. Generally speaking, a work permit is also required. Check with the embassy beforehand to be sure. These rules may change for other EU nationals when Hungary joins the European Union on 1 May 2004. To get a visa you need a passport valid for at least six months, a return ticket for the whole journey or ticket reservation, confirmation of accommodation reservation or a letter of invitation from your host and an official invitation letter from the Hungarian organisation. Many nationals (including citizens of the UK, New Zealand, US and Canada) do not require a visa for short holidays or business trips of less than ninety days. For more information check the website for the Hungarian Embassy in the UK, **www.huemblon.org.uk**. Call 09065 508 936 for the visa information telephone service (calls cost £1 a minute) or for visa application forms call 09065 266 662 (calls cost £1.50 a minute).

POLAND

Compared to other European countries, Poland has a much lower incidence of volunteering. According to Pawel Jordan who set up the National Volunteer Centre in Poland, this is partly down to the fact that in Poland the idea of volunteering has very negative connotations. Under the previous regime, citizens were forced into 'compulsory volunteering', performing tedious tasks for the public good such as harvesting vegetables at co-operative farms.

Despite this long tradition of working towards the common good, however, volunteering for the benefit of the local community is almost unheard of. Local community groups are few and far between, and the best way to find work is to go through one of the Western organisations that send volunteers on projects in Poland. These include the following: Across Trust, BTCV, Camphill Village Trust, Christians Abroad, Concordia, Gap Activity Projects, Global Volunteers, Intercultural Youth Exchange, International Voluntary Service, Prince's Trust, Quaker Voluntary Action, VSO, Youth Action for Peace and the Australian Involvement Volunteers.

Despite this, many expats report that Poland is a great place for networking, and spreading the word to a few useful contacts that you are looking for unpaid work may open some much-needed doors for you.

To find out about the few local voluntary opportunities that do exist, head for the Volunteer Centre in Warsaw (Centrum Wolontariatu, 00-150 Warszawa, ul. Nowolipie 9/11, Tel: 00 48 22 635 27 73, Fax: 00 48 22 635 46 02).

Two other organizations that may be of help are Volunteer Association, Stowarzyszenie 'Centrum Wolontariatu', ul. Nowolipie 9/11, 00-150 Warszawa, Tel: 00 48 22 635 27 73, Fax: 00 48 22 635 46 02, Email: wolontar@medianet.com.pl, and BORIS: Biuro Obslugi Ruchu Inicjatyw Samopomocowych, Support Office For The Movement Of Self-Help Initiatives, 01-011 Warszawa, Nowolipie 25B, Tel: 00 48 22 838 26 72, Fax: 00 48 22 838 39 82, Email: boris@medianet.pl.

You can also try the Anglo-Polish Universities Assisted Teaching Project, Tel: 020 7498 7680 or 0113 275 81217.

The Mlodziezowa Agencja Pracy (Young Persons' Work Agency) provides advice and information on seasonal work for students, including voluntary work, Tel: 00 48 22 628 92 81, ext 196, Address: 00-491 Warszawa, ul. Konopnickiej 6.

Unlike Prague and Budapest, Warsaw does not have many English-language newspapers. The *Warsaw Voice* may feature voluntary-work opportunities, while the national paper *Gazeta Polska* carries job vacancies and is known to be an excellent resource.

VISAS AND REGULATIONS
EEA and US citizens do not need a visa to enter the country but your stay will be limited from fourteen to ninety days depending on your nationality. British people have up to 180 days. In order to work you will have to get hold of a work permit from your country of origin before you leave. This usually requires proof of relevant qualifications and proof from your future employer. Before travelling to Poland, you must apply for a Polish residence visa if you intend to undertake paid employment in Poland. This requires possession of a Polish work permit. Given the dubious reputation of voluntary work, and Poland's high unemployment rate, you can assume that the same rules apply for unpaid work. However, contact your nearest Polish Consulate General for information and check the situation thoroughly.

VOLUNTARY OPPORTUNITIES IN OTHER EASTERN EUROPEAN COUNTRIES
Belarus: ATM Belorussian Association of International Youth Work, PO Box 64, 220119 Minsk, Belarus (Tel: 0172 278183, Fax/Tel: 0172 222714), organises a range of social and ecological work camps in Belarus for volunteers over eighteen years old.

Croatia: Adriatic Dolphin Project allows volunteers to take part in an ongoing study of the ecology of the bottlenose dolphin inhabiting the Cres and Losinj waters (Croatia, Northern Adriatic Sea). Volunteers spend twelve days in the field base in Lošinj and actively participate in the daily routine. This includes collecting data at sea, preparing boats and equipment, logging data into computers, preliminary data analysis, preparation of lecture materials and background reading. Contact Adriatic Dolphin Project, Blue World (Plavisvjet), Kastel 2, HR-51551, Veli Lošinj, Croatia, Tel: 00 385 (51) 236406, Email: adp@hpm.hr, website: **www.hpm.hr/adp**.

Romania: There are many charities set up to help the children of Romania. One of these is The Tanner Romania Mission which has opportunities for volunteers to serve within the foundation and its five children's homes. Volunteers need to commit to placements lasting between three and twelve months. Most of the time will be spent providing structured activities for the children, cleaning and cooking and providing whatever help is necessary. Volunteers are provided with free board and lodgings. Contact Bruce and

Sandie Tanner, com. Nicoresti, jud Galati, Romania, Tel: 00 40 236-867-185 or go to www.tannermission.org.

British Romanian Connections organises voluntary teaching in Romania. For more information contact British Romanian Connections, PO Box 86, Birkenhead, Merseyside CH41 8FU, Tel: 0151 512 3355 or email brc@pascutulbure.freeserve.co.uk.

AMURT (Ananda Marga Universal Relief Team) operates voluntary projects worldwide designed to improve the quality of life for the poor and underprivileged people of the world, and to assist the victims of natural and man-made disasters. The organisation runs short- and long-term projects in Romania which require professional volunteers, including children's homes, kindergartens and healthcare. For more information visit the website: www.amurt.net/ or contact Amurt Global Network, 7627 16th St. NW, Washington, DC 20012, USA, Tel: 00 1 202 829 8676, Fax: 00 1 202 829 0462 or contact the AMURT Romania office directly: Str. Romancierilor 2A Bl M17 Apt 65, Bucharest, Tel/Fax: 00 40 21 4135522.

Munich Wildlife Society and Romanian State Forest Administration (Str. Mare 887, RO-2241, Prejmer, Romania, Tel: 00 40 (94) 532798, website: www.clcp.ro) occasionally runs projects such as the Carpathian Large Carnivore Project, which studies wolves and bears through radio-tracking and care for captive wolves.

Slovenia: Zavod Voluntariat: Service Civil International Slovenia, Breg 12 Sl-1000 Ljubljana, Slovenia (Tel: 00 386-1-4258067, Fax: 00 386-1-2517208, Email: placement@zavod-voluntariat.sl, website: www.zavod-voluntariat.sl) organises short-, long- and medium-term voluntary projects in Slovenia. Projects can range from ecological summer work camps to working with Bosnian refugees. Workcamps include food and accommodation.

VOLUNTEER BUREAUX IN EASTERN EUROPE
Bulgaria: The Bulgarian Volunteers' database in Bulgarian and English allows you to search for volunteer opportunities in Bulgaria and worldwide. Go to www.nava-bg.org/vdb/en/default.asp.

Lithuania: Lithuania National Volunteer Centre, Jaksto 9-306, 2006 Vilnius, Lithuania, Tel: 00 370 526 18 874, Fax: 00 370 526 18 874, website: www.nisc.lt/savanoris.php.

The NGO Information and Support Centre (in Lithuanian and English) has plenty of information about volunteering in Lithuania as well as details of Lithuanian projects. Go to www.nisc.lt.

Bosnia: OSMIJEH, Naselje Lamele bb, 75320 Gracanica, Bosnia-Herzegovina, Tel: 00 387 35 787 281, Fax: 00 387 35 787 281.

Romania: Pro Vobis National Volunteer Centre, 3400 Cluj Napoca, Piata Mihai Viteazu nr. 33 ap. 40, Tel/Fax: 00 40 264 412 897, Mobile: 00 40 744 88 17 93, website: www.voluntariat.ro.

RUSSIA AND THE FORMER SOVIET REPUBLICS

Now that the former Soviet Union has opened up, travellers are flocking there to experience a diverse and fascinating glimpse into Baltic culture. Working in Russia is notoriously difficult, thanks to complicated laws and red tape. Volunteering, then, is seen as the perfect opportunity to experience working life and gain access into a tightly insulated community.

However, despite the fact that Russia has a long tradition of community life, the concept of volunteering is little understood in modern society. This is partly because the voluntary sector is still in its infancy; it is only in the last decade or so that not-for-profit and charitable organisations have been able to legally exist. The other reason is that, like Poland, the previous regime carried heavy obligations to give up free time to work towards 'the common good'. During Soviet times, everyone was required to spend their Saturdays taking part in work outside their own job, harvesting crops or doing other communal work. This work was generally seen as compulsory, despite the fact that there was no actual law in place.

Despite all this, however, there are plenty of opportunities for people to get involved in voluntary projects should they wish. Many of these programmes are organised by the Western organisations, but there are also some Russian projects requiring volunteers. Most of the work on offer is working in social humanitarian projects such as helping at orphanages, research and ecological programmes. There is also scope for volunteer English teachers.

VOLUNTARY ORGANISATIONS

Given the difficulties in obtaining visas to enter Russia, turning up and finding work is extremely difficult. The best way to experience voluntary work here, then, is to secure a place on one of the many volunteer schemes that operate here. Most of these are through Western agencies and include: VSO, Camphill Village Trust, Concordia, Earthwatch, Gap Activity Projects, Global Outreach Projects, International Voluntary Service, i-to-i, Prince's Trust, Youth Action for Peace and Youth With A Mission.

Another possibility is to post a message asking for work on one of the many travellers' websites that allow this, such as the discussion forum on **www.russia.com**.

You can try to fix up work yourself before you arrive by contacting the charities/not-for-profits in the big cities such as Moscow and St Petersburg, or search for Russian NGOs on the website **www.charitynet.org**.

To find out more about volunteer opportunities in Russia, it may be worth contacting the Moscow Charity House Volunteer Center, Novy Arbat 11, Offices 1728–1738 Moscow 515129, Russian Federation, Tel: 00 7 (095) 291 1473, Fax: 00 7 (095) 291 2004. If you understand Russian, you can also check out its website **www.volunteer.ru** (Russian only).

VOLUNTARY PROGRAMMES IN RUSSIA

Travellers' Worldwide runs teaching, conservation and work-experience placements in Russia. Contact them at 7 Mulberry Close, Ferring, West Sussex BN12 5HY, Tel: 01903 700 478, Fax: 01903 502595, Email: info@travellersworldwide.com. Prices start from £995.

Teaching & Projects Abroad runs medicine, teaching and journalism placements in Russia for suitable candidates. Prices for the Russian teaching and journalism placements are £1,295. The medicine programme is only open to medical students but, if you're a fledgling journalist, you could gain valuable experience working on a Russian newspaper with seasoned journalists who have previously had to work in an unfree world. Picture that on your CV! Contact Teaching & Projects Abroad, Gerrard House, Rustington, West Sussex BN16 1AW, Tel: 01903 859911, Email: info@teaching-abroad.co.uk.

The International Student Exchange Centre (Isec) has a number of opportunities. Not only does it recruit camp counsellors to work in children's summer camps in Russian and the Ukraine, but it also recruits qualified English teachers for language schools in Russia, Latvia and the Ukraine for a placement fee of around £100 (teachers should be qualified).

There is also a Work and Study Experience Russia programme which arranges work experience in a Moscow company, and other cities, for two to four months combined with a four-week Russian language course at a university. Wages are low by Western standards but include accommodation and the language course. Placement fee is £240. Contact International Student Exchange Centre, 35 Ivor Place, London NW1 6EA, Tel: 020 7724 4493, Email: outbounder@btconnnect.com, website: **www.isecworld.co.uk**.

Love Russia works within Russia to provide orphans with food, clothing, shelter and education. Contact Love Russia, Falcon House, 3 Castle Road, Newport, Isle of Wight, PO30 1DT, UK, Tel: 01983 530262, Fax: 01983 530262.

BSES Expeditions (The Royal Geographical Society, 1 Kensington Gore, London SW7 2AR, Tel: 020 7591 3141, Fax: 020 7591 3140, website: **www.bses.org.uk**) use a limited number of young volunteers to help with their adventure in wilderness expeditions in scientific fieldwork, research and conservation. Expeditions take place in Russia as well as other worldwide destinations (see Scandinavian Section).

Americans can contact Cross-Cultural Solutions, a non-profit-making organisation that sends volunteers abroad to provide humanitarian assistance to various countries in a range of long- and short-stay programmes. Its Russia programme operates in Russian orphanages or adult care homes. Contact Cross-Cultural Solutions, 47 Potter Avenue, New Rochelle, NY 10801 USA, Tel: 00 1 800 380 4777 or 00 1 914 632 0022, Fax: 00 1 914 632 8494, Email: info@crossculturalsolutions.org.

RUSSIAN ORGANISATIONS

Institute of Archaeology of Almaty, International Scientific Projects, Tole, Bi 21, Room 22, 480100 Almaty, Kazakhstan (Tel: 00 7-3272917338, Fax:

00 7- 3272 916111, Email: ispkz@nursat.kz) requires volunteers for summer fieldwork. Programmes cost US$250–300 (£175–210) per week. In return, volunteers will receive free food and accommodation.

The Russian Folkore Expedition requires volunteers to help in research to document Russian traditions in villages throughout rural Russia, using a variety of recording methods (field notes, audio records, video records, photographs). The kind of work involved ranges from conducting interviews (in English with a help of an interpreter), making audio records, taking photographs, copying embroidery and collecting facts on ethnography. The cost for the twelve- to fourteen-day expedition varies between US$900 and US$1,200 and covers: visa invitation, visa registration, transport, food and accommodation (including staying at the hotel in Moscow), excursion in Moscow, eight working hours per day of an interpreter and an expedition fee. It is not necessary to speak Russian. For more information, contact Yelena and Sergey Minyonok, Principal Investigators at msefolk@cityline.ru, Folklore Department, Institute of World Literature, Povarskaya st., 25A, Moscow 121069, Russia, Tel: 00 7 095 952 6583, Fax: 00 7 095 200 3216 or visit **www.russianexpedition.net/**.

Translators can polish up their skills through The German–Russian Exchange, which is looking for students and translators to work as volunteers for NGOs, as part-time or full-time volunteer translators, editors or proofreaders in Russia. The NGO translation service can present volunteers with letters of reference (in Russian, German, English) certifying their work with the programme. For more information, contact Ulrike Kaczinski, Deutsch–Russischer Austausch e.V., Brunnenstrasse 181, D-10119 Berlin, Germany, Tel: 00 49 (30) 44 66 80-27, Fax: 00 49 (30) 444 94 60, E-mail: assistenz@austausch.com or dra@austausch.com, website: **www.austausch.org**. Alternatively, contact the co-ordinator of the project in St Petersburg directly: Alexandre Sotov, Deutsch–Russischer Austausch e.V. St. Petersburg, E-mail: a.sotov@obmen.org or nro@obmen.org, website: **www.obmen.org**.

Baikal Volunteer Corp needs volunteers on a ecological project in the Baikal-Lena Nature Reserve developing a trail system, constructing huts, border marking, counting work and population census. Species are brown bear, roe deer, red deer and moose. Contact Baikal Centre for Ecological and Citizen Initiatives, PO Box 1360, Irkutsk, 6640000, Tel: 00 7 (3952) 381787, Email: irkutsk@glas.apc.org.

The Ecotourism Development Fund Dersu Uzala organises eco-tourism projects throughout nature reserves in Russia. Write to them at 6, Khamovnichesky Val Str., Moscow, Russia, Fax/Tel: 00 7 095 242 7406 or visit the website **www.ecotours.ru/english/about.htm**.

Union Forum, Lychakivskastr. PO 5327, lviv-10, Ukraine, 79010 (Tel: 380322 726934, Fax: 38 0322 759488, Email: ukrforum@ipm.lviv.ua), requires volunteers aged between 18 and 35 for summer environmental work. Food and accommodation is included.

VOLUNTEERS' STORIES

Alison Tapp volunteered in Russia for almost a year for a variety of charitable organisations. Her stay was originally funded by the VSO's Overseas Training Programme (now Youth for Development) as part of her three-year Russian literature degree. As part of the deal, however, Alison had to fix up the work herself – a daunting task in Russia. She started by sending out emails to NGOs she found through her network of university tutors. Out of twelve emails, she received only one reply. This was from Povoljze, an NGO resource centre in the city of Samara, about a thousand miles from Moscow.

She says: 'Originally I wanted to gain experience in NGOs so I could start a career in development. But I also wanted to get some solid workplace skills.' Alison was in luck. Povoljze offered her voluntary work translating Russian into English and teaching English to NGO representatives. The centre also helped Alison organise her accommodation, and soon she was living in Samara, with a 24-year-old student and her grandmother. 'Most visitors live with couples or old ladies who need the extra money to live off. You can live in rented flats, of course, but it's very difficult to fix up from England.'

The centre helped Alison obtain a visa by granting her the necessary invitation to work. This was relatively straightforward, but the labyrinth of Russian bureaucracy still got to her in the end: it took the entire three and a half months she was in Samara to obtain the necessary registration she needed. 'This involved frequent trips to the officials and hours of queuing. I saw people queuing up for hours to register births and deaths. The whole procedure was tedious, time consuming and slightly inhumane.'

After three and a half months, Alison left Samara and went to St Petersburg to study Russian literature. Once there, Alison fixed up more voluntary work – this time, by turning up at the main NGO resource centre and offering her services. It was a strategy that paid off. 'Because St Petersburg is a much bigger city, the resource centre was much better organised and offered very good support. I did some translation work on their website and they also put me in touch with other NGOs.' Alison knocked on a few different doors, targeting work on the NGOs. They were all very receptive, and pretty soon she was doing translation work for a variety of organisations.

The experience stood her in good stead – she is now back in the UK completing her Masters and getting ready to start her PhD in Russian literature.

She says, 'It's a lot easier to set up voluntary work once you are there, although you have to be brave and it can be costly. St Petersburg and Moscow are much more used to contact from Westerners so you are more likely to find voluntary work here. I'd also advise people to be realistic about their expectations. The working environment is very different to the UK – it could be a hangover from the Soviet times when there was full employment, but it's not unusual to see people with jobs that don't require them to do much and it can be very frustrating if you are trying to get things done.'

On the positive side, however, Alison says the Russian people are extremely hospitable. 'Once you get to know the Russians, they are very welcoming and friendly. Their attitude to literature and culture is also much more open than back in the UK and people would happily talk to me about Russian authors like Pushkin and Dostoyevsky. In fact, people will talk to you wherever you go. It's not unusual to meet people on trains who will want to talk to you and give you things or invite you to stay. There is a readiness to help and, as a result, there are very good networks.'

VISAS AND REGULATIONS

Applying for a visa to enter Russia can be a complicated affair, particularly as the regulations are constantly changing. Make sure the information is up to date before you send off your money as you may not be reimbursed if you fail to provide the correct documentation. British citizens should also note that the Russian Consulate in Edinburgh has a much better reputation than the London one – according to travellers, they are much more efficient, well-versed in the rules and friendly. The address is 58 Melville Street, Edinburgh EH3 7HF, Tel: 0131 225 7098, Fax: 0131 225 9587.

All foreign nationals are required to have entry visas to travel to the Russian Federation. Russian entry visas can be obtained at your local Russian Embassy or Consulate. Proper authorisation (invitation) from the Passport and Visa Department (OVIR) of the Ministry of Internal Affairs or specially authorised travel agencies is required. Check with the Russian Embassy or Consulate or go to the US-based **www.visatorussia.com** which has plenty of up-to-date advice, or try the website for UK nationals **www.russianvisas.org**. Once you are in Russia you will need to register your passport at the local OVIR office, although the company that gave you the visa will probably do this for you.

Applicants intending to stay for longer than three months may have to provide proof of a negative HIV test. Make sure you do this in time as the results take a couple of weeks to come through.

This is also one country where it may be worth spending the extra money to have the visa arranged by a private agent. This may be expensive but often cuts out the need for an invitation and can make things considerably more straightforward. Andrews Consulting (23 Pembridge Square, Notting Hill, London W2 4DR, Tel: 020 7727 2838, Fax: 020 7727 2848) is particularly well versed in providing visas for Russia and has an office in Moscow.

The good news for volunteers is that in most cases the organisation you are working for will set up the visa for you. If you are fixing up voluntary work through a Russian organisation, bear in mind that not all employers are legally entitled to apply for a work permit.

EMBASSIES

Bulgarian Embassy, 186–188 Queen's Gate, London SW7 5HL, Tel: 020 7584 9400, or 1621 22nd Street, NW, Washington, DC 20008, USA, Tel: 00 1 202 483 5885.

Czech Embassy, 28 Kensington Palace Gardens, London W8 4QY, Tel: 020 7243 1115, or 3900 Spring of Freedom St, NW, Washington, DC 20008, USA, Tel: 00 1 202 274 9100, website: **www.czech.cz/washington**.

Hungarian Embassy, 35 Eaton Place, London SW1X 8BY, Tel: 020 7235 2664, or 3910 Shoemaker Street, NW, Washington, DC 20008, USA, Tel: 00 1 202 362 6730.

Polish Embassy, 73 New Cavendish Street, London W1N 4HQ, Tel: 020 7580 0476, or Consular Division of the Polish Embassy, 2224 Wyoming Avenue, NW, Washington, DC 20009, USA, Tel: 00 1 202 234 2501.

Romanian Embassy, Arundel House, 4 Palace Green, London W8 4QD, Tel: 020 7937 9666, or 1607 23rd Street, NW, Washington, DC 20008, USA, Tel: 00 1 202 332 4848.

Russian Embassy, 5 Kensington Palace Gardens, London W8 4QX, Tel: 020 7229 2666, or 2650 Wisconsin Avenue, NW, Washington DC 20008, USA, Tel: 00 1 202 298 5700, website: **www.russianembassy.org**.

FRANCE VISAS AND REGULATIONS

13. FRANCE

France is a wonderful place to take part in volunteering projects and has plenty of interesting opportunities. From National Nature Reserves in the Jura region to restoring crumbling chateaux in the Dordogne or briefing journalists at film festivals in Clemont-Ferrand, the diverse range of voluntary opportunities available is enough to tempt even the most reluctant of Francophiles.

With a good network of volunteer bureaux, the range of voluntary opportunities in France is broadly similar to the UK, with voluntary agencies backing up government provision. France is also said to have more agencies sending volunteers overseas on aid, relief and sustainable development projects than any other country. Another thing worth knowing is that the French have two words for volunteering: 'bénévolat' and 'volontariat'. 'Bénévolat' refers to a part-time voluntary activity (a few hours per week, generally on a regular basis), while 'volontariat' implies a 'full-time' voluntary activity. This is important as 'bénévolat' has no legal status and therefore no social rights, whereas 'volontariat' does. Full-time volunteering or 'volontariat' in France refers to a number of activities including voluntary work in developing countries and voluntary firemen, which amazingly accounts for 90 per cent of firemen! These have legal status.

VISAS AND REGULATIONS

EU nationals require no work permit for employment in France and have up to three months to look for work (renewable so long as you can prove that you are purposefully looking for a job). Passports are still needed and, if you plan to stay for over three months, you will need to apply for a residence permit (*une carte de séjour*) from the town hall (*la mairie*) or local police station (*la préfecture de police*), which entitles you to various state benefits. This will require four passport photos, a birth/marriage certificate, original and translation, proof of residence, such as an electricity/gas/phone bill, and proof of employment/financial resources, such as a contract or bank statement.

Opening a bank account can be tricky and can only be done if you intend to stay for over three months. You can fix that up in the UK before you leave by popping along to a French bank such as Credit Lyonnais or BNP, or in France by showing your passport, *carte de séjour*, proof of address and birth certificate. You may also have to show proof of your income such as a contract and tax return.

NON-EU NATIONALS

Work permits are required for non-EU nationals, which must be obtained before they leave their home country. Work must be pre-arranged and their employer must prove that the post cannot be filled by a French or EU national.

The Council on International Educational Exchange (633 Third Avenue, 20th Floor, New York, NY 10017-6701, 00 1-888-COUNCIL) runs a scheme by which American students with a working knowledge of French are allowed to look for a job in France at any time of the year and work for up to three months on an *authorisation provisoire de travail*. Contact the Council on International Educational Exchange for more details.

FINDING WORK ON THE SPOT

EU citizens can enjoy all the benefits that EU membership affords and take part in pretty much whatever voluntary project they find, although never forget the importance of speaking good French in integrating into the community. Besides, you will need a decent smattering of French to be able to make the most of the state employment agency, ANPE, which occasionally carries details of projects requiring volunteers, and the network of volunteer bureaux.

FINDING WORK BEFORE YOU ARRIVE

Everything becomes much more complicated, of course, if you aren't an EU national. In these circumstances it's best to take advantage of any work-exchange schemes operating in your country or try to fix up work before you leave. Concordia, BCTV, European Voluntary Service, Archaeology Abroad and Camphill Communities all have projects in France, while Americans can try Volunteers for Peace, which runs 374 of its projects in France.

Americans can also take part in International Volunteers Programme (IVP), 7106 Sayre Dr, Oakland, CA 94611, USA, which offers a variety of volunteer placements including work in children's summer camps, homeless shelters, hospitals and other social service environments. The placements take place in all areas of France. Participants must be reasonably proficient in French. Go to **www.ivpsf.org** for more details.

VOLUNTEER BUREAUX

Contact the Centre National du Volontariat (CNV) which promotes and encourages volunteerism in France through its network of local volunteer centres: Centre National du Volontariat, 127, rue Falguière, 75015 Paris, Tel: 00 33 (0)1.40.61.01.61, Fax: 00 33 (0)1.45.67.99.75.

Association Montaigne, 83 Boulevard de Montmorency, 75016 Paris.

CIDJ, 101 quai Branly, 75740 Paris.

Co-ordinating Committee for International Voluntary Service, 1 rue Miollis, 75015 Paris, Tel: 00 33 (0) 1 56 82 73 11.

Jeunesse et Reconstruction, 10 rue de Trevise, 75009 Paris.

Message Mother's Support Group offers support and contact for English-speaking mothers who live in and around Paris. Volunteer positions include area leaders, project co-ordinators, speakers and newsletter journalists. Go to **www.messageparis.org** for more information.

WICE is a volunteer-run cultural association dedicated to providing high-quality, innovative continuing education courses to the English-speaking community in and around Paris. Work includes front desk, assistance, programme planning, fundraising, training, clerical help and developing the newsletter. Contact 20, bd du Montparnasse, 75015 Paris, France, Tel: 00 33 (0)1.45.66.75.50, Fax: 00 33 (0)1.40.65.96.53, website: **www.wice-paris.org/**.

VOLUNTARY ORGANISATIONS

There are also plenty of French organisations that require international volunteers to take part in community-based projects. Here are some indigenous projects:

La Sabranenque organises restoration projects in the beautiful region of Provence. Volunteers live in a small Mediterranean village working with nationals of many countries and doing work that typically includes stone masonry, stone cutting, tiling, paving and dry-stone walling. Contact La Sabranenque, rue de la Tour de l'Oume, 30290 Saint Victor la Coste, France, website: **www.sabranenque.com**.

Alpes de Lumière (Prieure de Salagon, Mane, 04300 France, Tel: 00 33 492 75 70 50 / 75 70 54, Fax: 00 33 92 75 70 51) organises several camps restoring historical buildings and creating cultural centres in the Provence area. Tasks can include construction, cooking and conservation, and workcamps take place around the summer. Food and accommodation is included.

Apcna (Hameau de la Pinede, Traverse Valette, 13009 Marseille, France, Tel: 00 33 491 25 05 30) requires volunteers to work as instructors for its two children's holiday camps in Marseille and Switzerland. Applicants should be over eighteen, speak fluent French and ideally have some experience looking after children. Accommodation is included.

The Association des Chantiers de Jeunes (ACJ) (BP 171, Salé-Medina, Morocco, Tel: 00 212 37 855350, Fax: 00 212 37 855350) organises workcamps in France, as well as local projects in Morocco.

Heritage Conservation in France runs youth volunteer camps all over France to preserve and restore French historical monuments. Work involves mainly traditional masonry, including earth moving and clearing vegetation, stone cutting and carpentry. Participants can register for a minimum of ten days. No skills or experience required, but basic French is a help. Volunteers pay their travel, insurance and a registration fee of ten euros daily and in return receive board and lodging. Contact Association CHAM, 5 et 7 rue Guilleminot, 75014 Paris, France, Tel: 00 33 (0)1 43 35 15 51.

OTHER USEFUL RESOURCES

The Centres d'Information Jeunesse (CIJ) dotted throughout the country can help people find jobs as well as accommodation and advice on temporary work. Not only do they publish advice leaflets on seasonal work (contact CIDJ at 101 Quai Branly, 75740 Paris Cedex 15, Tel: 00 33 (0)1.44.49.12.00, website: **www.cidj.asso.fr**), but they are also a good source for temporary vacancies.

Check out the French newspapers *Le Monde* and *Le Figaro* for job advertisements.

The Paris Job Site (**www.parisjobsite.com**) has information on careers fairs and relocating to Paris, as well as a job-search facility.

THE INTERNET

As always the Internet is your greatest ally in finding voluntary work. Just a few minutes surfing should throw up plenty of ideas. First stop, however, should be the Euro-Volunteers Information Pool. France is one of the five countries featured on the European Commission-funded website which includes a searchable database of voluntary initiatives in France, as well as Germany, Greece, Luxembourg and the Netherlands. Go to **www.euro-volunteers.org**.

VOLUNTEERS' STORIES

Lynne Moor was volunteering on a renovation project in Sommieres in the South of France when an unexpected flood turned the project into something drastically different. After one week renovating a volunteer centre, Le Cart, she found herself providing emergency assistance to the local community, along with the other Concordia volunteers from France, Germany, Japan, Russia, Turkey and Slovakia.

Lynne says, 'The rain started in their first weekend, the day after a trip to Nimes. On the Sunday, we had hoped to go hiking in the Cevenne mountains. However, our plans were stopped when it proceeded to rain all day. Instead, we spent the day playing cards, and having heated discussions about the way the group was working. That evening it was still raining and there was lots of thunder and lightning.'

The next morning the group awoke to find that it was still raining, and their leaders' cars were already one metre under water. Then came the news that they would have to open the gates of a nearby dam. The group quickly rallied round to stock up on food but, on their way into town, found that all the shops were closed. Meanwhile the rain was bearing down so hard that they had to wade home.

By the time they returned to the centre, the water was pouring down the main road heading for their door. Over the next two hours it rapidly rose. The town had no electricity and, when they went to bed that evening, the water had reached over three metres. The next morning, the group awoke to find the water gone and their surroundings in ruins. There was mud and dirt everywhere, and the once beautiful medieval town of Sommieres had been badly damaged. 'It seemed like nothing had escaped,' says Lynne. 'Shops, houses, and much more. The town was full of emergency services. With the Le Cart centre being so well placed and having many bedrooms and a restaurant, it quickly became like a refugee centre. People whose houses had been damaged stayed there and even the police and firemen from outside the area had meals in the centre. It provided an excellent service to the people of the town.'

The group helped the centre by clearing the mud and helping the kitchen and restaurant cater for over 200 people. 'This work was both physically and emotionally demanding as we were helping people who had lost everything. There had also been people killed.'

After Le Cart was cleaned out, the group went into the town to offer their services to the rest of the community. 'We worked like this for almost the rest of the two weeks, apart from the weekends when we organised trips to the beach, walks in the vineyards and a visit to the Pont du Gard.'

Despite the ordeal, Lynne says she still gained a lot from her time there. 'Working with no electricity, water or communications didn't particularly bother us. In fact, It was character building and helped us to appreciate things we had taken for granted at home. Even the way things turned out with the floods, I would do the whole thing over again in a shot.'

14. GERMANY

Finding voluntary schemes in Germany is much easier now thanks to a rise of interest in volunteering. This is partly due to the International Year of Volunteers in 2001, which gave volunteering a massive boost and encouraged the government to invest more money into setting up a well-co-ordinated infrastructure of volunteer bureaux. Since then, around 28 per cent of the population is said to be engaged in some form of voluntary work; in previous years, volunteers tended to be seen but not heard, and there were many complaints that they were not given the profile they deserved. Volunteering has also gained in popularity since the reunification of the two German states, when the government announced that the role of volunteers would be increasingly important.

Despite this growth, however, Germany is a prosperous country and not as many opportunities exist as there are in other European countries. However, there are still plenty of ways to get involved. The sectors of health and social work are top of the list, followed by sport and leisure activities. Most voluntary schemes are people-orientated, and there are several schemes for non-nationals wishing to work in social-care projects. These include working with the elderly, young, poor and refugees and immigrants who find it hard to adjust to the changes caused by the reunification of Germany. There is also voluntary work in sports associations and a strong green movement ensures plenty of opportunities exist in ecological and conservation work.

VISAS AND REGULATIONS

EU citizens have the right to live and work in Germany without a work permit, but, even if you are looking for work, you may have to prove that you have adequate means to fund both your stay and your return journey out of there. You must also have a residence permit if you intend to work. You will then have to start a complicated procedure which will involve registering at various places, usually in your town hall. If you are not staying in a hotel, you must register at the *Einwohnermeldeamt/Meldestelle* (Residents Registration Office) for a registration certificate. This is normally at the town hall, and you will need to take your passport, a copy of the lease or rental agreement and a completed registration form.

If you intend to spend more than three months in Germany, you must then register at the *Auslanderbehorde* (Foreign Nationals Authority) as soon as you have begun work. You will need to take with you proof of employment (a contract or letter of employment), two passport photos, a copy of your resident's registration and your passport.

NON-EU NATIONALS

Non-EU nationals must have a visa and permit to work. In the case of voluntary work, you must normally secure work before arriving, get written proof from your employer and approval from the aliens authority nearest to your intended place of work, and then you can apply to your embassy for your work/residence permit. The application process can take six weeks. Swiss and US citizens can apply after they arrive in Germany if they have not already started work.

The Council on International Educational Exchange runs a Work in Germany exchange programme for American students. Check out **www.ciee.org** for more information.

FINDING WORK ON THE SPOT
Germany has very few private employment agencies, but it does have an excellent state employment service, *Arbeitsamt*, in most towns, which has a reputation for helping foreigners. There is also a strong eco-movement so contacting the green organisations could be a good move. Voluntary agencies are said to run with all the efficiency that goes to make up the German national stereotype, so it pays to approach your search for voluntary work in as professional manner as possible. Applying in writing for jobs can pay dividends here – follow the protocol and emphasise valued attributes such as being hard working and reliable. Speaking good German will help things considerably, despite the fact that most Germans can speak excellent English. Germany also has good volunteer bureaux. Here are some:

Aufbauwerk der Jugendgemeinschaft für den Freiwilligen Interationalen Arbeitseinsatz, Bahnhofstrasse 26, 3350 Marug.

Bund der Deutschen Katholischen Jugend (BDKJ) Jugendferienwerk, Antoniusstrasse 3, Postfach 1229, 7314 Wernau/N.

You can also try Gute-tat.de (**www.gute-tat.de/**) the Plattform für Soziale Projekte (in German) to find voluntary opportunities.

FINDING WORK BEFORE YOU ARRIVE
Germany is well represented by the mainstream voluntary organisations, most of which organise projects here. This includes Concordia, International Voluntary Service, Quaker Voluntary Action, Gap Activity Projects, Global Outreach Mission, Archaeology Abroad, Prince's Trust, Camphill Village Trust, BTCV, ATD Fourth World and Youth Action for Peace.

It also has a strong green movement and has plenty of eco-projects. There are also several schemes which place volunteers in more long-term social settings such as hospitals and refugee centres. Bear in mind that hours can be long, and the work, although unpaid, can still be demanding.

VOLUNTARY ORGANISATIONS
For longer-term opportunities, the German Red Cross has recently allowed young British people to join its German Red Cross Voluntary Social Year, a national volunteering scheme which enables people to give a year's service in a social setting. This includes working for a wide range of causes, including addicts, AIDS/HIV, refugees and children in settings such as

hospitals, special schools and services for the elderly and disabled. Volunteers should be over eighteen and have a working knowledge of German plus an interest in social/care work. Contact Red Cross Voluntary Social Year, Youth and Schools Unit, British Red Cross Society, 9 Grosvenor Crescent, London SW1X 7EJ, UK, Tel: 020 7201 5179, Fax: 020 7235 7447.

IJGD organises workcamps and workshops in Germany for volunteers aged between 16 and 26, including renovating educational centres, assisting with city recreational activities and conservation work. Most camps last between two and four weeks and take place around Easter and from June to the end of September. Food and accommodation are provided. Contact IJGD (Internationale Jugendgemeinschaftsdienste Bundesverein eV – Gesellschaft fur Internationale und Politische Bildnung) Kaiserstr. 43, 53113 Bonn 1, Germany, Tel: 00 49 228 2280 00, Fax: 00 49 228 2280024, website: **www.ijgd.de**.

The Australian voluntary organisation Involvement Volunteers has an office in Germany and places volunteers on conservation, archaeology, history and social welfare projects in Germany. Projects cost around £200, which includes travel, visa, accommodation, advice and transport from the airport. Projects last from two to twelve weeks with some including free food and accommodation. Contact Involvement Volunteers – Deutschland, Naturbad Str. 50, 91056 Erlangen, Germany, Tel: 00 49 91 35 80 75.

Open House Network recruits about 100 volunteers every year on preservation and restoration projects in Eastern Germany. Projects last from two weeks to six months from May to October. Accommodation and food are provided free. Open House Network, Goetheplatz 9B, D-99423 Weimar, Germany, Tel: 00 49 (0) 3643 50 23 90, Fax: 00 49 (0) 3643 85 11 17.

Mountain Forest Project (Bergwald Projekt e.V., Sophienstr.19, 70178 Stuttgart, Tel: 00 49 (0) 711 607 55 09, website: **www.bergwaldprojekt.ch**) organises one-week forest conservation projects. German is widely spoken in the camps.

Internationaler Bund e.V, Freiwilliges Soziales Jahr, Rathenauplatz 2, 60313 Frankfurt am Main, Germany, Tel: 00 49 69 28 21 71, Fax: 00 49 69 91 39 63 65. Internationaler Bund places volunteers in hospitals, residential homes for the aged or homes for handicapped people. Programmes start in early April and September and last for six or twelve months.

Working Holidays (**www.workingholidays.de**) arranges jobs all the year round on German farms or in country hotels, living with the family, looking after children and/or horses and farm animals. The project Happy Hands is suitable for gap-year students from England, and all students from EU countries wishing to perfect their knowledge of the German language and help the families. Work typically lasts for three to six months and includes accommodation, meals and some pocket money.

To arrange voluntary work on an organic farm contact WWOOF which has a branch in Germany (WWOOF-Deutschland, Postfach 210259, 01263 Dresden, Germany).

EU national students can try looking at the *studentische Arbeitsvermittlung* in German universities, where they can find advertised casual work.

Fully qualified teachers may take part in an Anglo-German Teacher Fellowship organised by the British Council where teachers from England spend two weeks working at a German school and undertaking professional action research projects or developing curriculum materials. Contact Teachers Team, British Council Education and Training Group, 10 Spring Gardens, London SW1A 2BN, Tel: 020 7389 4447, Fax: 020 7389 4426, website: **www.britishcouncil.org**.

Inter Cultural Youth Exchange offers one-year placements in Germany or Austria under the European Voluntary Scheme to 18- to 25-year-old European nationals on a pocket money, board and lodging basis. See **www.icye.co.uk** for details.

USEFUL ADDRESSES
The German Embassy, 23 Belgrave Square, London SW1X 8PZ, Tel: 020 7824 1300 or Bundesverwaltungsamt, Marzellenstrasse 50-56, 50668 Koln, Tel: 00 49 221 7582748, Bundesverwaltungsamt, 50728 Koln (for postal enquiries).

OTHER USEFUL RESOURCES
Try all the databanks organised by the European Commission: Germany is one of the five countries featured on the European Commission-funded website for The Euro-Volunteers Information Pool. The website includes a searchable database of voluntary initiatives in Germany, as well as France, Greece, Luxembourg and the Netherlands. Go to **www.euro-volunteers.org**.

The Association of Voluntary Service Organisations (AVSO) is the European platform for not-for-profit organisations active in the field of longer-term voluntary work. Although it does not organise voluntary placements itself, it represents more than eighty organisations, most of which recruit volunteers. You can search for projects across Germany on its website **www.avso.org**.

You could also try the volunteerabroad.com website. Although this is primarily an American website, not all of the organisations listed are exclusively for those Stateside so it can bring up some useful information. Go to **www.volunteerabroad.com**.

15. GREECE AND TURKEY

GREECE

Despite a strong tradition of communal life and hospitality, volunteering is a relatively new concept in Greece. Organised social volunteering opportunities are hard to find, and young Greek people in particular are supposed to be resistant to the idea of volunteering. All this is set to change however. The Olympic Games in 2004 are actively looking for volunteers to help get involved with all stages of the event. At the time of writing they have already received 60,000 volunteer applications, with three-quarters of those interested under the age of 34, and experts say they hope the Games will encourage young people to get involved and build a volunteering consciousness for the future.

If you fancy volunteering for the Games yourself, contact: 0800-11-20041 (for residents of Greece) or 00 30 210-200-4000 (if you are calling from abroad). However, you will have to be quick: the deadline for volunteer applications is May 2004. People with languages or knowledge of specific sports will be more in demand, but the only requirement is that the person will be eighteen by 31 December 2004. There is no upper age limit but volunteers must be in reasonably good health and attend a training course prior to the games. Volunteers have to pay for their own transport and accommodation.

The website Go Greece has more information (**www.gogreece.about.com**). In fact, this website is a good starting point if you intend to travel to Greece. Not only does it have plenty of links to job-search websites, but you can also place an ad in its classified section.

VISAS AND REGULATIONS

As Greece is part of the EU, EU nationals don't need a working visa to work here. The official line is that you should register with the local police within eight days of arriving but, that said, many people work all summer without any kind of permit or registration. Once your first three months is up, you should do as you do in all EU member states, and apply for a residence permit from your local police station or Aliens Department (*Grafeio Tmimatos Allodapon*). Take with you your passport and a letter from your employer.

NON-EU NATIONALS

Non-EU nationals can obtain a work permit in Greece if a vacancy matching their qualifications exists. The work permit is valid for a specific period of time and only for a specific position. Contact your nearest Greek Consulate Office or Embassy for details.

Given the unclear concept of volunteering here, you will have to clarify if the same rules apply to voluntary work. Greece has been known to adopt a fairly relaxed attitude to 'unofficial' work without the necessary documentation, but it's best to err on the side of caution. Immigration officers do make checks – particularly in harvesting areas – and fines can be heavy if you do not have the right permit. Make sure you check your situation thoroughly with the consulate first.

FINDING WORK ON THE SPOT

Greece is not an easy place to turn up and find work as the voluntary service network is not very well developed. With more than 2,000 islands, Greece is also a scattered, disparate country – fascinating to travel around, but not so easy to establish reliable information. Despite the lack of official voluntary programmes, however, there are plenty of community projects around – it's just a question of finding them – and there is also a notoriously low cost of living. For these reasons alone Greece is one country where turning up to find work can pay dividends. The best thing is to head for the remote rural villages and turn up at the local square, which is often the centre of communal life. You may also be able to find farm work and casual agricultural labour, as well as getting involved with unpaid community projects. There are also plenty of archaeology and conservation projects. Head for the hostels where you are more likely to hear of any opportunities. In Athens, in particular, you may be able to find work helping out and cleaning in exchange for free board.

FINDING WORK BEFORE YOU ARRIVE

By far the best way to fix up work before you arrive is to go through one of the Western sending agencies. The following organisations send volunteers to work camps in Greece: BTCV, Concordia, European Voluntary Service, Global Outreach Mission UK, International Voluntary Service, Prince's Trust, Quaker Voluntary Action, Sierra Club, Youth Action for Peace and Youth Exchange Centre. Australians can take part in Involvement Volunteers programmes. The US-based organisation Global Volunteers run a Teach English in Crete volunteer scheme. Placements last for one to two weeks. Contact 375 E. Little Canada Rd., St. Paul, MN 55117, US, Tel: 00 1 800 487 1074, Fax: 00 1 651 482 0915. American citizens can also take part in archaeology, conservation, culture, environment and renovation projects in Greece organised by the CIEE, while the US organisation Volunteers For Peace runs 26 projects in Greece.

American high-school students can take part in the five-week American Farm School–Greek Summer Programme in Thessaloniki, Greece. Contact American Farm School–Greek Summer Program, 1133 Broadway Suite 1625, New York, NY 10010, USA, Tel: 00 1 212 463 8434, Fax: 00 1 212 463 8208.

VOLUNTARY ORGANISATIONS

There are very few indigenous programmes in Greece. However, Conservation Volunteers Greece (CVG) is one exception. This organisation holds summer workcamps in Greece, usually in remote areas in co-operation with forestry departments, local authorities and cultural associations. Projects range from nature conservation (forest-fire protection, tree-planting, footpath maintenance, construction and placement of signs) and cultural heritage (restoration of traditional buildings, ancient cobbled-stone footpaths and help in archaeological digs) to social benefit (restoration of school buildings, construction of playgrounds). Camps last for two to three weeks and include basic accommodation, usually in schools and community or youth centres. For more information, contact: Conservation Volunteers Greece (CVG), Omirou 15, GR-14562 Kifissia, Athens, Greece, Tel: 00 30 (1) 623 1120, Fax: 00 30 (1) 801 1489, website: **www.cvgpeep.gr** .

The Volunteers for Nature network, organised by the conservation organisation Arcturos, has thirty Greek NGO members that organise volunteer programmes for the protection of the natural environment. Its website contains details of volunteer projects as well as information about volunteering in general. For more information, go to **www.arcturos.gr/envolunter.htm** or contact Arcturos, 3, Victor Hugo str., 546 25 Thessaloniki, Greece, Tel: 00 30 31 55 46 23, Fax: 00 30 31 55 39 32, Email: volnat@the.forthnet.gr.

Archelon Sea Turtle Protection Society runs a rehabilitation centre and volunteer projects in various locations including Crete, Zakynthos, Athens and Peloponnesian coast. Go to **www.archelon.gr** to find out more.

The Lesbian Wildlife Hospital on the island of Lesvos welcomes volunteers to look after injured, sick or orphaned animals. Contact Joris en Ineke Peeters-Lenglet, os Christofa I Chatzigianni, Agia Paraskevi 81102, Lesvos, Greece, Tel: 00 30 2253032006.

Earth Sea & Sky organises conservation volunteer projects and green activities on the island of Zakynthos. For more information visit the website **www.earthseasky.org** or email anna@earthseasky.org or visit the information centre in Gerakas, Zakynthos.

OTHER USEFUL RESOURCES
Greece is one of the five countries featured on the European Commission-funded website The Euro-Volunteers Information Pool, which includes a searchable database of voluntary initiatives in Greece, as well as France, the Netherlands, Luxembourg and Germany. Go to **www.euro-volunteers.org**.

Athens has an English-language newspaper with a jobs section. You can also place an advert asking for work.

TURKEY

As Turkey stands as the cross-over between the East and West, it offers a fascinating glimpse into the way the two cultures merge and exist together. On one hand, you are living in a Muslim country and may encounter religious differences, while, on the other hand, you are faced with all the entertainment and tackiness of living in a vibrant global culture, surrounded by brands, consumerism and neon signs. Like Greece, Turkey is also a relatively cheap place to live.

Turkey has more NGOs than Greece, particularly in Eastern Turkey and inland areas. Most of the work is in social and health care, such as in hospitals, or looking after children and the poor. There are also many archaeological programmes. Other than that, volunteer projects are thin on the ground and the best way to find work in Turkey is to pre-arrange it through a Western sending agency. There are voluntary agencies in the UK who help with natural disasters such as the earthquakes in 1999, although these kinds of relief organisations are mostly interested in professional people with much-needed skills. There are also archaeology and excavation projects.

VISA AND REGULATIONS

Turkey is making considerable efforts to join the EU, but at the time of writing, Turkey is not an EU member. This means that EU nationals and non-nationals alike must get hold of a work visa from a Turkish Consulate in your country of residency before you leave in order to work here. This is required for all work including au pair and voluntary work.

Getting a work permit is not easy – you will need a contract of employment and in some cases a letter of approval from the relevant authorities. The processing time can take about two to three months so bear this in mind before booking your flight.

Once you arrive in Turkey, you must also obtain a residence permit from the local police within a month of your arrival. Any UK national is also advised to have a minimum of six months validity on their passports from the date of entry into Turkey. For more information contact your nearest Turkish Consulate or Embassy.

You will also need to check with your local travel clinic, or doctor, which injections are advised for travelling to Turkey.

FINDING WORK BEFORE YOU ARRIVE

Unfortunately, finding out about voluntary opportunities in Turkey is extremely difficult, as the network of agencies is not as developed as in other countries. The following Western organisations run projects in Turkey: BTCV, Concordia, Earthwatch, International Voluntary Service, Prince's Trust, Quaker Voluntary Action, Youth Action For Peace and Youth With A Mission. Volunteers For Peace, Global Volunteers, World Pulse and CIEE run projects for American citizens in Turkey, while Australians can fix up projects through Involvement Volunteers. You can also try writing to the Turkish charities and offering your services.

GSM Youth Activities Services runs nature and ecological volunteer projects and internships for teenagers. Contact the Director of International Programs, Bayindir Sokak No. 45/9, Kizilay, Ankara 06450 Turkey.

Ecovolunteers run conservation programmes protecting the endangered species of monkseals in the Karaburun Peninsula in Turkey. Volunteers help train locals, inform both locals (fishermen, villagers, young people, etc.) and tourists and lobby politicians. They also help maintain marine-conservation zones and monitor and study monkseals and their habitat. Go to **www.ecovolunteer.org**.

It's also possible to work voluntarily at diving resort centres along the south west coast where you can polish your diving skills. Although more in the field of adventure holidays, Bluedog Adventure can arrange unpaid work in Turkish diving resorts for which you can receive super-cheap diving training. Contact Bluedog, Amwell Farm House, Nomansland, St Albans, Herts AL4 8EJ, UK. Check out the websites **www.twarp.com/diving.htm** and **www.turizm.net/bluecruise/diving.html** for details of diving centres in Turkey.

USEFUL ADDRESSES
Embassy of Greece, 1a Holland Park, London W11 3TP, UK, Tel: 020 7229 3850, or 2221 Massachusetts Avenue, NW, Washington, DC 20008, USA, Tel: 00 1 202 939 5800, website: **www.greekembassy.org**.

Turkish Embassy, 43 Belgrave Square, London SW1X 8PA, UK, Tel: 020 7393 0202, or 1714 Massachusettes Avenue, NW, Washington, DC 20036, USA, Tel: 00 1 202 659 8200, website: **www.turkishembassy.org**.

OTHER USEFUL RESOURCES
To find work try the usual routes (see International Sections). The English-language newspaper the *Daily News* has a job classifieds section, where you can also place an advert.

16. ITALY

Despite the fact that Italy has good opportunities for volunteering, information can be a little hard to find. This is largely because the country doesn't have such a developed network of volunteer centres as other European countries. That said, there are plenty of organisations that run schemes and workcamps here, particularly in the less prosperous South where more voluntary help is needed. Most are concerned with alleviating poverty or with archaeology and conservation, and are often church based owing to the strong Italian Catholic tradition. Prospective volunteers are advised to speak reasonable Italian as English is not spoken as well or as widely as in other European countries. You should also make sure you have all the necessary documentation as the red tape can be time consuming and complicated, even for EU nationals.

VISAS AND REGULATIONS
If you hold an EU passport you are legally entitled to work in Italy. However, the complicated Italian bureaucracy might make things more time consuming than you expect. You will also need to apply for a temporary residence permit (*una Ricevuta di Segnalazione di Soggiorno*) at the main police station (*Questura Centrale*), which entitles you to stay for up to three months. For this, you will need to take a valid passport and some proof of employment or financial resources (e.g. bank statements, tax returns or a contract). If you wish to stay any longer you need to apply for a residence permit, *un Permesso di Soggiorno*.

NON-EU NATIONALS
Non-EU nationals will find the whole process much more difficult. The official line is that non-EU nationals can only get hold of work visas in their own country of residence and typically need an authorisation to work from the Ministry of Labour and from the local police. The red tape is complicated and procedure can vary, so travellers are advised to look into it in some detail first. Furthermore, despite the fact that unofficial work has been reported to be relatively easy in the past, a strict clampdown on illegal workers has made the situation much more risky now.

FINDING WORK ON THE SPOT
EU nationals may have some luck in turning up on the spot to find work, but non-EU nationals are in a much more risky position. Italy has strict immigration rules and has recently cracked down on illegal workers, threatening tough fines and a real risk of arrest and deportation. Volunteers are warned that what they might consider to be bona fide volunteer work, to the Italian authorities could be taking much-needed work away from locals. This particularly applies to farm work, and people are advised to go through an organisation such as WWOOF or EVS first. Stories abound of police

checking farms and other institutions to make sure they are not harbouring any illegal workers, including volunteers.

EU nationals who are perfectly entitled to be looking for work in the country should take advantage of Italy's strong church links, which are behind many indigenous voluntary schemes. If you speak good Italian, you can also try the state employment service, although word of mouth and having good contacts seem to be a more effective route here.

Try the volunteer bureau The National Centre for Volunteering (Centro Nazionale per il Volontariato, 55100 Lucca, Via A.Catalani, 158 – C.P. 202, Italy, Fax: 00 39 (0)583.419501, email: cnv@centrovolontariato.it.

Also check out Centro Servizi per il Volontariato (CSV), **www.volontariatossp.to.it/**.

There are a few online resources with information on volunteering in Italy. These are ANPAS (National Public Assistance Association) at **www.anpas.it** or Fondazione Italiana per il Volontariato with headquarters in Rome.

Wanted in Rome is a fortnightly publication that appears in newsagents in Rome and contains jobs for English speakers and other expatriates, which sometimes include voluntary work. See **www.wantedinrome.com**.

Informagiovani is a Youth Information Scheme that provides information on jobs, scholarships and enrolment to universities, as well as a database on the availability of work. It is accessible nationwide and on the Internet. A complete list of *Informagiovani* is available at the Italian Cultural Institute for consultation. Here is a list of the *Informagiovani* addresses in the main Italian cities:

Agenzia Informagiovani, Via Captain Bavastro, 94, 00154 Roma, Italy, Tel: 00 39 6 575 6759, Fax: 00 39 6 574 7623.

Informagiovani, Via Marconi, 1, 20123 Milano, Italy, Tel: 00 39 2 62085215, Fax: 00 39 2 865067.

Centro Informagiovani, c/o Centro Civico Lame Via Marco Polo 53, Quartiere Navile, 40131 Bologna, Italy, Tel: 00 39 51 6345550.

Servizio Informagiovani, Vicolo S. Maria Maggiore 1, 50123 Firenze, Italy, Tel: 00 39 55 218310, Fax: 00 39 55 292056.

FINDING WORK BEFORE YOU ARRIVE

As always, the best option is to fix up work before you arrive. Luckily, there are plenty of organisations that allow this. British citizens can take part in schemes organised by Concordia, BTCV, Across Trust, Archaeology Abroad, Earthwatch, International Voluntary Service, Prince's Trust, Quaker Voluntary Action, Sierra Club and Travel Active.

Americans can try Global Experiences, CIEE, Volunteers for Peace, World Pulse and the organisation Global Volunteers, which runs volunteer Teach English in Italy programmes. Australians can take part in schemes through Involvement Volunteers.

Europeans can also go through the European Voluntary Service (EVS) programme set up by the European Commission, as well as the European Commission's YOUTH programme which is open to thirty European countries. See International Section for more details.

VOLUNTARY ORGANISATIONS

Gruppo Archeologici d'Italia (Group of Archaeologists of Italy) is one of the largest Italian archaeological organisations and needs volunteers for excavations. Go to **www.gruppiarcheologici.org**. Contact Sede Legale, Sede Operativa, Segreteria Nazionale e Direzione Nazionale, Via degli Scipioni 30/a, 00192 Rome, Italy, Tel/Fax: 00 39 06-39734449, Tel/Fax: 00 39 06-3721935.

Italian League for the Protection of Birds (ILPB), V. Trento, 9, 43100 Parma (Tel: 00 39 0521 27 30 43, Fax: 00 39 0527 27 34 19, website: **www.lipu.it**) places 350–400 volunteers in environmental, conservation and education workcamps, as well as admin positions throughout Italy. Placements last for between one week and one month.

Agape Centro Ecumenico (10060 Prali, Turin, Italy, Tel: 00 39 12 180 7960, Fax: 00 39 12 180 7514, website: **www.chiesavaldes.org**) requires volunteers to help run its Christian conference centre in the Italian Alps from June to September, Christmas and Easter.

Tenuta di Spannocchia, a historic organic farm, educational centre and guest residence, often uses volunteers to assist with guest services. Contact Associazione Castello di Spannocchia, Tenuta di Spannocchia, 53012 Chisudino, Siena, Italy, Tel: 00 39 207-730-1154.

For farm work, send 25 Euros to WWOOF Italy for its up-to-date farm list, which includes biodynamic and organic farms and smallholdings. Contact WWOOF Italia, 109, via Casavecchia, Castagneto Carducci, 57022 (Li), Italy, Fax: 00 39-0565-765742 or visit its website **www.wwoof.it/**.

Servizio Civile Internazionale, Via Laterani, 28, 00185 Roma, Italy, Tel: 00 39 6 7005367.

Mani Tese (Via Cavenaghi 4, 10149 Milano, Italy, Tel: 00 39 2 46971888) organises international workcamps to raise funds for projects in developing countries.

Europe Conservation Italia (**www.agora.stm.it/eco.htm**) runs spring and summer conservation projects in Italy.

Summer Camps (**www.rosenet.it/summercamps**) runs a programme where people can provide an English-language immersion experience to Italian children who cannot afford to spend the summer in a foreign English-speaking country.

La Sabranenque organises restoration projects in small Mediterranean villages in Italy working with nationals of many countries and doing work that typically includes stone masonry, stone cutting, tiling, paving and dry-stone walling. Contact La Sabranenque, rue de la Tour de l'Oume, 30290 Saint Victor la Coste, France, website: **www.sabranenque.com**.

Oikos runs workcamps aimed at tackling environmental problems in big cities, especially Mediterranean ones. Volunteers can take part for a period of two weeks to some months in the outskirts of Rome. Board and lodging is free in exchange for twenty hours of work per week. Work consists mostly of biological horticulture and general maintenance. You can apply online or go to website **www.oikos.org** or write to Oikos, Via Paolo Renzi 55, 00128 Rome.

USEFUL ADDRESSES

Italian Embassy, 14 Three Kings Yard, London W1Y 2EH, UK, Tel: 020 7312 2200, website: **www.embitaly.org.uk** or 1601 Fuller Street, Washington, DC 20009, USA, Tel: 00 1 202 328 5500.

17. SCANDINAVIA

Scandinavia does not have many opportunities for voluntary work as people here pay the highest taxes in Europe and enjoy very good state provisions. There are some voluntary organisations, however, and a limited number of volunteer workcamps. The cost of living is also very high, which makes these countries an expensive prospect to travel around. Your best bet in finding projects is to either fix up work before you arrive, or arrive armed with some very reliable contacts. Although English is widely spoken in most parts of Scandinavia, a working knowledge of the language of the country is a strong first step. It's also wise to make the most of any Scandinavian business or personal acquaintances you have.

BSES Expeditions (The Royal Geographical Society, 1 Kensington Gore, London SW7 2AR, Tel: 020 7591 3141, Fax: 020 7591 3140, website: **www.bses.org.uk**) sends a limited number of young volunteers to help with their adventure in arctic wilderness expeditions in scientific fieldwork, research and conservation. Expeditions take place worldwide including Finland, Iceland, Norway, Russia and Sweden.

VISAS AND REGULATIONS
Denmark, Finland and Sweden are all members of the EU so, in theory, EU nationals can enjoy all the benefits their membership affords. Norway and Iceland are outside the EU but, as members of the EEA, EU nationals are still free to enter to look for work for three months.

All countries require you to apply for a residence permit from the local police once you have found work and got hold of a Confirmation of Employment from your employer.

Unfortunately, foreigners outside the EU and EEA have hardly any prospects of finding work. Not only will they have to obtain a work permit before leaving home, but this meets with some strict regulations. For more information contact the Department of Immigration or the consulate of the country you would like to visit.

VOLUNTARY WORK RULES
In Denmark and Norway the same rules apply for voluntary work that apply to paid employment. Although this is a good general rule to follow with most countries, there appears to be no hard or fast rule and the regulations may depend on your particular circumstances. According to the Finnish Embassy, for example, 'All non-EU nationals who wish to enter gainful employment in Finland need a work permit unless they belong to a group which is exempt. It is the responsibility of the prospective employer in Finland to find out from the local employment office whether a person needs a work permit or not and to get it for them as well. Voluntary workers don't generally need one but again the employer will confirm this. If the

stay exceeds three months they will need a residence permit which will have to be applied for before travel from the nearest Embassy of Finland.'

The visa regulations and the list of countries whose nationals need (or don't need) a visa for Finland can be found on the website **www.finemb.org.uk**. Another useful one for work and residence permit information is **www.uvi.fi**.

Despite these complications there are some programmes for non-EU nationals. Australians can apply for the Working Holiday Maker programme (WHM), which allows Australians to work legally for up to twelve months in eleven participating countries, including Denmark and Norway. Contact the Australian Embassy for details.

PROGRAMMES FOR US CITIZENS

Here are a few programmes that Americans can take advantage of:

AFS Intercultural Programs (**www.usa.afs.org**, Tel: 00 1 800 AFS-INFO) arranges short- and long-term study/volunteer work programmes in Scandinavia for American high-school students. Participants live with a host family.

Communicating for Agriculture (**http://ca.cainc.org/**, Tel: 00 1 218 739 3241, Fax: 00 1 218 739 3832) organises long- and short-term agriculture and horticulture programmes in Denmark, Finland, Norway and Sweden for people with relevant experience aged between 18 and 28.

InterExchange has opportunities available for short-term farming work in Norway for ages 18–30. (**www.interexchange.org/**, Fax: 00 1 212 924 0575.)

Volunteers for Peace oversees two to three workcamps in Scandinavia (Denmark, Finland, Iceland, Norway and Sweden) for anyone eighteen years old and above. (Tel: 00 1 802 259 2759, Fax: 00 1 802 259 2922.)

Council of International Fellowships (CIF) offers short-term, unpaid opportunities for field work and observation in human services in Finland, Norway and Sweden. Go to **www.cipusa.org/outsideus.html**.

To find out about volunteer opportunities, it may be a good idea to contact The American–Scandinavian Foundation (Exchange Division, 58 Park Avenue, New York, NY 10016, Tel: 00 1 212 879 9779, Fax: 00 1 212 249 3444, website: **www.amscan.org**), which offers training opportunities in Scandinavia for Americans aged 21 and over. There are short-term placements of two to three months during the summer for students majoring in certain fields, principally engineering, chemistry, business and computer science.

DENMARK

Given the fact that Danish people are said to pay the highest taxes in Europe and enjoy an extensive welfare state, the need for social voluntary work is much less acute than in most countries. However, there is still an active tradition of volunteering in Denmark and at least one-third of the adult population say they volunteer in formal organisations. Half of this work takes place within sports and cultural activities.

The following organisations arrange volunteer schemes and workcamps in Denmark: Across Trust, Camphill Village Trust, Concordia, European Voluntary Service, Global Outreach Mission UK, Intercultural Youth Exchange, International Voluntary Service, National Federation of City Farms, Prince's Trust, Quaker Voluntary Action, Sierra Club, Time for God Scheme, Youth Action for Peace, Youth Exchange Centre and Youth With a Mission.

Americans can take part in International Volunteer Projects and Service Civil International. The Council on International Educational Exchange (CIEE) (Tel: 00 1 212 822 2600) places volunteers, aged eighteen and up, in workcamps of two to four weeks in Denmark (and Finland). Room and board are provided.

The Danish Volunteer Centre is Center for Frivilligt Socialt Arbejde, Pantheonsgade 5, 3, Postboks 158 5100 Odense C, Denmark, Tel: 00 45 66 14 60 61, Fax: 00 45 66 14 20 17, website: **www.frivsocarb.dk** or **www.frivillighed.dk** (in Danish).

You can also try the youth information centre Uselt, Rädhusstraede 13, 1466 Copenhagen K (Tel: 00 45 33 73 06 20/ Fax: 00 45 33 73 06 49, website: **www.useit.dk**), which can provide some useful tips on finding work.

You should also be able to get hold of a copy of a free booklet, *Working in Denmark*, from Employment Service, Overseas Placing Unit, Rockingham House, 123 West Street, Sheffield S1 4ER.

The Danish branch of WWOOF is VHH. Contact: WWOOF Denmark, Bent & Inga Nielsen, Asenvej 35, 9881 Bindslev, Denmark, website: **www.wwoof.dk**. Membership is Dkr. 50 or Euro 10. Please include an addressed envelope (min 20 x 15 cm).

Swallows in Denmark (Østerbrogade 49, DK-2100, Copenhagen Ø, Denmark, Tel: 00 45 35 26 17 47, Fax: 00 45 31 38 17 46) is a non-profit organisation whose aim is to support grassroots movements in Bangladesh and India. The camp draws on twenty international participants aged eighteen over and lasts two to four weeks during the summer.

Mellemfolkeligt Samvirke (Stuosgade 20, DK-8000 Arhus C, Denmark, Tel: 00 45 81 69 77 66) places volunteers for international workcamps during the summer in Denmark and Greenland. Workcamps normally last two to three weeks and are community centred, such as conservation of playgrounds, renovation, conservation, archaeological work, nature protection, etc. Participants must pay for their own travelling costs, but food and accommodation are provided. Volunteers should be over eighteen. British applicants should apply through International Voluntary Service, IVS Field Office, Old Hall, East Bergholt, Colchester, Essex CO7 6TQ.

The European Diaconal Year Network (**www.timeforgod.org/edyn.htm**) organises Diaconal Year programmes in Denmark (as well as Austria,

Belgium, France, Germany, the Netherlands, Sweden and the UK). Volunteers are placed in children's homes, centres for persons with physical and learning disabilities, hospitals, social projects (drugs, homeless, refugees) and parish work for ten to twelve months of service each year.

FINLAND

Despite the high standard of living in Finland, volunteering is a popular activity and nearly every third Finn takes part in some type of voluntary work. In fact, more people volunteer in Finland than in most countries, seeing this kind of community activity as a way of strengthening social networks. The most popular voluntary activity is sport; the second most popular is healthcare and social work and the third is education.

Despite all this, however, there are very few opportunities for non-nationals to participate in volunteer schemes. The best bet is to head for one of the volunteer-sending organisations that place people on international workcamps.

The following organisations send volunteers to Finland on schemes and workcamps: Camphill Village Trust, Concordia, European Voluntary Service, Intercultural Youth Exchange, International Voluntary Service, Involvement Volunteers, Prince's Trust, Quaker Voluntary Action, Sierra Club, Time for God Scheme, Travel Active and Youth Exchange Centre.

Americans can take part in camps organised by International Volunteer Projects and Service Civil International. The Council on International Educational Exchange (CIEE), Tel: 00 1 212 822 2600, places volunteers, aged eighteen and up, in workcamps of two to four weeks in Finland (and Denmark). Room and board are provided. Involvement Volunteers organises placements in work camps for Australian citizens.

You can also try Finland's main volunteering bureau to see if it has any openings. Contact Finland Citizen Forum, Sörnäisten Rantatie, 27 A, 2nd floor, 00500 Helsinki, Finland, Tel: 00 358-9-7744080, Fax: 00 358-9-77440828, website: **www.kansalaisareena.fi/citizen.htm**.

The Finnish Family Programme is a scheme where native English-speaking families can live with a Finnish family for up to a year and teach English on a regular basis. For more information contact The Ministry of Labour, PO Box 30, 00100 Helsinki 10 or, in the UK, the Education and Training Group, 10 Spring Gardens, London SW14 2BN, website: **www.britishcouncil.org**.

The Centre for International Mobility specialises in study and training placements to Finland and runs a number of official EU programmes. Go to **www.cimo.fi** for more information.

The International Student Exchange Centre runs agriculture programmes in both Finland and Norway. Visit its website **www.isecworld.co.uk** for more information or write to them at 35 Ivor Place, London NW1 6EA, Tel: 020 7724 4493, Fax: 020 7724 0849.

NORWAY

Despite the fact that Norway has one of the wealthiest welfare states in the world, the spirit of community work (*dugnadsånden*) is part of the national identity and there is still an active contribution made in the field of voluntary work. However, owing to its wealth, the voluntary sector is not as vital as in other European countries. Many non-governmental organisations in Norway are involved in environment and development work. One of the biggest barriers to volunteering here is Norway's reputation for not exactly welcoming foreigners to work with open arms. Apart from EU nationals, who do not need a work permit to work here (despite the fact that Norway is not a member of the EU), foreign workers are banned and will have to go through an established programme if they want to volunteer.

The following organisations send volunteers to Norway on schemes and workcamps: BTCV, Camphill Village Trust, Concordia, European Voluntary Service, International Voluntary Service, Prince's Trust, Sierra Club, Time for God Scheme, Travel Active, Youth Exchange Centre and Youth with a Mission. Volunteers for Peace place US citizens on workcamps in Norway.

Norway's volunteer centre is Frisam, PO Box 8054 Dep NO- 0031 Oslo, Norway, Tel: 00 47 24 16 35 40, Fax: 00 47 24 16 30 02. Office address: Keysers gt. 13, website: **www.frivillig.no**.

Jøssåsen Landsby, N 7550 Hommelvik, Norway, Tel: 00 47 73 9799900, Fax: 00 47 73 978840. Jøssåsen Landsby is part of the Camphill Village Trust, an organisation catering for special needs. This village operates as a working community for people who are mentally and physically handicapped, and requires volunteers and workshop leaders to help with all aspects of working life. It is generally recommended that volunteers stay for at least one year, although there are working volunteer holidays in the summer.

The International Student Exchange Centre runs agriculture programmes in both Finland and Norway. Visitb its website **www.isecworld.co.uk** for more information or write to them at 35 Ivor Place, London, NW1 6EA, Tel: 020 7724 4493, Fax: 020 7724 0849.

The Atlantis Work Guest Programme offers farm work lasting for four to sixteen weeks for people aged between eighteen and thirty. Work is voluntary but comes with board, lodgings and some pocket money. Contact Atlantis-Norwegian Foundation for Youth Exchange, Director International Programs, Rolf Hofmosgate18, 0655 Oslo 6.

VOLUNTEERS' STORIES

Bob Randall took part in a BSES Expedition to Arctic Norway. On arriving home, he writes: 'I did it! I've survived six weeks in arctic conditions: sleeping in a tent, eating rehydrated food and trekking miles – crossing rivers, boulder fields and arctic tundra. It was great!'

Bob's adventure began in July 2002, when he met sixty people at Heathrow all heading for a valley just outside the tiny village of Nuvsvag in Finnmark, Norway's most northerly region. From there they travelled by air, bus and ferry to Oksjordjoklen. Their mission? To undertake research into arctic conditions for the Royal Geographical Society.

Bob says, 'The first couple of days were taken up by ferrying kit, ropes and rations to base camp and deciding what each "fire" (group) would be doing for the first three weeks. There were also briefings on medical procedures, crampon fitting, Global Positioning System, general campcraft and how to operate an EPIRB (Emergency Position Indicating Rescue Beacon), in case of emergency.'

Day Five saw the beginning of their ice training, learning how to fix anchor points in the snow and ice in case someone fell into a crevasse and needed to be hauled out. 'On day nine our "fire" set off on a five-day trek over a very steep and rocky pass into a different valley and down to the shore of another fjord, where we measured the flow of meltwater off the Oksfjord glacier.'

The expedition also involved some serious arctic trekking, and the group spent one week on the Oksfjord ice cap, camping on an isolated nunatak (rock outcrop).

Bob says, 'We travelled to the highest point on the ice, which is also the highest point in Finnmark, did some cross-country skiing, lowered each other into (and out of!) crevasses and took part in some serious extreme high-altitude sledding! Walking along ridges, sometimes less than one foot wide, was scary but definitely a highlight of the expedition.

'We also had a fair amount of free time in which we played games, fished or just recuperated after a few hard days' walking. For me the highlight of my time in Norway was sitting on the nunatak watching the midnight sun over the ice, the sky constantly turning into new shades of reds, oranges and greens, and seeing the pink snow and ice.'

SWEDEN

As with all Scandinavian countries, Sweden has a very strong welfare state that takes responsibility for most public services. In fact, although the Swedes are very civic minded and around 28 per cent actively give up their time voluntarily (in 2001 at least), there is a slight mistrust of the role of charity, fuelled by the belief that only strong government provision can deliver a fair and just society. For that reason it is best to fix up voluntary work before you arrive, through one of the listed voluntary organisations.

Like Denmark, volunteering activity in Sweden is focused on sports and recreation, with less emphasis on social welfare or civic volunteering.

The following organisations send volunteers to Sweden on schemes and workcamps: Camphill Village Trust, European Voluntary Service, Global Outreach Mission UK, Intercultural Youth Exchange, International Voluntary Service, National Federation of City Farms, Prince's Trust, Sierra Club, Time for God Scheme, Youth Exchange Centre and Youth With A Mission. Volunteers For Peace organises work camps for American citizens.

Sweden's national volunteer centre is Forum för Frivilligt Socialt Arbete, Starrbäcksgatan 11, 172 99 Sundbyberg, website: **www.socialforum.a.se**.

For farm work, contact the Swedish branch of WWOOF to obtain a list of farms in Sweden: Andeas Hedren, Palstorp Hunna, 340 30 Vislanda, Sweden, Tel: 00 46 0470 75 43 75.

US citizens can take advantage of the YMCA International Camp Counselor Program/Abroad (Tel: 00 1 212 727 8800, website: **http://ymcanyc.org/international/programs.html**) which places volunteers as summer camp counsellors in Sweden. The scheme is open to anyone aged eighteen to thirty and comes with free room and board.

Voluntary Year (Stor Sköndal, 128 85 Sköndal, Sweden, Tel: 00 46 8 605 0927) organises projects in Sweden in community work throughout the year. Projects last from 40 to 52 weeks and participants should be aged between eighteen and twenty-five.

Diakonala Aret is the Swedish branch of the Christian-based European Diaconal Year network. Volunteers give ten to twelve months of service to placements in children's homes, centres for persons with physical and learning disabilities, hospitals, social projects (drugs, homeless, refugees) and parish work. Contact: Diakonala Aret, Svenska kyrkans Forsamlingsnamnd, S-75170 Uppsala, Sweden, Tel: 00 46 18 16 95 00, Fax: 00 46 18 16 96 18.

IAL is a Swedish NGO working for a peaceful world by organising international volunteer workcamps in Sweden, and sending Swedish volunteers to such camps abroad. IAL is the Swedish branch of Service Civil International, SCI. Volunteers should be at least eighteen years of age. Internationella Arbetslag, IAL, Tegelviksgatan 40, Stockholm, 116 41, Sweden, Tel: +46-(0)8 643 0889, Fax: +46-(0)8 6431 8188.

EMBASSIES

Finnish Embassy, 38 Chesham Place, London SW1X 8HW, UK, Tel: 020 7838 6200, or 3301 Massachusetts Avenue, NW, Washington, DC 20008, USA, Tel: 00 1 202 298 5800, website: **www.finland.org**.

Swedish Embassy, 11 Montagu Place, London W1H 2AL, UK, Tel: 020 7917 6400, Email: embassy@swednet.org.uk, website: **www.swedish-embassy.org.uk/embassy/index.html**, or 1501 M Street, NW, Washington, DC 20005, USA, Tel: 00 1 202 467 2600, website: **www.swedenemb.org**.

Royal Danish Embassy, 55 Sloane Street, London SW1X 9SR, UK, Tel: 020 7333 0200, or 3200 Whitehaven Street, NW, Washington, DC 20008, USA, Tel: 00 1 202 234 4300, website: **www.denmarkemb.org**.

Royal Norwegian Embassy, 25 Belgrave Square, London SW1X 8QD, UK, Tel: 020 7591 5500, Email, morten@embassy.norway.org.uk, website: **www.norway.org.uk**, or 2720 34th Street, NW, Washington, DC 20008, USA, Tel: 00 1 202 333 6000, website: **www.norway.org**.

SPAIN

Spain has always had a reputation for being a difficult country in which to find voluntary projects, as the government has tended to fund initiatives that in other countries may have been left to the voluntary sector. However, since the International Year of Volunteering in 2001, volunteering has received a welcome image overhaul and is now fast becoming a mainstream activity. Young people under 25 are particularly getting involved, as well as retired people between the ages of sixty and eighty. In fact, volunteering is such a popular activity there are apparently two national volunteering magazines sold on the newsstands, so it's worth keeping your eyes open.

VISAS AND REGULATIONS

As Spain is part of the EU, all EU citizens are free to live, travel and work in Spain, although if you intend to stay for longer than three months you will have to get a residence card (*a tarjeta de residencia*). You can apply for these from the Foreigners' Department, *el Departamento de Extranjeros*, which should be done within thirty days of arriving. Forms are available from the Ministry of the Interior (**www.mir.es/extranje/guiap.htm**) – you will need a valid UK passport, four passport photos, a medical certificate from your home doctor, proof of financial resource (i.e. bank certificates from your home bank) and proof of health insurance.

If you're an EU national, your residence permit should entitle you to find employment so you won't need a separate work permit. For non-EU nationals it's a complicated and tricky procedure – first they must get hold of a *visado especial* from the Spanish Embassy in their country. This requires setting up work before they leave. In order to apply for the visa, they will need to provide a copy of their contract and documentation such as medical records and qualification certificates. To find out more, contact your Spanish Embassy.

FINDING WORK ON THE SPOT

Turning up to find work in Spain is a possible option if only because cold-calling in person is a more acceptable way of finding work in this country. There are also the two volunteering magazines sold on newsstands which should be a useful starting point, as well as English-language newspapers in tourist areas. That said, volunteer bureaux are thin on the ground and the state employment service CNC is reputed not to be particularly helpful towards foreigners. There are environmental and evacuation opportunities, however, according to a message posted on the website Wild-Spain.com: 'Conservation volunteering (*voluntariado medioambiental*) is a fairly new concept in Spain and programmes are sometimes vague and poorly publicised. There is no national registry of volunteer posts, although some of the regional governments (*autonomías*) do have better than average listings – Andalucía and Navarra, for example. Frustratingly, it is often easier to find out about past opportunities than future ones!'

A word of caution: under Spanish law, employers have an obligation to pay high social security contributions for paid workers and may be tempted to offer voluntary work to fill the same position. Non-EU nationals should be aware that, if you are working without the necessary permission, both you and your employer could face heavy fines.

FINDING WORK BEFORE YOU ARRIVE

Most volunteer opportunities in Spain come through the mainstream volunteer-sending agencies, such as Across Trust, Concordia, Archaeology Abroad, BTCV, Earthwatch, European Voluntary Service, Global Outreach Mission UK, International Voluntary Service, Intercultural Youth Exchange, Involvement Volunteers United Kingdom, National Federation of City Farms, Prince's Trust, Quaker Voluntary Action, Sierra Club, and Youth With A Mission.

American citizens can take part in schemes organised by International Volunteers Programme (IVP: 7106 Sayre Dr, Oakland, CA 94611), Service Civil International Voluntary Service, Earthwatch and Global Volunteers. The Australian organisation Involvement Volunteers Association places volunteers in Spain.

In addition, try the usual sources to find projects listed in the International Section, such as the website Working Abroad, and newspapers such as *Overseas Jobs Express*. Most of the voluntary work available in Spain is in workcamps usually run from April to October.

VOLUNTEER BUREAUX

The National Centre for Voluntary Work is Federació Catalana de Voluntariat Social, Pere Vergés 1, 11è, 08020 Barcelona, Spain, Tel: 00 34 93 314 19 00, Fax: 00 34 93 314 11 08, website: **www.federacio.net/en** (in Catalan, Spanish and English).

You can also try the Foundation for Solidarity and Voluntary Work of the Valencian Community, Calle Fuencaliente 1, 46023, Valencia, Spain, Tel: 00 34 96 330 11 09, Fax: 00 34 96 330 65 11.

You can search for volunteer opportunities in Spain (in Spanish) on **www.hacesfalta.org/index2.htm** or on the website for Servei Catalá **ww.voluntariat.org** (in Catalan).

You can also apply directly to one of Spain's numerous NGOs, such as The Cruz Roja Espanol, one of the largest voluntary organisations in Spain, which uses more than 200,000 volunteers and other personnel. Much of the work involves working with vulnerable people such as the elderly, refugees, young people at risk, disabled people, etc. Best's Volunteer and Train in Spanish NGO Programme arranges work experience in your professional field in one of Spain's many non-profit organisations. See Volunteer Programmes for more details.

VOLUNTEER PROGRAMMES

Instituto de la Juventud (Servicio Voluntario Internacional de España, c/Jose Ortega y Gassel 71, Madrid, Tel: 00 34 91 401 6652) organises 150 workcamps a year mostly for volunteers aged between eighteen and twenty-six.

Best's Volunteer and Train in Spanish NGO Programme arranges work experience in your professional field in one of Spain's many non-profit organisations. The programme starts off with a two-week intensive orientation Spanish course, followed by part-time volunteer internship in one of the divisions of a Spanish humanitarian organisation, such as press department, logistics, projects, legal, fundraising, volunteer recruitment, psychology. Your schedule will give you time to pursue other interests while in Spain like tourism, study and work. Placements are available all over Spain: Madrid, Barcelona, San Sebastian, Granada, Cádiz, Bilbao, La Coruña, Valencia, etc. The programme is open to American, Australian, Canadian, European, Kiwi and South African people over the age of eighteen with intermediate Spanish. Typical volunteer projects can include anything from working with people who have AIDS to reforestation or wildlife surveying. For more information contact Best Programs, Calle Solano 11, 3-C, Pozuelo de Alarcón, Madrid 28223, Spain, Tel: 00 34 91 518 7110, Fax: 00 34 91 518 7110, website: **www.bestprograms.org/**.

International Educational Services (**www.ies.ciberia.com**) runs study programmes in Valencia, while Centros Europeos Principe. S.L. (C/Principe, we, 6A – 28012 Madrid, Spain Tel: 00 34 91 532 72 30, Fax: 00 34 91 521 60 76) organises exchanges between Spanish and British students aged 12 to 25 for two to four weeks.

Americans can organise language-assistant programmes in Spain through InterExchange (161 Sixth Avenue, New York, NY 10013, website: **www.interexchange.org**).

CONSERVATION, AGRICULTURE AND WILDLIFE PROGRAMMES

The Spanish national parks network (Red de Parques Nacionales) organises volunteer programmes, in collaboration with conservation NGOs. For more information go to **www.mma.es/parques/lared**.

La Red de Voluntarios Ambientales del Litoral Andaluz organises wildlife volunteer projects. Contact La Red de Voluntarios Ambientales del Litoral Andaluz, Aula del Mar de Malaga, Avd. Manuel Agustin Heredia, 35, CP. 29001, Malaga, Spain, Tel: 00 34 952 229287, Fax: 00 34 952 219761, website: **www.juntadeandalucia.es/medioambiente/voluntariado/ voluntariado2002/act4.html**.

Grefa runs an animal hospital and has an active volunteer programme in the Madrid area. Its website **www.grefa.org/Voluntarios/voluntarios.html** has more information in Spanish. Contact Grefa (Grupo para la

Recuperación de la Fauna Autóctona y su Hábitat), Apto de Correos 11, 28220 Madrid, Tel: 00 34 91 6 38 75 50.

To obtain a booklet of alternative volunteer farm projects in Spain (Vida Alternativa en España) write to Dinah Faehre, Apdo 15, 43570 Santa Barbara, Tarragona, Spain, Tel: 00 34 77 261159.

The farm La Mohea runs farm work volunteer programmes – go to **www.lamohea.com** or write to the farm at Finca La Mohea, Genalguacil, 29492 Málaga, Spain, mentioning the following details: name, age and sex; relevant experience in sustainable agriculture, forestry or other outdoor work; related skills; aspects of sustainable agriculture that most interest you; any special dietary requirements.

Sunseed Desert Technology (**www.sunseed.org.uk**) organises volunteer placements to help with the charity's work on semi-arid land. Work includes research into appropriate technology, semi-arid land management and organic gardening as well as helping communities to live in such environments.

British Trust for Conservation Volunteers (**www.btcv.org.uk**) organises international conservation working holidays in both Spain and Portugal. Call 01491 821600.

Atlantic Whale Foundation (St Martins House, 59 St Martins Lane, Covent Garden, London WC2, website: **www.whalefoundation.f2s.com**) allows volunteers to help on whale and dolphin conservation and research projects in the Canaries. Participation costs £95 a week including half-board accommodation and training.

You can also try the website for Spanish Ornithological Society (SEO/BirdLife) (**www.seo.org/**), which sometimes has details of volunteer bird conservation projects. Another good resource is the website for Wild-spain.com (Information on Nature and Outdoor Travel: **www.wild-spain.com**); this lists the occasional volunteer project and is a good starting point for anyone interested in nature and conservation in Spain.

Here are some conservation organisations which sometimes require volunteers:

ANNA: Asociación Nacional Amigos de los Animals, Apto de Correos 335, 28100 Alcobendas, Madrid, Tel: 00 34 91 3 72 10 29/91 3 14 44 11, Fax: 00 34 91 6 61 08 00.

Consejo Ibérico para la Defensa de la Naturaleza: CIDN, Oficina de Coordinación Ibérica: C/ Montserrat, 16, Bajo B. 28015 Madrid, Tel: 00 34 91 5 41 98 19, Fax: 00 34 91 5 41 45 82, website: **www.bme.es/cidn/**.

Ecologistas en Acción, C/ Marqués de Leganés, 12, 28004 Madrid, Tel: 00 34 91 531 27 39, Fax: 00 34 91 531 26 11, website: **www.nodo50.org/ecologistas/**.

Fundación 2001 Global Nature Fund, Tel: 00 34 91 5 56 93 90, website: **www.fundacionglobalnature.org**.

Reforesta, Tel: 00 34 91 8 04 65 09, website: **www.reforesta.es**.

OTHER USEFUL RESOURCES

The *Entertainer*, a free newspaper published each Thursday, has a classified section covering Costa Almeria as well.

You can also try *Island Connections* (**www.ic-web.com**), an online version of the Canary Islands' fortnightly English-language newspaper, or *Island Sun* (**www.island-sun-newspaper.com**), a newspaper for the Canary Islands. The *Paper* (**www.thepaper.net**) and *Tenerife News* (**www.tennews.com**) are fortnightly Tenerife newspapers.

The website Spainalive (**www.spainalive.com**) also includes a Jobs in Spain section.

PORTUGAL

Portugal does not have a great tradition of voluntary work, and projects are difficult to find. It is also one of the least prosperous countries in Europe and what little voluntary work exists is mainly directed towards relieving poverty and working with the elderly, young people and disabled people. The best approach by far is to contact one of the main sending organisations such as Concordia to see what projects they offer. The following organisations send volunteers to projects in Portugal: Across Trust, Archaeology Abroad, BTCV, European Voluntary Service, International Voluntary Service, Prince's Trust, Sierra Club, Tearfund, Youth Action for Peace, Youth Exchange Centre and Youth With a Mission. Americans can go through Service Civil International Voluntary Service and Volunteers for Peace, which oversees 29 international workcamps in Portugal.

VISAS AND REGULATIONS

EU nationals are free to live and work here, although, as is usual, you will need a residence permit if staying longer than three months. For details and application form, contact your local immigration office (*Serviço de Estrangeiros e Fronteiras*), the British Embassy in Portugal, Rua de S.Bernardo 33, 1249-082 Lisbon, Tel: 00 351 21 392 40 00, Fax: 00 351 21 392 41 88) or your Portuguese Embassy or Consulate.

Non-EU nationals have to fix up work before being granted a residence visa – contact your nearest Portuguese Consulate for more information.

VOLUNTEER PROGRAMMES

There are two agencies in Portugal that appear to accept volunteers. ATEJ (Associacao de Turismo Estudentil e Juvenil, Apartado 4586, P-4009 Oporto, Portugal) places a small number of volunteers on farms, archaeological digs and projects with people with disabilities. The other agency is Turicoop (Rua Pascoal-Melo, 15-1DTO, P-1100 Lisbon, Portugal), which runs nature conservation and archaeological projects and workcamps.

ICA offers one-year volunteer placements with local development organisations in Portugal, with no formal skills or experience requirements.

The placements last for nine months to a year and include a volunteer orientation weekend and foundation course. Volunteers are responsible for meeting the expenses of all their pre-departure training and preparation, including travel and insurance, with support and advice from ICA. Contact ICA: UK, PO Box 171, Manchester, M15 5BE, England, Tel: 0161 953 4064.

The US organisation Habitat for Humanity International enables volunteers to build houses in 82 countries including Portugal, for anything from two weeks to three years. Contact Habitat for Humanity International, 121 Habitat Street, Americus, GA 31709, USA, Tel: 00 1 229 924 6935, website: **wwwhabitat.org**.

USEFUL ADDRESSES

Spanish Embassy, 39 Chesham Place, London SW1X 8SB, UK, Tel: 020 7235 5555, or 2375 Pennsylvania Avenue, NW, Washington, DC 20037, USA, Tel: 00 1 202 452 0100, website: **www.spainemb.org**.

Portuguese Embassy, 11 Belgrave Square, London SW1X 8PP, UK, Tel: 020 7235 5331, website: **www.portembassy.gla.ac.uk**, or 2125 Kalorama Road, NW, Washington, DC 20008, USA, Tel: 00 1 202 462 3726, website: **www.portugal.org**.

You can get a free booklet, *Working in Portugal*, from Employment Service, Overseas Placing Unit, Rockingham House, 123 West Street, Sheffield S1 4ER.

OTHER USEFUL RESOURCES

EU Nationals can try the state employment service (Minstério de Trabalho, Praça de Londres, 1091, Lisbon) or the national employment service, *Centro de Emprego*. Look in the Yellow Pages (*Las Páginas Amarelas*) for addresses.

You can find listings of charities in Portugal with possible voluntary opportunities on the Virtual Portugal website (look under the Master Directory, the Associations and Organisations, and then Charities): **www.portugalvirtual.pt/**.

The Hispanic and Luso Brazilian Council publishes a twelve-page leaflet called *Notes on Employment, Travel and Opportunities in Portugal* aimed at the younger worker/traveller. Contact Hispanic and Luso Brazilian Council, Canning House, 2 Belgrave Square, London SW1X 8PJ, Tel: 020 7235 2303, website: **www.canninghouse.com**.

Portuguese speakers can check out the online job site StepStone Portugal: **www.stepstone.pt**.

Check out the English-language papers such as *Anglo-Portuguese News* and the *Algarve* that both carry job adverts.

19. UNITED KINGDOM AND IRELAND

UNITED KINGDOM

The voluntary sector in the United Kingdom has grown steadily in recent years and now consists of around 200,000 voluntary organisations. These cover a huge range of areas, including social and healthcare, environmental and cultural projects, sports and recreation, and welfare of animals and young people, and the disabled and disadvantaged. Many of the agencies open to UK citizens are also there for non-nationals, particularly EU nationals who have the right to live and work here. It is a good idea, then, if you want to volunteer in the UK, to read the first half of this book which concentrates exclusively on voluntary opportunities within the UK. For the moment, however, you can rest assured that there are plenty of opportunities in the UK for you. The UK has an extensive network of volunteer bureaux and a wide range of voluntary agencies. There is also a growing interest in employee volunteering and virtual volunteering. See chapters three and five for more details.

VISAS AND REGULATIONS

EU nationals are free to work and live in the UK and the same freedom is extended to nationals of Iceland, Norway and Liechtenstein. Non-EU nationals will generally have to obtain a work permit to take up paid or unpaid employment, which includes volunteering. However, there are some exceptions. People on working holiday visas are permitted to volunteer, as are spouses of work-permit holders. Students from outside the European Economic Area no longer need permission to take part-time or holiday work, including volunteering. However, there is a limit of twenty hours per week during term time. Refugees are now allowed to volunteer – contact the Home Office for more details.

There are also other concessions. People from non-EU countries are allowed to volunteer if:

- **they volunteer with a registered charity.**

- **pocket money, board and accommodation may be provided, but no additional remuneration.**

- **the volunteer's work must be closely related to the aims of the organisation – they should be working with people rather than doing purely clerical, administrative or maintenance work (for which a work permit is required).**

- **the volunteer may be allowed to stay in the country for a maximum of twelve months.**

- **the volunteer must not seek or take paid employment whilst they are here.**

People from countries for which a visa is needed to travel to the UK must obtain one before travelling. To find out if nationals from your country require a visa to enter the UK (visa nationals) phone the Immigration and Nationality Department on 020 8606 7766 or go to **www.ukvisas.gov.uk**. If you are a visa national, you must have the appropriate visa. This is important to remember because you cannot volunteer on a tourist or visitor visa. If you wish to switch to a different visa you will have to return to your home country and apply from there.

NON-VISA NATIONALS

Non-visa nationals who have arranged their voluntary work before travelling to the UK can seek entry clearance before travelling. Although you will have to pay for the privilege, entry clearance is often a good idea as it can make your passage through immigration control easier and give you extra peace of mind. To apply for entry clearance, contact your British Embassy or High Commission.

Non-visa nationals can apply to the Home Office while in the UK to change their immigration status to allow them to volunteer. Application is made on Form FLR0 obtainable from the Application Forms Unit (0870 241 0645 or **www.ind.homeoffice.gov.uk**). You will need a letter from the organisation you are volunteering with and evidence of funds.

FINDING WORK ON THE SPOT

Providing you have checked the visa situation thoroughly, turning up to the UK to find voluntary projects is extremely plausible. The first place to head for is your local volunteer bureau, which can tell you what voluntary work is available locally and put you in touch with local organisations. Most areas have a volunteer bureau – look up your nearest volunteer bureau in the phone directory under 'V' or phone Volunteer Development England on 0121 633 4555. You can contact the National Association of Volunteer Bureaux (NAVB) for details of your local volunteer bureau by writing to NAVB, New Oxford House, 16 Waterloo Street, Birmingham B2 5UG, Tel: 0121 633 4555 or 0121 633 4043, Email: info@vde.org.uk.

Another excellent resource is the National Centre for Volunteering, Regent's Wharf, 8 All Saints Street, London N1 9RL, Tel: 020 7520 8900, Fax: 020 7520 8910, Email: Volunteering@thecentre.org.uk, website: **www.volunteering.org.uk**. As well as a volunteer magazine, it has a do-it searchable database of local opportunities by area and can provide information for employee volunteering.

If you are in Scotland contact: Volunteer Development Scotland, Stirling Enterprise Park, Stirling FK7 7RP, Tel: 01786 479593, Fax: 01786 449285.

For Wales, go to **www.wcva.org.uk**.

Students can try Student Volunteering UK, which gives information about volunteering opportunities within students unions. Visit **www.studentvol.org.uk** or freephone 0800 0182146. It also publishes a quarterly magazine, *Grapevine*, and a booklet, *The Art of Crazy Paving* (free to students, otherwise £10), which has advice on using volunteering to get on in the job market.

The National Association of Councils for Voluntary Service is the umbrella body for 300 local Councils for Voluntary Services. Go to **www.nacvs.org.uk** to find your local CVS and volunteering opportunities in your region. They are sometimes known by a different name, so look in the telephone book or Yellow Pages under 'Council', 'Volunteers' or 'Voluntary'. If you live in a rural area, try the Rural Community Councils. Alternatively, contact the NACVS at 177 Arundel Street, Sheffield S1 2NU, Tel: 0114 278 6636, Fax: 0114 278 7004.

The organisation Timebank will match your interests and skills with volunteering opportunities in your area. It also produces a volunteer guide and newsletter, as well as regular updates about volunteering opportunities. To register call 0845 601 4008 or for general enquiries 0207 401 5438. Alternatively, register online at **www. timebank.org.uk**.

Older volunteers can contact Retired and Senior Volunteer Programme (RSVP), c/o CSV, 237 Pentonville Road, London N1 9NJ (Tel: 020 7278 6601); or REACH (Bear Wharf, 27 Bankside, London SE1 9DP, Tel: 020 7928 0452), which specialises in finding voluntary schemes for retired professionals and executives.

FINDING WORK BEFORE YOU ARRIVE
There are plenty of workcamps and projects available to work on in Britain including those run by BTCV, Across Trust, Camphill Village Trust, European Voluntary Service, EIL and Earthwatch. People wishing to volunteer in the UK are advised to get hold of a copy of *Worldwide Volunteering for Young People*, which has extensive listings of voluntary opportunities in the UK. If cost is an issue, then applying through these organisations will, in most cases, ensure you have free board and lodging provided as part of the scheme. If you have contacts in the UK who can put you up for a while, or have the money to fund travelling and accommodation, then contact one of the charitable organisations. Many of these have a wide range of opportunities, such as the National Trust and Addaction, which uses volunteers to help in projects each year. See chapter three for more information on working for charities and, for professional volunteer opportunities, look at chapter two.

The US organisation International Volunteers Programme (IVP) allows American citizens over the age of eighteen to take part in six-week summer volunteer programmes. Participants work on six-week assignments at not-for-profit organisations. Tasks include office work; hospital assistance; work in tourism offices; and work with children, the elderly or people with disabilities, among others. Contact IVP, 7106 Sayre Dr, Oakland, CA 94611, USA or go to **www.ivpsf.org**.

Community Service Volunteers places 3,000 volunteers each year on projects throughout the UK, including overseas visitors. Work includes working with elderly or homeless people, young people at risk, and people with disabilities, learning difficulties or mental illness. Board and lodging are provided. Contact CSV, 237 Pentonville Road, London N1 9NJ, UK, Tel: 020 7278 6601, Fax: 020 7837 9621, website: **www.csv.org.uk**.

The Northern Ireland branch of BTCV is Conservation Volunteers Northern Ireland, 159 Ravenhill Road, Belfast, Co. Antrim, BT6 0BP, N. Ireland, Tel: 028 9064 5169, Fax: 028 9064 4409, website: **www.cvni.org.uk**. This registered charity runs projects throughout Northern Ireland. Projects include a diverse variety of activities such as tree-planting, dry-stone walling, path creation, river clearance and pond construction as well as office work.

For lists of farms requiring voluntary help, contact WWOOF (Willing Workers on Organic Farms), PO Box 2675, Lewes, East Sussex BN7 1RB, Tel: 01273 476286.

The Seasonal Agricultural Workers Scheme (SAWS) is a British government-sponsored scheme that enables full-time students of Eastern and Central European countries to carry out harvest work including fruit-picking jobs on farms throughout Great Britain. The scheme is operated on behalf of the government by organisations such as Concordia and HOPS. If your university does not have an arrangement with one of these organisations, the British Embassy may be able to put you in touch with local agents. There is a limited number of places available and they are filled very quickly. You usually need to apply in October or November to have any chance of obtaining a place for the following year.

The British Trust for Conservation Volunteers runs week- or weekend-long conservation projects in Britain. Write to British Trust for Conservation Volunteers, 36 St Mary's Street, Wallingford, Oxfordshire OX10 0EU, Tel: 01491 821600, Fax: 01491 839646, website: **www.btcv.org**.

British Waterways (Willow Grange, Church Road, Watford WD17 4QA, Tel: 01923 201 120, website: **www.britishwaterways.com/site**) maintain Britain's old industrial canals and have voluntary work opportunities.

OTHER USEFUL RESOURCES

In addition to the volunteer bureaux, there are plenty of other resources to help you in your job search. *The Guardian* newspaper has a jobs section on Wednesdays which often features about 100 volunteering opportunities.

Try the notice boards at public libraries or ask if they have a file of information on voluntary work. Some of them also contain published directories on voluntary work such as *The Voluntary Agencies Directory*.

Local hospitals often take volunteers, particularly if you are looking to start a career in one of the caring professions.

The website for YouthNet UK (**www.Do-it.org.uk**) has a database of local volunteering opportunities in the UK and is searchable by postcode, type of work and type of organisation.

The state job centre may have details of any local schemes you can join.

The website Going Green has a directory of voluntary organisations and campaigns you can get involved with. Go to **www.goinggreen.net**.

Also look out for Volunteers' Week which runs in June each year. It is hosted by the National Centre for Volunteering and lists events going on around the UK to celebrate volunteering.

If you are an overseas student studying in the UK, check out your university careers library which is bound to carry some useful information. Also keep a watchful eye on notice boards.

IRELAND

Like the UK, Ireland has a thriving voluntary sector and 33 per cent of the adult population currently volunteers. Many of the charitable organisations are religiously based with most work aimed at promoting the health and welfare of children, the elderly and disabled. There are also environmental projects.

VISAS AND REGULATIONS

As volunteering is outside the realm of paid work, prospective volunteers do not need to obtain work permits. However, there are no 'volunteer visas' and ordinary immigration/visa rules apply. EU and EEA nationals are allowed to work and live and move freely around Ireland. Many nationals outside the EU, however, must obtain a visa in order to enter the country. These requirements change all the time. For a current list of countries whose passport holders do not need visas to enter Ireland, see the Department of Foreign Affairs website **www.irlgov.ie/services/visas**. There are also reciprocal agreements with USA, Canada, Australia and New Zealand.

FINDING WORK ON THE SPOT

Providing you are eligible to work and travel here without a permit, Ireland is a good option for the travelling volunteer. Like the UK, it has a good voluntary infrastructure with plenty of charitable organisations that are in need of volunteers. The first place to head for is the national volunteer bureau, Volunteering Ireland, which runs a placement service matching volunteers to non-residential opportunities. Its website (**www.volunteeringireland.com/**) also has an online searchable database of opportunities. The address is Volunteering Ireland, Coleraine House, Coleraine Street, Dublin 7, Republic of Ireland, Tel: 00 353 1 872 2622 Fax: 00 353 01 872 2623.

Tallaght Volunteer Bureau can put you in touch with voluntary opportunities as well as advising you on all forms of voluntary work. Go to **www.volunteertallaght.ie/** or call 00 353 1 462 8558. The address is Tallaght Volunteer Bureau, 512 Main Street, Tallaght, Dublin 24, Ireland.

Travellers may be particularly interested to hear about a new project launched by Volunteering Ireland to promote volunteering for groups that 'are traditionally underrepresented or may require a degree of support to pursue and sustain voluntary work'. According to the centre, such groups may include travellers, as well as people with physical disabilities, learning difficulties or mental illness, and the long-term unemployed and asylum seekers. The project aims to develop four pilot projects and to publish a resource/training pack for both volunteers and volunteer-using organisations. For more information look on the website **www.volunteeringireland.com/**.

Another option is to try and find work on the many farms. Paid work is not easy to find, but some farms provide free board or camping in exchange for work. Keep an eye open for messages on notice boards in the hostels.

You can also obtain a farm list from Ireland's WWOOF branch (Willing Workers on Organic Farms). Contact the Irish Organic Farmers and Growers Association, Organic Farm Centre, Harbour Road, Kilbeggan, Co. Westmeath, Ireland, Tel: 00 353-506-32563, Fax: 00 353-506-32063, website: **www.irishorganic.ie**.

Simon Community of Ireland requires volunteers to work alongside homeless men and women in Ireland in Cork, Dundalk, Dublin and Galway. Contact Simon Community of Ireland, St Andrew's House, 28–30 Exchequer Street, Dublin 2, Ireland (Tel: 00 353 (0)1 671 1606, website: **www.simoncommunity.com**).

Travellers can offer assistance at youth hostels throughout Ireland, which may offer free board in exchange for unpaid work. Óige, the Irish Youth Hostel Association, requires voluntary help for many of its 32 youth hostels located through Ireland's countrywide. Volunteers, including voluntary managers, help with office work, maintenance and conservation, etc. Go to An Óige, 61 Mountjoy Street, Dublin 7, Tel: 00 353 (01) 830 4555, Fax: 00 353 (01) 830 5808 or the website **www.irelandyha.org** for more details.

Many of the charitable organisations in Ireland require volunteers. To find links to Irish charities, visit the website for the Carmichael Centre for Voluntary Groups, a resource for voluntary organisations and part of Volunteering Ireland, **www.carmichaelcentre.ie**. The centre also has non-residential employment projects for volunteers.

You can also find links to voluntary organisations that have major volunteer input on the National Committee for Volunteering website **www.ncvireland.ie/linka.html**.

FINDING WORK BEFORE YOU ARRIVE

Ireland has plenty of workcamps and residential opportunities to offer volunteers. The following organisations run voluntary schemes in Ireland: Across Trust, BTCV, Camphill Village Trust, European Voluntary Service, Global Outreach Mission UK, Global Volunteers, International Voluntary Service, Prince's Trust, Quaker Voluntary Action, Sierra Club, Time for God Scheme, Youth Exchange Centre and Youth With a Mission.

The Volunteering Ireland website has lists of residential programmes, while Voluntary Service International also publishes a guide to International

Voluntary Work Projects each spring (cost €4). This also lists workcamps of between ten days and four weeks held each summer throughout Ireland. Contact Voluntary Service International, 30 Mountjoy Square, Dublin 1, Ireland, Tel: 00 353 1 8551011, Fax: 00 353 1 855 1012.

The Volunteer Development Agency produces a good guide to Residential Volunteering Opportunities in Northern Ireland, covering all types of voluntary work. Volunteer Development Agency, Annsgate House, 70–74 Ann Street, Belfast BT1 4EH, Tel: 028-9023 6100 (from Republic of Ireland: 048 - 9023 6100), Fax: 028-9023 7570 (from Republic of Ireland: 048 - 9023 7570).

Groundwork runs environmental work camps for volunteers from all over the world to spend one or two weeks working and living in Ireland. The cost is €25.50 for one week (€38.00 for two) including food and accommodation. The remaining cost is subsidised by Dúchas (the National Parks and Wildlife Services). Contact Groundwork, Irish Wildlife Trust, Garden Level, 21 Northumberland Road, Dublin 4, Ireland, Tel: 00 353-1-6604530, Fax: 00 353-1-6604571, website: **www.groundwork.ie**.

The Barretstown Gang Camp runs short-term therapeutic activity programmes for seriously ill Irish and other European children between seven and sixteen years old. Volunteers are needed for the spring and autumn (minimum ten days) to organise and participate in a range of activities and to be responsible for the day-to-day care of the children. Contact The Barretstown Gang Camp, Barretstown Castle, Ballymore Eustace, Co. Kildare, Ireland, Tel: 00 353 45-864115, Fax: 00 353 45-864711, website: **www.barretstowngc.ie**.

Caring and Sharing Association (CASA) offers care to people with disabilities in two breakhouses in Dublin. Both short- and long-term volunteers are required, from two months to one year. Contact Caring and Sharing Association, 15 Ard na Mara, Malahide, Co Dublin, Tel: 00 353 1-845 4841, Email: anclanncasa@eircom.net.

CVI organises weekend- and week-long conservation breaks throughout Ireland. Volunteers normally stay in hostel accommodation and undertake a range of practical conservation tasks, such as tree planting and dry-stone walling. A cost of €40 upwards covers all transport, accommodation and food. Conservation Volunteers Ireland, 65a Harold's Cross Road, Dublin 6W, Ireland, Tel: 00 353 1-495 2878, Fax: 00 353 1-495 2879, Email: info@cvi.ie.

Friends of the Elderly provides full-time internships lasting from six months to one year for international volunteers to work with older people. Contact Friends of the Elderly, 25 Bolton Street, Dublin 1, Ireland, Tel: 00 353 1-873 1855, Fax: 00 353 1-873 1617.

The Galway County Association seeks female volunteers to live with one person with learning disabilities for around one year. Accommodation is free. Contact Galway County Association, Blackrock House, Salthill, Galway, Ireland, Tel: 00 353 91-528122, Fax: 00 353 91-528150.

Glencree Centre for Reconciliation requires volunteers to undertake practical work in the kitchen and garden, as well as programme work on peace issues and with community groups. Most placements last a year and start in September, but there are opportunities for shorter placements, including weekends. Contact Glencree Centre for Reconciliation, Glencree, near Enniskerry, Co. Wicklow, Ireland, Tel: 00 353 1-282 9711, Fax: 00 353 1-276 6085.

Knockadoon Camp is a children's summer camp in Ballymocada, Co Cork, with a Catholic ethos, run solely by volunteers. Contact Knockadoon Camp, St Malachy's Priory, Anne Street, Dundalk, Co Louth, Ireland, Tel: 00 353 42-933 4179, Fax: 00 353 42-932 9751, Email: bulmanj@iol.ie.

Society of St Vincent de Paul (SVP) organises holidays for underprivileged children and young people from the Dublin area. Voluntary 'stewards' are required during the summer months for the week-long Sunshine House holidays in Balbriggan, Co Dublin, and the Teenhols at an outdoor educational centre in Birr, Co Offaly. Society of St Vincent de Paul, 18 Nicholas Street, Dublin 8, Ireland, Tel: 00 353 1-454 9922/0317/0319 [Sunshine], Tel: 00 353 01-454 0317/9 [Teenhols], website: **www.svp.ie**.

USEFUL ADDRESSES
British Embassy, 3100 Massachusetts Avenue, NW, Washington, DC 20008, USA, Tel: 00 1 202 588 6500, or Employment Service, Glen House, 22 Glenthorne Road, London W1 0PP, UK, Tel: 020 8210 8184.

Irish Embassy, 17 Grosvenor Place, London SW1X 7HR, UK, Tel: 020 7235 2171, or 2234 Massachusetts Avenue, NW, Washington, DC 20008, USA, Tel: 00 1 202 462 3939.

The booklet *Working in Ireland* is available from the Overseas Placement Service from Employment Service, Overseas Placing Unit, Rockingham House, 123 West Street, Sheffield S1 4ER.

Get hold of the booklet *London, Edinburgh and Dublin Guide* published by the London-based travel magazine *TNT* (TNT Guides, 14–15 Child's Place, London SW5 9RX, Tel: 020 7373 3377); send an SAE with 70p. Look out for their free pocket-sized regional guides at airports, stations and backpackers'hostels.

OTHER USEFUL RESOURCES
In addition to Volunteering Ireland, EU nationals can use Ireland's state employment service: FAS (Foras Aiscanna Saothair). The European Employment Services Eures may also have details of opportunities. The Irish Eures branch is at 27–33 Upper Baggot Street, Dublin 4 (Tel: 00 353-1-6070500, website: **www.fasjobs-ireland.com**).

Uslt Now (19–21 Aston Quay, O'Connell Bridge, Dublin 2) has a notice board advertising jobs.

All the major papers carry classified job ads such as the *Irish Times*. The *Evening Herald* newspaper has a job section each day, while other papers feature jobs on certain days.

The website **www.ireland.com** has a good jobs section and links to the *Irish Times*.

REST OF THE WORLD

20. AFRICA AND THE MIDDLE EAST

AFRICA

Africa has huge potential for finding voluntary work. Much of the continent is still heavily reliant on aid work, and there are numerous opportunities with charities and religious organisations from helping farmers to teaching English. There is also a huge need for long-term professional skilled staff to work for the large NGOs or aid and development organisations (see Working in Aid for more details). However, those without professional skills can still find work, mainly through the gap-year organisations.

CULTURE SHOCK

Turning up in most African countries without a voluntary placement organised is not really advisable. There are some countries, such as Nigeria, which are extremely dangerous to travel around. It is also worth reiterating that conditions throughout the continent are amongst the most shocking in the world. Some countries have an extremely low standard of sanitation and healthcare, where people have to cross borders even to find hospitals, and infectious diseases are rampaging through the countries leaving thousands sick or dying in their wake. It is therefore essential to take all the health and safety precautions you can (see Health Section).

All of this isn't to put you off. Volunteering in developing countries can give you a sense of reward and achievement hard to beat anywhere else, but it is important that you thoroughly think about committing yourself to living in such testing conditions. It is also a good idea to check out the organisation sending you. While most NGOs and volunteer-sending agencies are extremely well organised, I have heard tales of volunteers being sent out on projects in dangerous countries such as the Sudan where civil war has been raging for the last twenty years, without the necessary support or orientation. One volunteer found herself in the middle of an anti-western riot complete with tear gas and found the experience extremely disturbing. For the occasional scare story like this, however, there are countless other more heart-warming anecdotes. One woman I know gives up all her time to work for a grassroots organisation in Nigeria, installing education and IT programmes. Although she does most of her work in the UK, sourcing ideas and materials, she travels frequently to Nigeria to work with the indigenous people. She became directly involved with the project after her friend, the founder of the project, an educated Nigerian man who emigrated to the UK, was murdered in the country by thieves. Despite the tragic circumstances, you only have to speak to her for a few moments to realise how passionate she is about her work, and how much satisfaction and pleasure she derives from her relationship with her Nigerian colleagues. It is clear that, however upsetting her introduction was, the project now gives great meaning and joy to her life.

FINDING WORK

The website **www.idealist.org** has a huge database of volunteer organisations and also runs a subscription-only newsletter with details of up and coming volunteer work.

VIA Africa, 'Visionaries In Action – Across Africa', is an Africa-based network with 'the vision of creating an enabling environment for volunteering in the continent'. In 2000, the organisation launched the first ever African portal to link potential volunteers with a diverse range of volunteer opportunities for children, youth, adults and older people. For more information, go to **www.volunteer.co.za/asp/about_volunteering.asp**.

Another website worth visiting is The Africa Centre, which carries listings of voluntary opportunities. Go to **www.africacentre.org/**.

You can also try writing to volunteer agencies and NGOs in Africa, although be prepared for delays in communication. The organisations listed at the end of this section should be able to tell you of available volunteer opportunities.

SKILLED LONG-TERM PROJECTS

Skilled professionals are particularly in need in this continent, including dentists, doctors, engineers, IT experts, mechanics, nurses, opticians, teachers, scientists, builders, horticulturists, librarians, accountants, administrators and business people. Most of these are required in projects working directly with indigenous communities, with the emphasis on teaching people to 'help themselves'. Sustainability is a key concept in development projects and many experts are employed in training, passing on vital skills to local workers who can then continue the work long after the project has finished. Many of the organisations sending professional volunteers are religiously motivated, although few are likely to be actively spreading the message of their faith. Projects tend to be long term, usually one or two years, but come with advantages such as paid travel, insurance, visa and accommodation. Some posts are salaried, although the payment is usually small in accordance with the local rates.

These professional placements are not only a fascinating option for those who want to broaden their experience and have a cultural insight into a country they would never otherwise be exposed to, but it can also help develop their careers. Frequently people find themselves taking on duties that may well go beyond what they would be obliged to do at home, being required to manage teams and cross over into other departments.

PROFESSIONAL ORGANISATIONS

In addition to the organisations listed under Professionals in the directory, including VSO, Beso, United Nations, The Red Cross, Volunteers

International, Médecins Sans Frontières and International Health Exchange, the following organisations require professional volunteers in Africa. Some of them require professional volunteers worldwide too:

Action Partner Ministries (Bawtry Hall, Bawtry, Doncaster DN10 6JH, Tel: 01302-710750, Fax: 01302-719399, website: **www.actionpartners.org.uk**) is a Christian organisation that places professionals for one year and upwards in sub-Saharan Africa. Volunteers are needed in medical work, teaching and engineering.

Amazon-Africa Aid Organisation (PO Box 7776, Ann Arbor, M1 48107, USA, Tel: 00 1 734 769 5778, Fax: 00 1 734 769 5779, website: **www.amazonafrica.org**) sends volunteer physicians, gynaecologists, dentists and family practitioners to work at medical clinics in the Amazon. Minimum stay is one month.

Skillshare Africa (126 New Walk, Leicester LE1 7JA, UK, Tel: 0116 254 1862, Fax: 0116 254 2614, Email: info@skillshare.org, website: **www.skillshare.org**) organises two-year voluntary placements for skilled people in Botswana, Lesotho, Mozambique, Namibia, Swaziland, South Africa, Tanzania and Uganda. Development workers and health trainers work in areas such as agriculture, community development, education, engineering, environmental conservation, healthcare, HIV/AIDS and vocational training.

GAP-YEAR ORGANISATIONS

Those with no solid professional experience can find plenty of scope to volunteer in Africa courtesy of the huge range of gap-year organisations that run projects here. Work can include anything from teaching (English or other subjects) to working on game reserves to conservation work studying bio-diversity. Most gap-year placements will charge a fee which can range from a few hundred to £2,000 but, on the upside, will include orientation, accommodation, food, transport, visa and insurance. Make sure you check all these details before committing.

Bunac's Volunteer Ghana programme places volunteers in community-based projects for three to six months. Candidates should be aged between 18 and 35 and have been in full-time university education within the last six months. Go to **www.bunac.org** for more details.

In addition to the voluntary organisations listed throughout the book such as Concordia and Global Outreach Mission UK, the following organisations send volunteers to Africa: Cross-Cultural Solutions, Student Partnership Worldwide, Gap Activity, Gap Challenge, Global Volunteers, Volunteers For Peace, Project Trust, Teaching and Projects Abroad, and Travellers Worldwide. WWOOF requires volunteers for work in Ghana and Togo.

Africa and Asia Venture sends hard-working students to Africa and Asia to spend four to five months teaching or working on conservation projects, followed by an exciting safari. Go to **www.aventure.co.uk** for more information.

EIL also organises voluntary and community placements in Argentina, Ecuador, Guatemala, Ghana, Nigeria, Mexico, EVS, Chile, Ireland and Great Britain.

Irish citizens can take part in the programme through UsIt Now. Go to **www.usitnow.ie**. UK citizens can apply through EIL Britain, 287 Worcester Road, Malvern, Worcestershire WR14 1AB, Tel: 0168 45 62577, Fax: 0168 45 62212, website: **www.eiluk.org**. US citizens should contact Federation EIL International Office, Worldwide Network of The Experiment in International Living, PO Box 595, 63 Main St., Putney, VT 05346 USA, Tel: 00 1 802 387 4210, Fax: 00 1 802 387 5783. Other nationalities should look at EIL's website **www.experiment.org/**.

Greenforce places volunteers on wildlife research projects in Fiji, Bahamas, Borneo, Peru and Zambia, such as helping to conserve endangered habitats. Go to **www.greenforce.org** for more information.

Quest Overseas specialises in combining exciting, worthwhile projects and expeditions in Africa and South America. Go to **www.questoverseas.com** for more information.

African Conservation Experience (**www.afconservex.com**) runs varied voluntary work on game reserves in southern Africa. Tasks may include game capture, wildlife veterinary work and alien plant control.

Save the Earth Network (PO Box CT 3635, Cantonments-Accra, Ghana, West Africa, Tel: 00 233-21-236362, Fax: 00 233-21-231485) organises voluntary work in Ghana for maths and English teachers, tree nursing and planting in the tropical rainforest, and conservation work on agro-forestry farms or harvesting fruit.

Volunteer Africa (PO Box 24, Bakewell, Derbyshire DE45 1TA, website: **www.volunteerafrica.org**, Email: admin@volunteerafrica.org) places volunteers in community-based initiated projects in Tanzania. Volunteers work alongside villagers in community projects, such as building primary schools.

Africa Inland Mission (2 Vorley Road, Archway, London N19 5HE) provides English teachers.

VOLUNTEERS' STORIES

Hugh Burnham Slipper has been teaching in Eritrea in Africa for two years with VSO. Hugh says, 'I wasn't a teacher, until I hit the tarmac on Asmara airport, but now I am. We had about ten days' training, which was pretty hard work, but it set us up well, and taught us how to write lessons and do exams and discipline. I came here expecting to teach rows of happy children with shiny white teeth and pens that worked and an insatiable thirst for learning. It was a little naïve perhaps.'

Hugh says school didn't so much start as evolve. A month passed between the official first day to his first lesson when the students actually turned up. This struggle for motivation was a problem throughout and, as a novice teacher, he found his first few months challenging. 'Everything I did for the first three months was communicated in mime, a bit like teaching in a school for the deaf, or more accurately a Punch and Judy show. We got there, though, and the kids were laughing most lessons, with me and not at me.'

There were problems, however. 'The teaching methods I used, which is how you and I were taught in school, are quite different from the standard Eritrean model of chalk and talk. This caused a lot of upset, because the kids thought that they were not learning if they were not copying reams of notes off the board.'

Generally, however, Hugh has relished his experience and he is now applying to extend his two-year stay. 'Two years is a good time, because the first year you're basically learning how to live in a strange land and having digestive problems (I have had to abort a class rather hastily once or twice in order to go and find a clean pair of trousers), and then in the second year you actually do the job that you were sent out to do. Though we have committed ourselves for two years, there is the option to duck out whenever you want. I think globally in VSO the early return rate is about 15 to 20 per cent.'

Hugh praises VSO for its ongoing support and says they do everything possible. 'We get a salary to live like an Eritrean would, and similar conditions, plus medical expenses, bike, bed, mosquito net and well-deserved pork chops in the Ambassador's garden once in a while. Oh, and a whopping great end-of-service grant – a couple of grand, which will do very nicely, thank you very much.'

Overall, he counts his experience as a milestone in personal development. 'Being a volunteer is approximately a million times better than an expat, because I'm living at the same level as the Eritreans and making friendships that would not be possible if I was earning bucketloads. Being part of the community is by far the best reward I have received. Then there's stuff like the scenery and whizzing through Africa in the back of a pickup, and lots of sunshine (bit too much at the moment) and generally being healthier and browner than your average Brit. I'm also much more confident than before I left and, as that plate in my grandmother's sitting room says, I "Know Thy Self".'

Hugh's volunteering has also shaped his future choice of career. 'It has strengthened my resolve to do more useful work back in the UK. I don't think I would be able to be an investment banker and sleep easy at night – or an interior designer, given that there are a lot of people who don't even have a house.'

SOUTH AFRICA

Since the end of the Apartheid era in 1994, numerous social and development projects have sprung up in South Africa as the country gets to grips with its new democratic culture. Conditions are still volatile – many people can't read or write, and thousands of them live in abject poverty, and, thanks to an exodus of doctors, teachers, nurses and IT people lured to the UK, there is a shortage of skilled workers. There is therefore much work to be done. However, international volunteering is still a very new idea for South Africa and, at present, there is not much of an infrastructure – the only volunteer centre is in Cape Town. But, with the rise of interest in South Africa as a tourist destination, international volunteer programmes are on the rise, and look set to develop further.

VISAS AND REGULATIONS

Work permits for non-nationals are hard to come by with so many natives unemployed. Applicants must have fixed up work first, and the prospective employer must prove that no South African can undertake the work.

FINDING WORK ON THE SPOT

With no real voluntary infrastructure in place, it is better to pre-arrange work instead of turning up to find projects on the spot. That said, many travellers work on a three-month tourist visa. Backpacker hostels are said to be a good place to find 'unofficial' work which could include voluntary projects. However, given the harsh reprisals for illegal work (some casual workers face prosecution or deportation), it is wise to be very careful about working without the necessary permission.

The South Africa Volunteer Centre serves the Western Cape and recruits and informs volunteers on the basic concept of volunteering. It also places volunteers with 150 member organisations. South Africa Volunteer Centre – The Volunteer Centre, Western Cape, Somerset Hospital, Helen Bowden Residence Private Bag, Green Point, 8051 Western Cape.

FINDING WORK BEFORE YOU ARRIVE

In addition to the organisations listed above for Africa, the following organisations organise voluntary projects in South Africa: Camphill Village Trust, Concordia, Gap Activity Projects, Gap Challenge, Global Outreach Mission UK, Institute of Cultural Affairs, Project Trust, Quaker Voluntary Action, Travellers, Youth Action for Peace, Youth With A Mission, i to i International Projects, Alliances Abroad, Earthwatch, InterExchange, Involvement Volunteers and Volunteer For Peace.

The agency Foreign Placements can arrange short-term casual work in South Africa as well as contracts for medical staff and skilled workers. Contact Foreign Placements CC: PO Box 912, Somerset West 7129, South Africa.

JCR SA Intercultural Exchange Programs (Pty) Ltd is a cultural exchange organisation in South Africa and offers student exchange programmes for most nationalities wishing to visit South Africa. For more details, check out their website **www.jcr.co.za** where you can also apply online.

Sports Science Institute of South Africa (SCORE: Boundary Rd, Newlands 7700, South Africa, Tel: 021 689 69680) organises summer programmes for self-funding volunteers to coach sports in deprived communities and initiate community sporting activities.

International Veterinary Students Association (VSA) provides opportunities to work with animals in South Africa. Some veterinary experience and skills required. Contact KVL, DSR, Dyrlaegevej 9, DK-1870 Frederiksberg, Denmark, Fax: 00 45 3528 2152, website: **www.ivsa,org**.

Bunac runs a volunteer South Africa programme for volunteers between the ages of 18 and 35 who have been in full-time university education within the last six months. Call 020 7251 3472 or go to **www.bunac.org** for more details.

The SASTS (South African Student Travel Service) offers an eight-week volunteer programme to South Africa. Projects last for two months. Accommodation and meals are included while you are on the project. If you decide to stay on to explore South Africa further, hostel accommodation will cost you about 200 rand per week. No work permit is necessary for Volunteer South Africa. Participants enter South Africa on a ninety-day visitor's visa. Irish citizens can take part in the programme through UsIt. Go to **www.usitnow.ie**, while other citizens can apply through EIL (see directory for more details).

Volunteers are needed to take part in tree planting and gardening projects throughout South Africa. Contact Africa Tree Centre, PO Box 90, Pessislaer 4500, Natal, South Africa.

VOLUNTEER BUREAUX IN AFRICA

Mauritius: Halley Volunteer Centre Halley Movement, PO Box 250, Curepipe, Mauritius, Tel: 00 230 674 6504, Fax: 00 230 677 8544, website: **www.halleymovement.org**.

Nigeria: National Volunteer Centre: 14 Bende, Umuahia, Abia State, Nigeria, Tel: 00 234 88 221 900, Fax: 00 234 88 221 900.

Sierra Leone: Africa Voluntary Service of Sierra Leone, PMB 717, Freetown, Sierra Leone.

Zaire: Zaire Volunteer Cooperation for Development, Covozade: 7 Rue Medeo, Zone de Ngaliema, BP 3410 Kinshasa/Gombe, Zaire.

Zambia: NGOCC, Non Governmental Organisations Co-ordinating Committee Zambia, 1st Floor, Bible House, PO Box 37879, Freedom Way, Lusaka, Zambia.

Zimbabwe: National Association of Non Governmental Organisations (Nango), 19 Selous Avenue, 3rd Street, PO Box CY 250, Causeway, Harare, Zimbabwe, Tel: 00 263 4 708 761, Fax: 00 263 4 794 973, website: **www.nango.org.zw**.

Egypt: Arab Network for NGOs (Shabaka), 5 Bahaa El-Din Karaqoush, Samalek, PO Box 15 Orman, Cairo, Egypt, Tel: 00 202 735 8011, Fax: 00 202 735 8013.

THE MIDDLE EAST

Most countries in the Middle East have little need for voluntary help, and opportunities are slim, particularly with the troubled relations between Israel and Palestine. There are a few exceptions, of course, most notably kibbutzim in Israel. This popular form of voluntary work places volunteers in a self-sufficient communal society for usually around eight weeks. Most volunteers receive free room and board and a small amount of pocket money in return for the labour. In order to take part, you will need a B4 Volunteer Visa, which you can apply for in Israel once you have found work. The visa expires after three months and can be renewed only once (under current regulations) allowing you to stay for a maximum of six months. The website **www.kibbutz.org.il** has details of agencies all over the world which can fix up kibbutz placements, as well as extensive information on life as a kibbutz volunteer. In the UK, contact Kibbutz Representatives: 1A Accommodation Road, London NW11 8ED (Tel: 020 8458 9235) to organise a placement. Cost £60 for administration fee and pay for your own flights.

American applicants can contact the Kibbtuz Aliya Desk (633 3rd Avenue, 21st Floor, New York, NY 10017, Tel: 00 1 212 318 6130). Some agencies offer a package including flights, placement, insurance, transport to the kibbutz and the B4 visa for around £400.

Alternatively, you can turn up and find work at one of the kibbutzim agencies in Tel Aviv. There is also the official Kibbutz Program Centre where you can visit its Volunteer Department (18 Frishman Street, Cnr. 90 Ben Yehuda Street, Tel Aviv 61030). You will have to pay for registration (around $60) and supply various documents such as passport, proof of insurance, return air flight tickets and a medical certificate.

OTHER OPPORTUNITIES
Beyond this, the following organisations organise voluntary projects in Israel and the occupied territories: Across Trust, Archaeology Abroad, Earthwatch, Christians Abroad, Gap Activity Projects, Travel Active and Youth Action For Peace. Christians Abroad, Global Outreach Mission, Project Trust, Institute of Cultural Affairs, Tearfund and Involvement Volunteers have sent volunteers to Jordan and Lebanon. Be aware that the availability of projects may vary according to the current political situation.

Friends of Birzeit University (21 Collingham Road, London SW5 0NU, Tel: 020 737 8414, Fax: 020 7835 2088) organises two international workcamps every summer. Work ranges from helping in refugee centres to helping local farmers, with the focus on providing support to the local community and experiencing life here firsthand.

Friends of Israel Educational Trust (PO Box 7545, London NW2 2QZ, Tel: 020 7435 6803, Fax: 020 7794 0291) offers short-term placements for eighteen- to twenty-year-olds working in a range of areas from EFL to workcamps.

Unipal (Universities' Education Trust for Palestinians: BCM Unipal, London WC1N 3XX, Tel: 020 8299 1132, Fax: 020 8299 1132) sends volunteers to the Israeli-occupied Gaza Strip and West Bank to work on short-term projects during the summer. Work mostly consists of teaching English but there are other opportunities. There are also longer placements lasting six months. Volunteers should be at least twenty years old.

Medical Aid for Palestinians (33A Islington Park Street, London N1 1QB, Tel: 020 7226 4114, Fax: 020 7226 0880) requires qualified medical professionals for placements lasting for 26 to 52 weeks.

VOLUNTEER BUREAUX
National Council for Voluntarism, Mailing Address: PO Box 20428, 67012 Tel-Aviv, Israel. Street Address: Ha'arbaa Street 4, 64739 Tel-Aviv, Israel, Tel: 00 972 3 561 41 44, Fax: 00 972 3 561 33 43, website: **www.volunteering.iol.co.il**.

Jordan: The General Union of Voluntary Societies in Jordan, PO Box 910236, Amman, Jordan, Tel: 00 962 6 634 001, Fax: 00 962 6 659 973.

Lebanon Association for Volunteer Services, PO Box 136104, Beirut, Lebanon, Tel: 00 961 01 797 247, Fax: 00 961 01 797247.

Palestine: Palestinian Association for Voluntary Efforts, PO Box 1828, Nablus, Palestine, Tel: 00 9729 237 6655, Fax: 00 9729 237 6655.

VOLUNTEERS' STORIES

Ellie Sandercock volunteered to teach English for five weeks in Palestine in 2000 through the organisation Unipal. With four other volunteers, she taught boys and girls in strictly segregated schools in a Palestinian refugee camp in Jenin. Ellie says the main objective was to teach in schools run by Unwra, a United Nations relief agency for Palestinian refugees, but it was as much about allowing British people the opportunity to experience Palestinian life. She says, 'We were only there for five weeks but it was the most intense integration into a community I have ever had. There was a real sense of being accepted. The people were unbelievably welcoming. As soon as they realised that we weren't Israeli spies, they invited us into their homes and it got to the point where we didn't have to buy any food because we were being invited out to meals three times a day. We got a lot of marriage proposals too but they were more like formal negotiations.'

Ellie found that, as women in a Muslim society, there were certain concessions they had to make. 'It was a very tight-knit community so as outsiders we were incredibly noticeable, particularly as we didn't wear headscarves, which all the other women did. We got a bit of hassle in town for this, but it was usually good-natured. The Jenin camp was very conservative so we had to wear long straight skirts to cover our legs, tops with long baggy sleeves and done up to the neck, and baggy wide-legged trousers.' The girls at school were particularly hard working. 'If they don't do well, they are more likely to be married off – there were a couple of girls in my class who were engaged at thirteen.'

The most testing condition, she says, was living with four volunteers plus one group leader in a three-bedroomed apartment. 'The buildings were really close so we were overlooked all the time and, because it was so hot, everyone had their windows open and people could see into the flat. There was absolutely no privacy and the only way we could deal with it was to make sure we went away at the weekends to meet other volunteers.'

Ellie sums her time up as 'fantastic, but challenging'. The experience opened her eyes to the reality of life for a Palestinian refugee. 'Most camps were separate from local towns and weren't camps as such. They had hastily erected buildings but there was little in the way of basic amenities and not much to do. It was peaceful when I went as it was before the suicide bombings had started, but there were terrible restrictions. It gave me a good insight into what the media tends to demonstrate as irrational terrorist behaviour. I didn't meet any terrorists but I did meet people who were driven to breaking point with frustration from the constant restriction and constant injustice. Palestinian refugees feel incredibly isolated and are very restricted in movement. We had to apply for a permit just to take the schoolchildren to Jerusalem for the day, and everywhere you went there were Israeli roadblocks.'

EMBASSIES

Kenyan High Commission, 45 Portland Place, London W1, UK, Tel: 020 7636 2371.

Kenyan Embassy, 2249 R. Street, NW, Washington, DC 20008, USA, Tel: 00 1 202 387 6101, website: **www.kenyaembassy.com**.

Nigerian High Commission, Nigeria House, 9 Northumberland Avenue, London WC2, UK, Tel: 020 7839 1244.

Nigerian Embassy, 1333 16th Street, NW, Washington, DC 20036, USA, Tel: 00 1 202 986 8400.

South African High Commission, South Africa House, Trafalgar Square, London WC2, UK, Tel: 020 7312 5000.

3051 Massachusetts Avenue, NW, Washington, DC 20008, USA, Tel: 00 1 202 232 440, website: **www.southafrica.net**.

Zimbabwe High Commission, 429 Strand, London WC2, Tel: 020 7836 7755.

1608 New Hampshire Avenue, NW, Washington, DC 20009, USA, Tel: 00 1 202 332 7100, website: **www.zimweb.com/Embassy/Zimbabwe**.

Zambian High Commission, 2 Palace Gate, Kensington, London W8 5NG, UK, Tel: 020 7589 6655.

Zambian Embassy, 2419 Massachusetts Avenue, NW, Washington, DC 2008, USA, Tel: 00 1 202 265 9717, website: **www.statehouse.gov.zm**.

Egyptian Embassy, 2 Lowndes Street, London SW1X 9ET, UK, Tel: 020 7235 9777, website: **www.egypt-embassy.org**.

3521 International Court NW, Washington, DC 20008, USA, Tel: 00 1 202 966 6342.

Moroccan Embassy, 49 Queen's Gate Gardens, London SW7 5NE, UK, Tel: 020 7581 5001.

1601 21st NW, Washington, DC 20009, USA, Tel: 00 1 202 462 7979.

Israel Embassy, 2 Palace Gate, London W8 4QB, UK, Tel: 020 7957 9500, website: **www.Israel-embassy.org.uk/London**.

Israel Embassy, 3514 International Drive, NW, Washington, DC 20008, USA, Tel: 00 1 202 364 5500, website: **www.israelemb.org**.

USEFUL WEBSITES
www.africaonline.com has job listings and links to other African job-listings sites. It also has the latest visa requirements for each African country.

www.africaguide.com/work has job vacancies and links to websites on working in Africa.

OTHER USEFUL RESOURCES
World Volunteers, edited by Fabio Ausenda and Erin McCloskey (published by Green Volunteers Publications), is a highly comprehensive directory of volunteering organisations in developing countries.

21. ASIA

With all the contrasts and variations that Asia offers, volunteering opportunities here are a mixed bag. Depending on whether you fancy sampling the wealth and industry of the Far East economies, or witnessing the poverty and squalor of India and Nepal, you could find yourself nursing orphaned babies in India or gardening and sipping green tea in the Japanese pastures of idyllic Hokkaido. Whatever you choose, there are plenty of voluntary opportunities in Asia, particularly in the developing countries.

JAPAN

With Japan's strong emphasis on corporate social responsibility, it's not surprising that the voluntary sector in Japan is reasonably well developed. Unlike other Asian countries, there is a national network of local and regional volunteer centres that are affiliated with the government. Volunteering is also being encouraged amongst young people, and some universities and Tokyo high schools have set up volunteer centres on campus to support and stimulate voluntary activities.

There is also a special visa volunteer scheme, where British people can come to Japan and take part in voluntary activities for a year. The Working Holiday Maker visas also make volunteering here a distinct possibility for many other nationalities.

VISAS AND REGULATIONS

In order to obtain a work permit, you must have a position secured before entering the country. However, there are Working Holiday Visas available for British, Australian, Canadian and New Zealand passport holders. These must be applied for at the Japanese Embassy of your home country. The rules are generally the same as Australian Working Holiday Visas and are intended primarily for holiday purposes for twelve months from date of entering the country. However, they are single entry so, if you leave Japan, you must obtain a re-entry permit before leaving to re-enter the country. In addition, from 1 May 2003, the Government of Japan has now started a Volunteer Visa scheme, which allows British Nationals to undertake voluntary work for charitable organisations in Japan for a period of up to one year. Volunteers can work for a registered charity and proposed work should be closely related to the aims of the organisation. The work is on a voluntary basis, although payment of a limited allowance for board, accommodation and pocket money is permitted. Within ninety days of arrival in Japan, Volunteer Visa holders must apply for alien registration at the Local Government Office near to where they are staying. Arriving in Japan, Volunteer Visa holders should register with the British Embassy in Tokyo or the British Consulate-General at Osaka.

FINDING WORK ON THE SPOT

Provided you have enough money to tide you over in a notoriously expensive country, turning up on the spot to find work is a plausible adventure in Japan. Make sure you can speak some Japanese. First stop should be the Japan International Volunteer Center, 6F Maruko Bldg., 1-20-6 Higashiueno, Taito-ku, Tokyo, Japan 110-8605 (five minutes' walk from JR Okachimachi or Ueno station), Tel: 00 81 3-3834-2388, Fax: 00 81 3-3835-0519, Email: jvc@jca.apc.org, website: **www1.jca.apc.org/jvc/**.

Another useful resource is the National Volunteer Activity Promotion Center (NVAPC), Shin-Kasumigaseki Bldg., 3-3-2, Kasumigaseki, Chiyoda-ku, Tokyo, Japan, Fax: 00 81 3 3581 7858.

Volunteers are always needed at the Community House and Information Centre (CHIC) in Kobe. CHIC is a non-profit community service organisation that aims to meet the needs of the international community in Kobe. Contact Community House and Information Centre, RIC Central Tower 3F, 5–15 Koyocho-Naka, Higashinada-ku, Kobe, Japan 658-0032, Tel: 078-857-6540 (international: 00 81-78-857-6540), Fax: 078-857-4789 (international: 00 81-78-857-4789). For more information go to the website: **www.chickobe.com/**, which also has directions for people who are already in Kobe.

Japanreference.com have a Japan Forum where members can post messages. Go to **http//forum.japanreference.com**.

To find listings of Japanese NGOs go to the website for Japan Information Network **www.jinjapan.org** and click on Japan Directory and look under Society, NGOs and Volunteer Groups.

FINDING WORK BEFORE YOU ARRIVE

The following organisations run volunteer schemes in Japan: BTCV, Christians Abroad, Earthwatch, Concordia, Gap Activity Projects, Institute of Cultural Affairs, International Voluntary Service, Project Trust, Quaker Voluntary Action, Youth Action For Peace, Youth With A Mission, Volunteers For Peace and Involvement Volunteers.

The Japan Youth Volunteer Association (3-1 Yoyogi-Kamizono-cho, Shibuya, Tokyo, Japan 151-0052, Fax: 00 81 3 3460 0386) invites young Asians to come over to Japan and volunteer for a year.

English-speaking student volunteers are needed to act as cultural assistants for Japanese schoolchildren at an English Camp in Hakuba. Contact English Camp in Hakuba, 22387 Kamishiro Hakuba, Nagano 399-9211, Japan, Tel: 00 81 090 9987 6530, Fax: 00 81 261 75 4321.

The Shin Shizen Juku (SSJ) New Nature School needs volunteers to help teach English to both children and adults, as well as helping out with gardening, farming, cooking and general assistance. Volunteers must be over eighteen and can stay from six weeks to the whole year. They are particularly needed between January and March. Board and lodging is provided and some volunteers receive Japanese lessons. Write to Shin

Shizen Juku, Tsurui Mura, Akan Gun, 085-1207 Hokkaido, Japan for more details.

The address for WWOOF Japan is Japan Office, Kita 16-jo Higashi 16-chome 3-22, Higashi-ku Sapporo 065-0016 Japan, Fax: (011) 780-4908, Fax (international): 00 81-11-780-4908, website: **www.wwoofjapan.com**/.

The organisation Gap has voluntary opportunities in Japan teaching English, working in hospitals, mainly with the Japanese Red Cross, and other caring institutions such as old people's homes. A six-month Gap placement in Japan costs £1,150, excluding flights, for which you receive full board and lodging and some pocket money. Contact Gap, Gap House, 44 Queens Road, Reading, Berkshire RG1 4BB, Tel: 0118 959 4914.

INDIA AND NEPAL

A huge number of Western organisations place volunteers in India and Nepal. Many of these are religious organisations and in particular require skilled professionals in the fields of health and medical care, aid/relief assistance and sustained development, etc. (See the Africa section for a list of organisations requiring professional people to work on development projects, and the Directory at the back.) There are also plenty of opportunities to be found through the gap-year organisations, particularly working in orphanages, taking part in community projects in remote rural villages, and the perennial favourite of the international traveller – teaching English. Unemployment is huge in India, and speaking English is seen as the gateway to bolstering your status in the job market. With poverty levels so high, most Indian people lack the financial clout to pay for lessons, however, and volunteer teachers are in high demand.

The following organisations run voluntary schemes in India: Africa and Asia Venture, BSES Expeditions, Camphill Village Trust, Christians Abroad, Cross Cultural Solutions, Earthwatch, Gap Activity Projects, Gap Challenge, Global Outreach Mission UK, Global Volunteers, Greenforce, ICA, International Voluntary Service, Involvement Volunteers, i to i international Projects, Teaching and Projects Abroad, Student Partnership Worldwide, Tearfund, Travellers, Voluntary Service Belfast, Youth With A Mission and VSO.

Beyond these Western organisations, there are numerous grassroots projects that you may stumble across by chance during your travels. Although you may strike lucky just by turning up and offering your assistance, many of these schemes are operating in extremely haphazard conditions, and may not be willing to take on board inexperienced volunteers. You will also have to fund yourself, and arrange your own accommodation. Some people manage to volunteer at children's homes, hospitals and orphanages by showing up in person. Jilly Coombes offered her services just by turning up at one orphanage and spent six months living close by and helping out every morning. Many people help out at Mother Teresa's Missionaries of Charity in Calcutta. You can either turn up and speak to one of the Sisters at Shishu Bhavan, 78 AJC Bose Road, Calcutta, or contact the London office at 177 Bravington Road, London W9 3AR (Tel: 020 8960 2644) for more information.

Despite the huge array of volunteer projects at work in India, there appears to be only one organisation overseeing volunteers: India Association of Volunteer Effort, People's House Paryavaran Complex, Shidulla Jab, New Delhi, India 110030, Tel: 00 91 11689 5091, Fax: 00 91 11 689 4407.

Here are some voluntary projects:

Global Hands, Nepal arranges short-term voluntary opportunities in Nepal and India for people to take part in community-service projects. Participants can work in a variety of capacities, including admin, development, fundraising, teaching, technical skills and befriending, for a variety of causes (healthcare, teaching or working with the poor, children, the disabled or homeless). Contact Global Hands, Nepal, PO Box 489, Zero k.m., Pokhara, Kaski, Nepal, Tel: 00 977 61 30266.

Bharat Sevak Samaj uses some volunteers for its nursery schools, child welfare centres and family planning camps, as well as relief work. Contact Bharat Sevak Samaj (BSS), Nehru Seva Kendra, Gugoan Bye Pass Road, Mehrauli, New Delhi 30, India, Tel: 00 91 11 685215.

Calcutta Rescue Fund (PO Box 16163, Clapham, London SW4 7ZT) uses volunteer health professionals in its clinics, schools and training projects for the destitute and socially disadvantaged. Placements last for nine months to a year and include a contribution to living costs if necessary.

India Development Group (UK) (68 Downlands Road, Purley, Surrey) organises sustainable development placements in India.

Indian Volunteers for Community Service (IVCS) (12 Eastleigh Avenue, Harrow, Middlesex, HA2 0UF, UK, Tel: 020 8864 4740, website: www.ivcs.org.uk) gives volunteers the opportunity to spend up to six months on rural development programmes in India. Causes covered include children, healthcare, teaching and helping the poor and homeless.

Student Action India (SAI: c/o HouseNet, Office 20, 30–38 Dock Street, Leeds LS10 1JF, UK, Tel: 07071 225 866, Fax: 07072 225 866) helps volunteers find placements in development projects in India.

Discover Nepal is an NGO that places volunteer teachers in schools in Nepal. Contact Discover Nepal, GPO Box 20209, Kathmandu, Nepal, Tel: 00 977 1 416326, Fax: 00 977 1 255487, website: www.discovernepal.com.np.

Volunteer Nepal places volunteers on a variety of community programmes including working with addicts/ex-addicts, AIDS/HIV, children, the disabled and the homeless. Volunteers stay with a Nepali family and at the end of the project receive free trekking, jungle safari and white-water rafting. To find out more, go to www.volunteernepal.org.np, or contact Volunteer Nepal, GPO Box 11535, Dilli Bazar, Kathmandu, Nepal, Tel: 00 977 1 426996, Fax: 00 977 1 416417/428925.

Voluntary Work Opportunities in Nepal (VWOP) provides voluntary opportunities throughout Nepal on a range of projects including teaching in schools and environmental, health and agricultural programmes. Voluntary Work Opportunities in Nepal, GPS Box 11969, Kathmandu, Nepal, Fax: 00 977 1416144, Email: vwop2000@hotmail.com.

Rural Community Development Programme – Nepal places volunteers on a variety of programmes, including teaching in schools and orphanages, taking part in local community forestry and conservation projects and, for medical students, working at hospitals. Contact Rural Community Development Programme – Nepal, Kalani-14, Kathmandhu, Nepal, Tel: 00 977 1 278305, Fax: 00 977 1 415679, website: **www.rcdpnepal.com**.

VISAS AND REGULATIONS

Under Indian visa regulations, all non-Indian nationals should have a tourist visa before entering the country. If you are planning to stay over three months the official line is that you register with the Foreigners' Regional Registration Office within fourteen days of arrival and provide evidence of how you intend to support yourself. However, one expat, who has a work permit and has been living there for a year, says she still hasn't registered at the Foreigners' Regional Registration Office. 'India is very bureaucratic but nobody bothers to follow the rules.'

For voluntary work under three months, most people work under a tourist visa. For over three months, however, you must send details of the scheme to the India Consulate when applying for a visa at least two months in advance.

If you intend to take up paid employment, you should have a valid work permit before you enter the country. Apply to the nearest Indian Consulate, enclosing a copy of your contract.

CHINA

As China makes the transition from a planned to a market economy, voluntary organisations and help are seen as fulfilling an important role. Voluntary work and community solidarity have always been vital components of China's two major religions, Buddhist and Confucius teaching, and the tradition still exists today, with many community projects actively working on the streets in different neighbourhoods. The government is also actively encouraging volunteers to get involved and international volunteers have been welcomed to take part in local projects.

The following organisations place volunteers in China: Project Trust, Christians Abroad, Earthwatch, Gap Activity Projects, Global Volunteers, i to i International Projects, Raleigh International, ICA, Teaching and Projects Abroad, VSO, WorldTeach and Youth With A Mission. Projects Abroad places people on a diverse range of volunteering placements in China, from medical help to working on a daily newspaper, teaching English or working in The Shanghai Wildlife Park.

For China's national volunteer centre, head for Beijing International Volunteer Association. Contact Address: No.18, Bei San Huan Zhonglu, Beijing, P.R.China, Zip Code: 100011, Tel: 00 86 010 62380891/62355771, Fax: 00 86 010 62380927/62355771, website: **www.civa.org.cn**. The website also has listings of Chinese member NGOs and voluntary organisations. Two organisations that may be of use are the China Young Volunteers Association and China Youth Development Foundation.

Another one worth contacting is Volunteer Action Centre, 1/F., Yuen Fai Court, 6 Sai Yuen Lane, Sai Ying Pun, Hong Kong, Tel: 00 852 2546-0694, Fax: 00852 2559-5142.

Agency for Volunteer Service, 602, Duke of Windsor Social Service Bldg., 15 Hennessy Road, Wanchai, Hong Kong, Tel: 00 852 2527-3825, Fax: 00 852 2866-2721, website: **www.avs.org.hk**.

International China Concern (PO Box 20, Morpeth, NE61 3YP, UK, Tel: 01670 505622, website: **www.intlchinaconcern.org**) sends twenty to thirty volunteers each year to assist in projects in China's government orphanages. Professionals in the following areas are required: admin, accounts, physical and occupational therapy, special needs and nursing.

The CIEE run a Teach in China scheme for graduates. Placements last between five and ten months and cost £625 plus flights, which includes one-week training on arrival in Beijing. In the UK, email TiC@councilexchanges.org or call 020 7478 2018 for further details.

VOLUNTEERS' STORIES

Karen Harrison spent a gap year volunteering in Indonesia with the organisation Project Trust before starting university. Matched with another volunteer, she worked for the first eight months in a university English department teaching conversational English to mature students and business people, and then spent the rest of the time working at an institute for the blind. She says, 'The whole experience was challenging. I was seventeen and had never been away from home, and there were a lot of cultural differences living in a Muslim country. It was quite difficult being away from home for the first time. But I gained a lot of confidence and, by the time I started at university, I felt I was much more mature than I would have been if I hadn't have done it.'

Karen describes it as a 'big challenge, culturally'. 'Basically, we were going out as two white young females in a developing area where people had certain perceptions of Western women. This was mainly a product of the way we are portrayed in the media and in Hollywood films, and extended to a misunderstanding of all Westerners – people thought the life we led was extremely affluent and didn't realise that even in the UK we have problems such as homeless people and poverty. But the attitudes towards us as young Western women were particularly challenging. We might get propositioned in the street and we would often get men touching our knees on local transport. We just had to push them aside – it made me more confident as we just had to learn how to deal with it.'

The work was good, however. 'There were lots of teaching material left by previous Project Trust volunteers which was useful as we had no previous teaching experience. The blind institute was really interesting – the ages ranged from seven to young adults and beyond, and basically they were disabled people who ended up here as there were very little provisions in the way of training them or integrating them into society. Some would possibly stay in the home for life. Most of our work was providing activities to entertain them, including taking them swimming once a week.'

Karen gained a huge amount from the experience. 'It made me the person I am today. I had to grow in confidence to deal with different situations. At seventeen you are usually not very aware of your abilities and strengths, but going abroad made me see what I enjoy. I also formed lifelong friendships with the people I was matched with.'

CONSERVATION PROJECTS IN ASIA

There are also numerous conservation projects in Asia, ranging from protecting endangered species such as tigers to studying biodiversity in the rainforest. In most cases, no former experience or qualifications are required, although experts are particularly in demand for research projects. The following organisations run conservation programmes in Asia:

Coral Cay Conservation (The Tower, 13th Floor, 125 High Street, Colliers Wood, London SW19 2JG, Tel: 0870 750 0688, website: **www.coralcay.org**) sends volunteers to Fiji, Honduras and the Philippines for marine and rainforest conservation expeditions.

Greenforce (11–15 Betterton Street, Covent Garden, London WC2H 9BP, Tel: 020 7470 8888, website: **www.greenforce.org**) organises Work on the Wild Side conservation projects around the world in the Amazon, Africa, Malaysia and South Pacific, ranging from monitoring marine life to working with wild animals. Placements last from ten weeks. No experience needed.

Trekforce Expeditions (34 Buckingham Palace Road, London SW1W 0RE, Tel: 020 7828 2275, website: **www.trekforce.org.uk**) sends people on eight- to twenty-week expeditions in conservation projects in South East Asia (and Central America), concentrating on working in the rainforest and with local communities.

Frontier sends 300 volunteers a year on conservation expeditions in remote and unexplored areas throughout the world, including Vietnam in Asia. Projects last from ten to twenty weeks and include work on coral reefs and in rainforests. (There are also projects in Tanzania and Madagascar on game reserves.) Contact Frontier, 50–52 Rivington Street, London EC2A 3QP, Tel: 020 7631 2422, Fax: 020 7613 2992, website: **www.frontier.ac.uk**.

Wild Animal Rescue Foundation of Thailand (WAR) recruits paying volunteers to help with its many conservation projects caring for abused wild animals such as bears and tigers in need. One such project is the Phuket Gibbon Rehabilitation Project on the island of Phuket. Volunteers can stay for three or eight weeks. Contact Wild Animal Rescue Foundation of Thailand (WAR), 235 Sukhumvit 31, Bangkok 10110, Thailand, Tel: 00 662 662 0898, Fax: 00 662 261 9670, website: **www.war-thai.org**.

OTHER PROJECTS

Korean International Volunteer Association (KIVA) organises volunteer placements throughout Korea, including teaching English and working in orphanages. Contact: Korean International Volunteer Association (KIVA), 11th Floor Sekwang B/D, 202 Sejong-ro, Congro-gu, Seoul, South Korea 110-050, website: **www.kiva.or.uk**.

Bangladesh Work Camps Association organises international workcamps for volunteers in rural and urban Bangladesh. Go to the website **www.mybwca.org** for more information or write to: Bangladesh Work Camps Association, 289/2 Work Camp Road, North Shajanahpur, Dhaka-1217, Bangladesh.

VOLUNTEER BUREAUX IN ASIA

Bangladesh: Center for Development Services (CDS), 38/1 Block-F, Ring Road, Shyamoli, Dhaka, Bangladesh 1207, Fax: 00 880 2 8115 512.

Bhutan: Volunteers in Bhutan, website: **www.undp.org.bt/**.

Cook Islands: Cook Islands Association of NGOs: Post Office Box 733, Rarotonga, Cook Islands, Tel: 00 682 29420, Fax: 00 682 28420.

Indonesia: Jakarta International Association for Volunteer Effort (JIAVE), Bina Murni Oannekia Educational Foundation, Binataro Java, Jakarta Selatan, Indonesia 15221, Tel: 00 62 21 735 9061, Fax: 00 62 21 572 7409.

Korea: Korea Council of Volunteer Organisations (KCVO): 100-043, 32-3 Ka, Nam-San-Dong, Choong-Ku, Seoul, Korea, Tel: 00 82 2 755 6734, Fax: 00 82 2 755 6735.

Korea Youth Volunteer Centre (KYVC), 142 Woomyeon-Dong, Seocho-ku, Seoul, Korea 137-715, Tel: 00 82 02 578 4104, Fax: 00 82 02 2188 8889.

Korean Association of Volunteer Centers (KAVC), c/o Songpa-GU Volunteer Center, 62-2 Samjeon-Dong, Songpa-Gu, Seoul, Korea 138-180, Tel: 00 82 2 410 37978, Fax: 00 82 2 2202 1104.

Volunteer 21, Pangbae-bon-dont 779-1 3f, Seochu-gu, Seoul, Korea, Tel: 00 82 2 599 6576, Fax: 00 82 2 599 6580, website: **www.vol21.peacenet.or.kr**.

Malaysia: National Nongovernmental Organisation Resource Center, c/o FOMCA, 8 Lorong, SS 1/22A, 47300 Petaling Jaya, Selangor, Malaysia.

Papua New Guinea: National Volunteer Service, PO Box 4073 Bokoko, Bokoko, Papua New Guinea, 111 NCD, Fax: 00 675 325 8756.

Republic of Fiji Islands: National Volunteer Center of the Council of Social Services (FCOSS), 256 Waimanu Road, PO Box 13476, Suva, Fiji Islands, Tel: 00 679 312 649.

Republic of the Philippines: Philippine National Volunteer Service Coordinating Agency (PNVSCA), Room 301, Cabrera Building 1, 130 Timog Avenue, Quezon City, Tel: 00 63 2 922 8635.

Singapore: National Volunteer Center Singapore, 7 Maxwell Road 05-01 Annex B MND Complex, Singapore 069111, Fax: 00 65 221 0625, website: **www.nvc.org.sg**.

The Volunteer Action and Development Center (VACD): 11 Penang Lane, 238485, Singapore, Fax: 00 65 339 6859.

Taiwan: Asia-Pacific Public Affairs Forum, 28 F, 55 Chung-Cheng 3rd Road, Kaohsiung City, Taiwan 800, Tel: 00 886 7 2274736, Fax: 00 886 7 227559, website: **www.appaf.nsysu.edu.tw**.

IAVE Taiwan is the National Representative of the International Association for Volunteer Effort. The website carries details of the national volunteer centre, voluntary opportunities and voluntary organisations in Taiwan. Go to **www.iavetaiwan.org**.

Thailand: National Council on Social Welfare of Thailand under Royal Patronage, Mahidol Building, Rajavithi Road, Bangkok 10400, Thailand, Tel: 00 66 2 246 0077, Fax: 00 66 2 247 6279.

EMBASSIES

Bangladesh Embassy, 28 Queens Gate, London SW7, UK, Tel: 020 7584 0081.

Chinese Embassy, 31 Portland Place, London, UK, Tel: 020 7631 1430, or 2300 Connecticut Avenue, NW, Washington, DC 20008, USA, Tel: 00 1 202 328 2500, website: **www.china-embassy.org**.

Indian Embassy, India House, Aldwych, London WC2, UK, Tel: 0906 8444 544, or 2107 Massachusetts Avenue NW, Washington, DC 20008, USA, Tel: 00 1 202 939 7000, website: **www.indianembassy.org**.

Indonesian Embassy, 38 Grosvenor Square, London, UK, Tel: 020 7499 7661, or 2020 Massachusetts Ave NW, Washington, DC 20036, USA, Tel: 00 1 202 939 7000, website: **www.indianembassy.org**.

Japanese Embassy, 101–104 Piccadilly, London W1V 9FN, UK, Tel: 020 7465 6500, or 2520 Massachusetts Avenue, NW, Washington, DC 20008, USA, Tel: 00 1 202 238 6700, website: **www.embajapan.org**.

Korean Embassy, 60 Buckingham Gate, London SW1E 6AJ, UK, Tel: 020 7227 5500, or 2450 Massachusetts Avenue, NW, Washington, DC 20008, USA, Tel: 00 1 202 939 5600, website: **www.mofat.go.kr/en-usa-html**.

Malaysian Embassy, 45 Belgrave Square, London WC2N 5DU, UK, Tel: 020 7235 8033, or 2401 Massachusetts Avenue, NW, Washington, DC 20008, USA, Tel: 00 1 202 328 2700.

Nepal Embassy, 12a Kensington Palace, London W8, UK, Tel: 020 7229 6231.

Philippine Embassy, 9A Palace Green, London W8 4QE, UK, Tel: 020 7937 1600, or 1600 Massachusetts Avenue, NW, Washington, DC 20036, USA, Tel: 00 1 202 467 9300.

Sri Lankan Embassy, 13a Hyde Park Gardens, London W2, UK, Tel: 020 7262 1841.

The Royal Thai Embassy, 29–30 Queensgate, London SW7, UK, Tel: 020 7589 2944, ext.117.

The Royal Thai Embassy, 1024 Wisconsin Avenue, NW, Washington, DC 20007, USA.

Vietnamese Embassy, 12–14 Victoria Road, London W8, UK, Tel: 020 7937 3222.

22. AUSTRALIA AND NEW ZEALAND

AUSTRALIA

With one in five people in Australia reported to be volunteering every week, Australia carries an extensive range of volunteering opportunities. The situation is said to be broadly similar to the UK with volunteer agencies supplementing good state provision. Community work is popular here, and can include anything from working in donkey sanctuaries to taking part in urban projects designed to help the poor, dispossessed, elderly and disabled. There are also plenty of opportunities for conservation and agricultural work, particularly in the bush and more remote areas.

VISAS AND REGULATIONS

One of the main drawbacks in gaining voluntary work in Australia is the restrictive visa situation. Every nationality except New Zealanders needs a visa to enter Australia, which in order to work legally is notoriously hard to obtain. People between eighteen and thirty are at an advantage here as they can make the most of the Working Holiday Maker visa. The main purpose of the visa is for holiday and travel so you are not entitled to work at one job or undergo studying or training for longer than three months, although you can still find work through the same agency. The visa can only be issued once and entitles you to stay for a maximum of twelve months (starting from the day you enter Australia). If you break the conditions of your visa, you may be asked to leave. It is also worth noting that, if you leave Australia within the twelve months of the visa's permit, your visa still expires on the original date, so don't expect to recover any months you were absent from the country.

In order to be eligible for the Working Holiday Maker visa you must be aged between eighteen and thirty (inclusive) at the time of the application, have no dependent children with you, and hold a valid passport from one of the following countries: the UK, Canada, the Netherlands, Ireland, Japan, Korea, Malta, Germany, Sweden, Denmark, Norway and Hong Kong. However, Australia is currently negotiating the same working holiday arrangement with other countries – to check which ones, look on the DIMA website **www.immi.gov.au** or check with your nearest Australian Government Office. Once you have turned 31, you are no longer eligible for a Working Holiday Maker visa, and can only work there if you meet the requirements for another type of temporary residence visa. Broadly speaking this operates under a point system, where certain professions are awarded points depending on the demand.

HOW TO APPLY FOR THE WORKING HOLIDAY MAKER VISA

Application for the visa must be lodged outside Australia, where you should also be granted it. Fill in Form 1150 available from the Australian Consulate, Embassy or High Commission. Since November 2001, applications for Working Holiday Maker visas cannot be lodged in person at the Australian High Commission in London, and can only be lodged by post. It can also be downloaded from the Australian Department of Immigration and Multicultural Affairs' website (**www.immi.gov.au**) or call the Australian Citizenship Information Line on 09065-508900 (calls charged at £1 per minute). For more information contact the Australian Government Offices.

How long will it take and what evidence will I need? Begin the application process well in advance of your travels as, because Australia is such a popular destination, there can be a limit on the number of Working Holiday Maker visas issued. Generally the process takes four to five weeks and it's recommended that you don't book your flight until your visa has been granted. You don't need to show a return ticket but proof will be asked that you have sufficient money for a return or onward journey (around £2,000 for UK citizens). There are also strict health standards and, in exceptional circumstances, you may be asked to have a medical examination or X-ray as part of your application.

Once you have been granted the visa, you have twelve months to travel to Australia. You can apply for another visa while you are in Australia, should you meet the requirements. Working Holiday Maker visa holders may be able to apply for a visitor visa to enable a longer stay in Australia but only in exceptional circumstances.

TOURIST VISAS

If you are not eligible for a WHM visa, or are only travelling for a short time, you are in theory entitled to undertake voluntary work on a tourist visa. Like all visa applications in Australia, this comes under certain conditions: namely, that you can prove you have sufficient funds to support you during your visit, and that you meet certain medical standards. Thirty-two nationalities (including EU/EEA countries, Canada, USA, Hong Kong, Singapore, South Korea, Japan and others) can undertake voluntary work on a Visitor/Tourist ETA. (ETA stands for Electronic Travel Authority where the visa is stored as an electronic record rather than stamped on your passport.) This is granted under three main conditions:

- **your main purpose in visiting Australia is tourism, and any voluntary work remains incidental to this. Voluntary work schemes must not, in other words, become a way of dodging the general work prohibition that applies to the visitor visa.**

- **the work involved would not otherwise be undertaken in return for wages by an Australian citizen or resident.**

- **the work activities are genuinely voluntary.**

Passport holders from countries where ETAs are not yet available will still have to apply for a visitor visa through an Australian Embassy, High Commission or Consulate, which will cost $A60.00 for a Visa Application (go to **www.immi.gov.au** for more information).

FINDING WORK ON THE SPOT

Once you have worked out which particular visa is appropriate for you, you have two options for finding voluntary work. The first is to head out on a WHM visa and pick up work as you travel around, a popular and feasible option. In this instance, your first line of enquiry should be Volunteering Australia, the national peak body working to advance volunteering in the Australian community. Its website **www.VolunteeringAustralia.org** has plenty of information on volunteering in Australia plus advice on rights and visas. You can also write to or visit Volunteering Australia, ABN: 23 062 806 464, Suite 2, Level 3, 11 Queens Road, Melbourne, Victoria, 3004, Tel: 00 61 03 9820 4100, Fax: 00 61 03 9820 1206.

Most regions have voluntary bureaux or agencies (such as Volunteering NSW, Volunteering Queensland, etc.) that will match you to local voluntary opportunities. Some of these include Volunteering New South Wales, Volunteering Queensland, Volunteering Northern Territory, Volunteering Western Australia, Volunteering South Australia, Volunteering Tasmania, Volunteering Victoria and Volunteering Australian Capital Territory.

Volunteering Australia has also started an online voluntary recruitment site called Go Volunteer (**www.GoVolunteer.com.au**), which provides volunteers with all they need to find out about volunteer opportunities. It also helps them make the best match possible between their personal requirements and choice of volunteer work.

Make sure you follow the advice regarding finding all kinds of work, which means going out of your way to speak to other travellers and locals who may be able to put you in touch with any volunteer opportunities around. Australia has a vast network of hostels to serve the backpacking community and these are famously a great way of hearing about work.

Not only is staying in hostels the fastest way to meet people and create networks, but farmers and project leaders frequently advertise any vacancies on the hostel notice boards. Many hostels also offer free board and lodging in return for helping out with chores around the site – such as cleaning, looking after reception and working behind the bar, etc.

Make sure you try all the usual lines of enquiry as for paid work. Australia's vibrant backpacking scene ensures that it is well served in agencies, publications and websites advertising jobs. Some of these occasionally carry details of voluntary work so keep your eyes peeled. Before leaving, register free with **www.gapwork.com** which has regularly updated lists of vacancies for working holidaymakers.

Some other useful employment websites are:

Employment.com.au
MyCareer.com.au
www. backpackingaround.com
www.greyhound.com.au
www.waywardbus.com.au/seaswork
www.countrylink.nsw.gov.au
www.yha.com.au

www.backpackers.com.au
www.immi.gov.au/allforms/temo.whm.htm

The other thing to do is read the classifieds in the main Australian newspapers and magazines – the *Advertiser* (Adelaide), the *Age* (Melbourne), the *Australian, Australian Financial Review, Canberra Times* (Canberra), *Courier Mail* (Brisbane), the *Mercury* (Tasmania), *Sydney Morning Herald* (Sydney) and *Queensland Country Life* magazine (Queensland).

FINDING WORK BEFORE YOU ARRIVE

The second option is to pre-arrange work through a sending organisation. This can curtail any visa complications as often the agency will arrange it for you, complete with flights and orientation courses. Luckily, there are many organisations that organise placements in Australia including BSES Expeditions, BTCV, Earthwatch, Gap Activity Projects, Gap Challenge, Global Outreach Mission UK, Institute of Cultural Affairs, International Voluntary Service, i to i International Projects and Travel Active.

There are also plenty of locally based projects worth contacting. Here is a selection:

WWOOF Australia provides voluntary work with more than 1,600 hosts including 1,200 traditional organic farms around Australia. Food and accommodation is provided in exchange for four to six hours' work per day. Contact Willing Workers on Organic Farms (Australia): Buchan 3885, Victoria, Australia (Tel: 00 61 3 5255 0218, Fax: 00 61 3 5155 0342, Email: wwoof@net-tech.com.au, website: **www.wwoof.com.au**).

Australian Trust for Conservation Volunteers is Australia's largest practical conservation organisation and completes more than 1,500 conservation projects in Australia every year. The Trust welcomes volunteers aged between fifteen and seventy to take part in projects typically involving tree planting, restoring damaged habitats, monitoring endangered fauna, creating wetlands and building paths. Volunteers are provided with food, accommodation and transport, but must bring their own sleeping bag and work boots. Projects last for at least six weeks and volunteers make a contribution of A$20 per day. The six-week package costs A$840. Contact: Head office, PO Box 423, Ballarat, Victoria 3353, Australia, Tel: 00 61 3 5333 1483, Fax: 00 61 3 5333 2166, website: **www.actcv.com.au**.

The Australian Koala Foundation uses volunteers to assist on fieldwork trips throughout the year, which usually last for two weeks. They can also assist with general office duties from March to October. For more information, contact The Australian Koala Foundation, Level 1, 40 Charlotte Street, Brisbane, Queensland 4000, Australia, Tel: 00 61 7 3229 7233, Fax: 00 61 7 3221 0337, Email: research@savethekoala.com, website: **www.savethekoala.com**.

The Big Swamp Wildlife Park is maintained by volunteers. Contact: Big Swamp Wildlife Park, Prince Philip Drive, PO Box 21, Bunbury, 6230 Western Australia, Tel: 00 61 8 9721 8380, Fax: 00 61 8 9721 7509.

Kids' Camps Inc employs volunteer camp leaders to take part in residential camps for schoolchildren with intellectual disabilities aged between six and eighteen. Contact Kids' Camps: Camps for Students with an Intellectual Disability Inc., Po Box 170, Ledderville, 6065 Western Australia, Tel: 00 61 8 9420 7247, Fax: 00 61 8 9420 7248.

VOLUNTEERS' STORIES

Kate Marshall found voluntary work in Australia as part of her mammoth eighteen-month trip, incorporating the United States, Australia, New Zealand and Thailand. Kate landed in Sydney and, after six months working for a publishing company in paid employment, she headed for Darwin. 'We were looking for something to do, so went to a national park in the Bush and met some guides. They told us that the aboriginal owners were looking for a couple of travellers to work in the Bush so we volunteered immediately.'

For three months, Kate lived in the Bush, working on a campsite. Work ranged from the mundane – collecting money from the campers, cooking and cleaning – to the exotic, and they spent their days making didgeridoos and boomerangs for the tourists and taking them to natural hot pools nearby. Kate says, 'It was an amazing experience – every night we slept on paper bark from the trees, and went fishing in the billabongs and cooked on an open fire in the evenings. I'll never forget it.'

OTHER USEFUL RESOURCES

The Australia Work and Travel (AUSWAT) Programme helps British, Canadian, Dutch and Irish citizens resident in the UK to travel and support themselves in Australia. It assists in all stages from obtaining visas to finding work and accommodation. Contact: Council on International Educational Exchange (CIEE), 52 Poland Street, London W1F 7AB, Tel: 020 7478 2022, Fax: 020 7734 7322, Email: auswat@councilexchanges.org.uk, website: **www.councilexchanges.org**.

Bunac arranges a work and travel scheme to Australia, organised by International Exchange Programme, for up to a year for eighteen- to thirty-year-olds (inclusive). The package includes a round-trip flight, Working Holiday Maker visa, two nights' accommodation in Sydney, and guidance on jobs, accommodation, health, etc. The programme is open to British, Irish, Canadian, Dutch, Swedish, Norwegian or Danish passport holders. Contact Work Australia, Bunac, 16 Bowling Green Lane, London EC1R 0QH, Tel: 020 7251 3472, Email: downunder@bunac.org.uk, website: **www.bunac.org**.

NEW ZEALAND

New Zealand has a strong tradition of volunteering and is well served by volunteer bureaux and agencies. Opportunities for voluntary work exist in a range of diverse areas, including sport and recreation, emergency services, childcare and young people, caring for sick people or people with disabilities. There are also opportunities with Maori community activities, churches, women's refuges, culture and heritage, and citizens' advice.

The country also offers plenty of opportunities for conservation work, and volunteers may be able to stumble across eco projects during their travels. Many of these projects are aimed at protecting the thousands of hectares of land badly in need of help with much native wildlife disappearing. Conservation work is a particularly good option as New Zealand boasts good budget accommodation and free camping on beaches and woodland.

VISAS AND REGULATIONS

The good news for citizens of the UK, Ireland, US and most European countries is that they do not need a visa for tourist and business trips of up to three months (for UK citizens this extends to six months). On arrival they must have valid passports, return tickets and evidence of sufficient funds. However, all nationals except Australians must have a work permit or visa in order to work and this applies to any form of work, including internships, jobs which are paid in board and lodging (such as working on a farm) and, yes, voluntary work. The work should normally be obtained before entering the country, and usually a New Zealand work visa will only be granted if you have provided a written offer of employment for which you are qualified.

You can apply for a work visa or permit by completing the Application to Work in New Zealand and downloading the application form for work visas and permits from the New Zealand Immigration Service (NZIS) website. Processing time takes normally three weeks if you have provided all the relevant documentation. People on working holidays can now apply to extend their stay or even residence without leaving the country. Applicants with skills in demand – such as doctors – may apply for a new work permit option that will be valid for up to six months at one of the seven Immigration Services offices in New Zealand.

FINDING WORK ON THE SPOT

Once you have cracked the visa situation, New Zealand's extensive infrastructure of volunteering agencies makes finding work on the spot an easier option than in many other countries. One of the first places to head for is Volunteering New Zealand (**www.volunteeringnz.org.nz**), which has agencies operating all over the country, which can put you in touch with volunteering opportunities. Call 0800 VolCntr (0800 865 268) for details of your local centre. You can also try the website **Volunteernow.org.nz** which allows you to search for a volunteer project.

FINDING WORK BEFORE YOU ARRIVE

The New Zealand Department of Conservation has a wide range of opportunities for volunteers to help in projects conserving the country's natural, cultural and historic resources, with a particular emphasis on Maori values. For more information go to **www.doc.govt.nz/community/006~volunteers/index.asp**, which has details of available projects as well as addresses of its regional offices.

WWOOF-New Zealand (PO Box 1172, Nelson, New Zealand, Tel/Fax: 00 64 03 544 9890, Email: wwoof-nz@xtra.co.nz, website: **www.wwoof.co.nz**) has 550 farms around New Zealand where volunteer farm labourers can work for free food and accommodation.

The New Zealand Trust for Conservation Volunteers offers international volunteering opportunities to overseas visitors, some of which include accommodation. Go to **www.conservationvolunteers.org.nz**. For more information call: 00 64 09 415 9336.

The US-based organisation Explorations In Travel runs voluntary projects for people from all over the globe in Australia and New Zealand (as well as a raft of other countries). Contact Explorations In Travel, 2458 River Rd, Guilford, VT 05301, Tel: 00 1 802 257 0152, Fax: 00 1 802 257-2784, Email: explore@volunteertravel.com, website: **www.volunteertravel.com**.

THE NEW ZEALAND–UNITED KINGDOM WORKING HOLIDAY SCHEME
The Working Holiday Scheme is similar to the Australian WHM and enables young people aged between eighteen and thirty from New Zealand and the United Kingdom to undertake working holidays in each other's countries. There is an annual quota of 8,000 visas available for British applications, starting on 1 September.

To apply you need the right Application for Work Visa form, your UK passport, the fee of £30 and evidence of a return ticket and proof of NZ$4,200 (about £1,200). This scheme doesn't require proof of a job offer and allows you to pick up work as you travel around. However, work permits obtained under this scheme have a few limitations. Holders of working holiday permits may not reapply for subsequent permits and may not undertake permanent employment. Working holiday permits are supposed to be restricted to temporary, casual and part-time work.

To apply call the NZIS UK call centre: within the UK, Tel: 09069 100 100 (calls charged at £1 per minute). From outside the UK, call 00 44 1344 71 61 99, or download an application form from the New Zealand Immigration website: **www.immigration.govt.nz**.

Alternatively, you can turn up in person along with your current passport and £30 application fee, and have your visa issued on the spot.

OTHER WORKING HOLIDAY SCHEMES
There are also a number of Working Holiday Schemes open to citizens of the Netherlands, Canada, Malaysia and Singapore who, since April 2001, do not need to be resident in their home country in order to apply. A similar Working Holiday Scheme is open to the Irish but application must be made to the London branch of the NZIS in New Zealand House. For more information visit the Immigration Service website: **www.immigration.govt.nz**.

Bunac (16 Bowling Green Lane, London EC1R 0QH, UK, Tel: 020 7251 3472, Email: downunder@bunac.org.uk, website: **www.bunac.org**) runs a Work

New Zealand programme which allows British passport-holders aged between eighteen and thirty (inclusive) to spend up to one year working and travelling there. The package includes a round-trip flight, stop-over in Bangkok, first night's accommodation and a three-month tourist visa for Australia.

American students can apply for a six-month work permit from Council Exchanges or Bunac USA to work between 1 April and 21 October.

CCUSA at 2330 Marinship Way, Suite 250, Sausalito, CA 94965 USA (Email: outbound@campcounselors.com, website: **www.campcounselors.com/australia.html**) runs a three-month work-experience programme (June to September).

VOLUNTARY ORGANISATIONS

You can also try some of the local organisations and agencies, which should be able to fix up placements even if you are not a native New Zealander. If you are working on a tourist visa, however, be aware that there may be visa complications.

New Zealand's branch of The Trust for Conservation Volunteers employs thousands of volunteers to maintain and improve New Zealand's ecology, including natural bush areas, parks, reserves, wildlife, waterways, walkways, urban and rural landscape, and countrywide projects. Go to **www.conservationvolunteers.org.nz** for more information or call Tel/Fax: 00 64 09 415 9336.

The New Zealand YMCA is a community organisation, based on Christian principles, which aims to enable individuals and families to develop physically, mentally and spiritually and enjoy a healthy quality of life. To find out about volunteering opportunities, contact your regional office or the national office: YMCA National Office, Level 1, 69 Tasman Street, PO BOX 6832, Marion Square, Wellington, Tel: 00 64 04 802 5524, Fax: 00 64 04 802 5514, website: **www.ymca.org.nz**.

The Royal New Zealand Foundation of the Blind uses over 2000 volunteers to assist blind people and offer support in a number of roles including puppy walking, taking members shopping, being a home visitor or phone buddy, producing audio cassettes, Braille and electronic books, and helping with fundraising events. For all general enquiries call (in NZ) 0800 24 33 33 or go to **www.rnzfb.org.nz/directory.html** for details of their offices based all over New Zealand.

Children's welfare organisation World Vision New Zealand needs volunteers at its national office in Auckland and district offices for running events, administration and promoting Third World issues. Contact World Vision New Zealand, Private Bag 92078, Auckland, Toll Free: 0800 800 774, Tel: 00 64 09 377 0879, Email: cs@worldvision.org.nz.

USEFUL ADDRESSES

Commissioner: Mr Michael L'Estrange, Australian High Commission, London, The Strand, London WC2B 4LA, UK, Tel: 020 7379 4334, Fax: 020 7240 5333.

Australian Honorary Consul, Scotland, Mr William Roxburgh, 37 George Street, Edinburgh EH2 3HN, UK, Tel: 0131 624 3333, Fax: 0131 624 3701.

Australian Honorary Consul, Manchester, Mr Rupert Nichols, First Floor, Century House, 11 St Peter's Square, Manchester M2 3DN, UK, Tel: 0161 237 9440, Fax: 0161 237 9135.

New Zealand Immmigration Service, Mezzanine Floor, New Zealand House, 80 Haymarket, London SW1Y 4TE, UK.

New Zealand applicants for the UK Working Holiday Programmes should contact The British High Commission, 44 Hill Street, PO Box 1812, Thorndon, Wellington, NZ, Tel: 00 64 4 495 0889, Fax: 00 64 4 473 4982, website: **www.brithighcomm.org.nz**.

Get hold of the booklet *Australia & New Zealand Guide*, published by London-based travel magazine *TNT* (14–15 Child's Place, London SW5 9RX, Tel: 020 7373 3377); send an SAE with 70p. Look out for their free pocket-sized regional guides at airports, stations and backpackers' hostels.

Call Tourism New Zealand's General Information Line on 09069 101010 (calls cost £1 per minute) for a brochure. You can also get a wide range of free brochures from the Information Point on the Ground Floor of New Zealand House, 80 Haymarket, London SW1Y 4TE (open 9am–5.30pm, Monday to Friday). Tel: 020 7930 1662, Fax: 020 7839 8929.

The website **www.workingin.com** lists job vacancies and produces a recruitment magazine, *Working In*, PO Box 3394, Shortland St, Auckland, Tel: 00 64 09 425 9540.

23. LATIN AMERICA

Latin America is in dire need of help from the voluntary sector and, with little backing from their own governments, is well served by a great number of Western voluntary organisations. There are also indigenous programmes, often organised by religious groups, but these tend to lack the resources needed to advertise themselves and bring in help from overseas. Most of the voluntary work is aimed at tackling the effects of poverty in all its different guises, and there is a desperate need for help in all social areas, such as welfare of the young, elderly, disabled and poor, as well as aid work for natural disaster relief. Many conservation programmes are organised here: eco-tourism is a growing market and there are several opportunities for trekking, exploration and guiding. Several gap-year programmes are springing up which offer a combination of the traditional voluntary experience and the exhilarating challenges of an adventure holiday.

One such organisation is Ventureco Worldwide, which runs four-month gap-year programmes in South America (and Asia) and includes cultural orientation, aid project work and a long-range expedition. Projects in South America could include trekking to Machu Picchu as well as caring for orphans. Contact Ventureco Worldwide, Pleck House, Middletown, Moreton Morrell, Warwickshire CV35 9AU, UK, Tel: 01926 651 071, Fax: 01926 650 120, website: **www.ventureco-worldwide.com**.

Language holidays promote voluntary social placements as the perfect way to practise and polish your foreign-language skills. Cactus Language runs volunteer programmes throughout South America, in Guatemala, Costa Rica, Peru, Ecuador, Bolivia, Argentina and Brazil, which include studying Spanish (or Portuguese in Brazil) at one of its approved schools and then taking unpaid work with a local organisation. The placement operating in Argentina when I checked the website was volunteering with a ten-year-old Catholic organisation that works with poor and street children, in Unquillo, a suburb about thirty minutes from Córdoba in the foothills of the Sierras of Córdoba. Tasks involved included caring for children, cooking, cleaning, shopping and gardening, etc. Contact Cactus Languages, No 4 Clarence House, 30-31 North Street, Brighton, East Sussex BN1 1EB, Tel: 0845 130 4775, Fax: 01273 775868, website: **www.cactuslanguage.com**.

Many Latin American countries have a huge demand for English teachers, so there is also scope for voluntary teaching positions. The International Student Exchange Centre (Isec) sends volunteer teachers to Latin America. Contact International Student Exchange Centre, 35 Ivor Place, London NW1 6EA, Tel: 020 7724 4493, website: **www.isecworld.co.uk**.

Casa Alianza (**www.casa-alianza.org**) offers six- to twelve-month placements for Spanish speakers to work with street children in Guatemala, Honduras, Mexico and Nicaragua.

VOLUNTARY ORGANISATIONS

The following voluntary organisations also run programmes in Latin America:

The Experiment for International Living (EIL) organises voluntary and community placements in Argentina, Ecuador, Guatemala, Mexico and Chile (as well as Ghana, Nigeria, Ireland and Great Britain). UK Citizens can apply to EIL Britain, 287 Worcester Road, Malvern, Worcestershire WR14 1AB, Tel: 0168 45 62577 Fax: 0168 45 62212, website: **www.eiluk.org**.

US citizens should contact Federation EIL International Office, Worldwide Network of The Experiment in International Living, PO Box 595, 63 Main St., Putney, VT 05346 USA, Tel: 00 1 802 387 4210, Fax: 00 1 802 387 5783.

Other nationalities should look at EIL's website **www.experiment.orgAmeriSpan**, PO Box 58129, Philadelphia, PA 19102-8129, USA, Tel: USA & Canada: 800 879 6640; Worldwide: 00 1 215 751 1100; Fax: 00 1 215 751 1986, E-mail: info@amerispan.com, website: **www.amerispan.com**.

Association of American Schools in South America (AASSA), 14750 NW 77th Court, Suite 210, Miami Lakes, FL 33016, Tel: 00 1 305 821 0345, Fax: 00 1 305 821 4244, Email: info@aassa.com, website: **www.aassa.com**.

Australian Volunteers International Office, National Office: 71 Argyle Street (PO Box 350), Fitzroy, Victoria 3065, Tel: 00 61 03 9279 1788, Fax: 00 61 03 9419 4280, Email: avaenq@ozvol.org.au, website: **www.ozvol.org.au**.

Inter-Cultural Youth Exchange (ICYE UK), Latin America House, Kingsgate Place, London NW6 4TA, Tel/Fax: 020 7681 0983, website: **www.icye.org**.

Latin Link Britain & Ireland, 175 Tower Bridge Road, London SE1 2AB, Tel: 020 7939 9000, Fax: 020 7939 9015, website: **www.latinlink.org**.

FINDING WORK ON THE SPOT

There are also more locally based programmes, although voluntary or community projects in Central and South America are rarely as organised as they are in the West, and can be difficult to find. While fixing up work before arriving in South America is usually the best option, given the cash-strapped nature of indigenous organisations it is unlikely you will be able to arrange work before you set out. Intrepid explorers may wish to try to find projects as they travel around, and there are several voluntary bureaux listed at the end of this section which may be able to help you in your search. As always the key is to ask the locals and keep an eye open in tourist offices or hostels. The jungles of Bolivia, Peru, Ecuador, Venezuela and even Colombia can also offer many opportunities in the way of eco-voluntary work – particularly for biology, pharmacy, medical and anthropology students or graduates. The South American Explorers (**www.samexplo.org**) has a list of many organisations where you can find work from trekking elephants to studying freshwater dolphins to working with and protecting indigenous tribes. Of course, jungle life is not for everyone – conditions can be difficult, humid and downright dangerous at times, so think carefully before rushing into a commitment.

VOLUNTEERS' STORIES

Twenty-year-old Clare Lewis spent two weeks volunteering in the jungle in Peru, helping to set up a jungle research community. She found the work after she and her boyfriend were forced to stop a sponsored cycle through Peru when they were mugged at knifepoint. Clare describes her journey. 'We were cycling 1,200 miles from La Paz, the capital of Bolivia, to Lima, the capital of Peru, to raise money for Christie's Against Cancer. Most of the journey was spent cycling through small rural villages, and we found rooms for the night just by turning up and asking. The people were lovely, really friendly, and they willingly put us up in front rooms, barns, farms or hotels. Some people didn't want money, although we obviously tried to pay them for their hospitality.'

Clare and her boyfriend ran into a few problems when wild dogs almost chased them off the road. Shocked and tired, they nearly aborted their trip, but carried on regardless, cycling thirty miles a day through beautiful scenery. Four weeks into their journey, however, they hit another crisis. They were just leaving the Inca tourist hot spot Cusco, cycling through the slums, when five men came out of nowhere and blocked them in the road. 'At first we thought they were joking, but then this guy hit me and knocked me off my bike. Suddenly they were bearing down on us. They grabbed us and had machetes at our neck, and the next thing we were thrown into a ditch so the passing cars couldn't see. The men took our passports, money, plane tickets – everything. The only thing they didn't take was the credit cards we had hidden beneath masking tape at the bottom of the panniers on our bikes. This proved a life-saver. We would have been lost without them – you need money to even renew your passport.'

Shocked and scared by the ordeal, Clare and her boyfriend were warned by the local police not to continue their cycling trip. 'They said there were pockets of Peru which are very dangerous and next time we might be killed.'

Duly warned, the couple went back to Cusco and soon found a notice board in a tourist office asking for volunteers to help out setting up a jungle research centre. 'The centre was in the middle of nowhere – we had to take a plane and then an eight-hour boat journey to get there.' Once there, they stayed for two weeks, trail clearing with machetes, varnishing buildings, gardening and doing general odd jobs – for which they received free meals and accommodation. On the way back, the couple decided they would forgo the plane and travel like the locals – 48 hours on the back of petrol tanks. 'It was a killer,' Clare says with a laugh. 'It was so bumpy, both of us were sick, but we saw some amazing scenery.'

Clare says volunteering opportunities are easier to find than people think. 'Often it's just a case of asking around and getting to know the locals.'

BRAZIL

Brazil appears to have the most extensive infrastructure of volunteering in the Latin American countries and there are many voluntary organisations working to tackle the country's shocking social problems, such as the high child-mortality levels.

Programa Voluntarios (**www.programavoluntarios.org.br**) offers a good introduction to volunteering in Brazil, with plenty of information and articles on voluntary work as well as information on the initiatives of the regional volunteer centres. Meanwhile, the Volunteer Centre of Recife (**www.voluntario.org.br/**) is actively working to increase the volunteerism culture in the region of Recife, in the Brazilian Northeast, and matches volunteers to many NGOs and community organisations on social, cultural and environmental projects. Contact Recife Voluntário – The Volunteer Center of Recife, Av. Visconde de Suassuna, 255 – Boa Vista Recife, PE – Brazil Postal Code: 50.050-540, Tel/Fax: 00 55 81 3221-7151 or 3221-6911/Tel: 00 55 81 9945-4211.

If you can understand Portuguese, it may be work checking out **www.voluntariar.org.br**, the website for Central de Voluntariado de Itajai, or Portal do Voluntário (**www.portaldovoluntario.org.br**) which lists voluntary opportunities. The website for Rio Voluntário (**www.riovoluntario.org.br**) offers details of voluntary opportunities in Rio de Janeiro and should soon be available in English.

Another Brazilian organisation is Seja um Voluntário (in Portuguese), which promises to match volunteers with opportunities, although non-nationals may find the placements are open only to Brazilians.

Despite these resources, however, the best way to find placements is to go through one of the many Western organisations that operate here. These include Christians Abroad, Camphill Village Trust, Earthwatch, Gap Activity Projects, Global Outreach Mission UK, Intercultural Youth Exchange and Youth With A Mission.

Task Brazil runs programmes designed to help 'street children', providing health and medical care, psychological support, drugs awareness, training, etc., as well as publicising the cause. Potential volunteers should contact Task Brazil, PO Box 4901, London SE16 3PP, UK, Tel: 020 7394 1177, Fax: 020 7394 7713, website: **www.taskbrasil.org.uk**.

ARGENTINA

Despite the fact that Argentina is well served by the Western agencies, it is very difficult to find out about indigenous projects. There also appears to be no real network of volunteer bureaux, so the best approach is to organise a placement in your home country first. Most of the organisations listed above operate programmes in Argentina, as do the following: Cat Survival Trust, Christians Abroad, Earthwatch, Gap Activity Projects, Involvement Volunteers and UNA Exchange. One project that does exist is Changemakers, which employs volunteers to work together in a project called The Centre of Culture (formed by the Humanist Movement) that aims at 'building bridges among the different cultures recognising diversity as something positive, as a contribution every culture can make to a new way of life'. To find out more contact: Javier Tolcachier/Conny Henrichmann, Email: connyh@arnet.com.ar, Tel: 00 54 351 4519552.

MEXICO

To work in Mexico, try the following organisations: Christians Abroad, Earthwatch, Gap Activity Projects, Global Outreach Mission UK, Global Volunteers, Institute of Cultural Affairs, Intercultural Youth Exchange, Involvement Volunteers, Quaker Voluntary Action, Travel Active, UNA, WorldTeach, Youth Action for Peace and Youth With A Mission.

Piña Palmera, a rehabilitation centre for disabled people, requires medical and healthcare volunteers, as well as building and construction workers, particularly from March to September. Centro de Atencion Integral, Piña Palmera A.C., Apdo Postal 109, Carretera hacia Mazunte s/n, Playa Zipolite, Pochutla, Oaxaca, 70900 Mexico, Tel/Fax: 00 52 958 40342/43113, website: **www.laneta.apc.org/pina**.

ECUADOR

Jatun Sacha place volunteers on conservation projects throughout Ecuador. Contact Jatun Sacha, Eugenio de Santillán, N34-248 y Maurian, Quito, Ecuador, Tel: 00 593 2 432 246, Fax: 00 593 2 453 583.

Fundación, Golondrinas needs volunteers to help on a local farm planting, farming, harvesting and doing general maintenance. Contact Fundación, Golondrinas, Avenida Isabel de Católica 1559, Quito, Ecuador, Tel: 00 593 226 602, website: **www.ecuadorexplorer.com/golondrinas**.

Rainforest Concern has a year-round volunteer programme in Ecuador to protect the rainforest and undertake research and physical conservation labour. It also places volunteers on short projects in a coastal reserve in Costa Rica between March and July protecting the leatherback turtle. Contact Rainforest Concern, 27 Landsdowne Crescent, London W11 2NS, UK, Tel: 020 7229 2093, Fax: 020 7229 4094, website: **www.rainforest.org.uk**.

HCJB UK (131 Grattan Road, Bradford, West Yorkshire BD1 2HS, Tel: 01274 721 810, Fax: 01274 514960) requires committed Christian volunteers to help with projects on media and medical ministries in Ecuador. Jobs include audio and broadcasting engineers, announcers, scriptwriters and other communication experts, doctors, nurses and laboratory technicians, youth workers, printers, secretaries and admin workers.

PERU AND COSTA RICA

Tambopata Jungle Lodge needs volunteer nature guides to lead nature walks for tourists at a jungle lodge in the Southern Peru rainforest. Contact Tambopata Jungle Lodge, PO Box 454, Cusco, Peru, Tel: 00 51 84 225 701, Fax: 00 51 84 238 911.

Teaching and Projects Abroad sends volunteers to Peru on projects including medical, teaching, journalism, conservation, engineering and accountancy.

Caledonia Languages Abroad organises volunteer placements in Peru and Costa Rica teaching English or taking part in community or tourism work. Volunteers should usually speak intermediate Spanish and are required to take a Spanish course in the country first. Placements last from four weeks to six months. Caledonia Languages Abroad, The Clockhouse, Bonnington Mill, 72 Newhaven Road, Edinburgh EH6 5QG, Tel: 0131 621 7721/2, Fax: 0131 621 7723, website: **www.caledonialanguages.co.uk**.

The Spanish-based organisation Don Quijote offers opportunities to study Spanish in an immersion setting and to volunteer in a variety of interesting places in Peru. Contact Don Quijote Salamanca, S.L. (B-37263621), Placentinos 2 - 37008 – Salamanca, España, Tel: 00 34 923 268860, Fax: 00 34 923 260651, website: **www.donquijote.org**.

Rainforest Concern places volunteers on short projects in a coastal reserve in Costa Rica between March and July protecting the leatherback turtle. Contact Rainforest Concern, 27 Landsdowne Crescent, London W11 2NS, UK, Tel: 020 7229 2093, Fax: 020 7229 4094, website: **www.rainforest.org.uk**.

THE CARIBBEAN

Caribbean Volunteer Expeditions need volunteers to assist with researching and documenting historic buildings for one to two weeks. No experience is required but architecture, photography and surveying are helpful skills. Contact Caribbean Volunteer Expeditions, Box 388, Corning, NY 14830, USA, Tel: 00 1 607 962 7846, Fax: 00 1 607 936 1153, website: **www.cvexp.org**.

VOLUNTARY BUREAUX

Chile: Chile's national volunteer organisation is Voluntar. Contact: Jean-Marc H. Zuczek, Programme co-ordinator, General Salvo 20, Providencia Santiago, Chile (02) 264 9437, Tel: 00 56 22096408, Fax: 00 56 22096408.

Argentina: Consejo de Coordinacion de Obras Privadas (CONDECOORD), Avenida Santa Fe 3114, 3fl. B, Buenos Aires 1425, Argentina.

Colombia: Corporacion Colombiana De Trabajo Voluntario (CCTV), Avenida Caracas No 63 32 Torre Oeste, Oficina 301 y 301 A, Sante Fe de Bogota, Colombia, Tel: 00 57 1 235 01 56, Fax: 00 57 1 640 54 93.

Costa Rica: Asociacion Federacion de Organizaciones Voluntarias (FOV), Calle Prinera Avenida 13, Apartado 7-3070, San Jose, Costa Rica, Tel: 00 506 222 1815, Fax: 00 506 223 1341.

Ecuador: Fundación Ecuatoriana de Trabajo, Quito y Ricaurte (esquina), Casilla 13-01-131, Ecuador, Tel: 00 593 5 639 20, Fax: 00 593 5 631 351.

Venezuela: Federación de Instituciones Privadas de Atención a Ninos, Edificio Las Fundaciones, Piso 7, Avenida Andres Bello, Caracas, Venezuela, Tel: 00 582 578 0028, Fax: 00 582 578 0948.

Jamaica: The CVSS United Way of Jamaica, 122–126 Tower Street, Kingston, Jamaica, website: **www.unitedwayja.org**.

Mexico: Centro Mexicano para la Filantropia (CEMEFI), Cerrada de Salvador Alvarado No. 7, Colonia Escandon, Distrito Federal, Mexico CP 11800.

Puerto Rico: Centro de Voluntarios, Fondos Unidos de Puerto Rico, Calle Los Angeles final/parada 26 1/2 Santurce, San Juan, Puerto Rico, Tel: 00 787 728 8500, Fax: 00 787 728 7099.

Trinidad and Tobago: Service Volunteered for All (SERVOL), website: **www.icd.org.uy**.

VISAS AND REGULATIONS

Central and South America have little in the way of a volunteering infrastructure, so it's no surprise that solid, reliable information on visa regulations for voluntary work is hard to find. The official line is that you will need a working visa to work in all of the listed countries. These are notoriously hard to obtain but, if you organise your placement through a sending agency, they should take care of the visa applications, which in most Latin American countries can be a minefield. Working visas should be obtained from the consulate in your country before you arrive. You will often need proof of contract, proof of funds and a raft of other complicated paperwork. However, many people turn up on three-month tourist visas, even to work, which they then renew by leaving the country and re-entering at the borders. This isn't exactly legal in the case of paid employment but, for some jobs, such as teaching, it seems the only way that foreign teachers can actually work in some countries (Brazil, for example). Whatever you decide, you may be subjected to tough questioning at immigration. Make sure you have proof of funds, a return flight (if possible) and details of where you will be staying.

USEFUL ADDRESSES

Argentinian Embassy: 65 Brook Street, London W1M 5LD, UK, Tel: 020 7486 7073, or 1600 New Hampshire Avenue, NW, Washington, DC 20009, USA, Tel: 00 1 202 939 6400, website: **www.embajadargentina-usa.org**.

Brazilian Embassy: 32 Green Street, London W1Y 4AT, UK, Tel: 020 7499 0877, website: **www.brazil.org.uk**, or 3006 Massachusetts Avenue, NW, Washington, DC 20008, USA, Tel: 00 1 202 238 2700, website: **www.brasil.emb.nw.dc.us**.

Chilean Embassy: 12 Devonshire Street, London W1N 2DS, UK, Tel: 020 7580 6392, or 1732 Massachusetts Avenue, NW, Washington, DC 20036, USA, Tel: 00 1 202 785 1746.

Mexican Embassy: 42 Hertford Street, Mayfair, London W1Y 7TF, UK, Tel: 020 7499 8586, or 1911 Pennsylvania Avenue, NW, Washington, DC 20006, USA, Tel: 00 1 202 728 1600, website: **www.embassyofmexico.org**.

Venezuelan Embassy: 1 Cromwell Road, London SW7 2HW, UK, Tel: 020 7584 4206, or 1099 30th Street, Washington, DC 20007, USA, Tel: 00 1 202 342 2214, website: **www.embavenez-us.org**.

24. UNITED STATES AND CANADA

UNITED STATES

It's not for nothing that the United States is seen as the trailblazer in voluntary work. Whatever you wish to do, the US has a strong infrastructure to support volunteering and actively encourages its citizens to take part. Volunteers are needed and well used in many sectors – including special needs, working with the poor and dispossessed, conservation, restoration and monitoring wildlife.

The US is also the pioneer behind corporate social responsibility, the movement that encourages the private sector to play a more responsible, active role in creating a fairer society. Indeed, the recent interest in employee volunteering which has seen such a massive growth in the UK first flourished on the other side of the Atlantic. The country was also the pioneer of online or virtual volunteering.

There is, of course, a darker side to all this enlightened altruism. The US has one of the greatest contrasts between the rich and the poor and, critics argue, uses voluntary work to right social ills that politicians fail to address.

THE DOWNSIDE

Despite the abundance of volunteering opportunities, however, working in American isn't easy. The US has strict immigration rules where working without a work permit carries heavy fines, and securing a work permit or residency is extremely difficult. The situation is made even more tricky as there are only a small number of volunteer agencies who send people to the States. Even working for your keep on farms is counted as employment by immigration officials, so organisations such as the US WWOOF (North East Workers on Organic Farm, Box 608, Belchertown, MA 01007, website: **www.smallfarm.org**) say they only place American citizens.

However, there is good news. If you are a young person or student, there are some good work-travel schemes that can provide you with the necessary work permit. Other people may have to use some ingenuity. Your best bet is to contact the US voluntary agencies first in writing and offer your services. Alternatively, if you have contacts already in the country, ask them to keep their ears to the ground for details of any voluntary projects where you could simply turn up. There are plenty of unofficial, less structured projects around; it is simply a question of rooting them out.

There are, of course, numerous chances for unpaid work outside the voluntary sector. Working on summer camps where you receive minimal pocket money and free board and lodging in return for acting as a camp instructor teaching special skills is a hugely popular option. There are also chances to train as a soccer instructor and teach soccer to children on camps, staying at natives' homes.

VISAS AND REGULATIONS

Despite all this, however, there is some good news for the States-bound volunteer. The first is that many volunteers on short-term projects (lasting less than three months) take part in schemes under the visa waiver scheme, which allows British citizens and those of 28 other countries to enter the US visa-free for up to ninety days. Valid for one entry, the visa waiver must be obtained when you arrive. If you plan to stay any longer, you must obtain a tourist visa in advance from the embassy.

For longer periods, or if are not eligible for this visa, there are several other visas around. The Q visa, (the International Cultural Exchange Visa) allows you to work for up to fifteen months if you can argue that you will be providing practical training or sharing the culture, history and traditions of your country with the Americans (if you do a mean Yorkshire pudding, for example). Another one is the J-1 visa which can only be obtained if you are taking part in an Exchange Visitor Programme, such as the Work and Travel Programmes and Summer Camp schemes listed below, and allows you to undertake any paid work.

By far the most relevant to volunteers, however, is the B-1 'Voluntary Service' visa which you can get if you are to do charitable voluntary work, for no payment, and have been sponsored by a charitable and religious organisation. If your proposed activities as a voluntary worker do not exactly meet the requirements for the B-1 visa, you will require either an exchange visitor (J-1) or temporary worker (H-2B) visa.

When applying for entry into the United States as a voluntary worker with a visa or under the VWP, you should also include a letter from your US sponsor which contains the following information: your name and date and place of birth; your foreign permanent residence address; the name and address of initial destination in the US; and the anticipated duration of your assignment.

WORK AND TRAVEL PROGRAMMES AND INTERNSHIPS

There are many work and travel programmes which operate in America and enable participants, usually students, to work virtually anywhere in the country by fixing them up with a J-1 visa. Many of these also allow voluntary work, so whether you fancy dancing with wolves in Colorado or planting trees in California, there are plenty of opportunities.

Work America is a work and travel programme for students run by Bunac. The programme enables students to take virtually any work in the US. The programme is only open to British university or college students studying for a degree (or equivalent), and gap-year students who have already received an unconditional offer at a university. To help applicants find work, Bunac publishes a directory listing jobs you can apply for before you leave.

The Work and Travel USA programme administered by CIEE allows you to work 'for just about any employer in the US'. The programme enables full-time students aged over eighteen to work and travel in the US from early June to mid-October. Check out its website **www.councilexchanges.org.uk** to search through over 18,000 jobs and download documents. Contact

Council on International Educational Exchanges, 52 Poland Street, London W1F 7AB, Tel: 020 7478 2020.

Alliances Abroad (702 West Avenue, Austin, TX 78701, Tel: 00 1 512 457 8062/1 888 622 7623, website: **www.alliancesabroad.com**) runs internships with practical training experience in Denver, San Francisco and Washington, DC.

Work Experience USA (see address for Camp Counsellors in Summer Camp section). This programme enables students between 20 and 28 years old to work in the US between June and September. Visit the website **www.ccusa.com** for more details.

InterExchange (161 Sixth Avenue, New York, NY 10013, Tel: 00 1 212 924 0446, Fax: 00 1 212 924 0575, website: **www.interexchange.org**) runs a Work and Travel Programme offering foreign university students the opportunity to live and work in America, filling positions in hotels, inns, amusement parks, country fairs, national parks, campgrounds, restaurants and resorts for up to four months during their summer break.

CIEE (7 Custom House Street, 3rd Floor, Portland, ME 04101, Toll-Free: 1-800-40-Study, Fax: 00 1 207 553 7699, website: **www.ciee.org**) also runs a number of schemes.

Here are some other agencies that can help you fix up a J-1 visa for work and travel in the USA:

Apex USA (**www.apexusa.org**)

Association for International Practical Training (**www.aipt.org**)

For Canadian Citizens: Student Work Abroad Program (**www.swap.ca/english/html/home**).

FINDING WORK BEFORE YOU ARRIVE

Despite the fact that the US is a difficult place to get work in, there are some opportunities to find some really interesting community projects. Typical areas range from conservation and environmental work in national parks and forest to urban renovation or working with disabled children. Find out which agencies send volunteers to the States by getting hold of a copy of *Worldwide Volunteering for Young People*.

The following organisations send volunteers on US projects: UNA Exchange, YAP (Youth Action for Peace) UK, Gap Activity Projects, Earthwatch, Global Volunteers and Quaker Voluntary Action.

Volunteers For Peace organises 2,000 international workcamps in eighty countries. In addition to placing volunteers on international workcamps all over the world, Volunteers for Peace have incoming programmes where volunteers from overseas can take part in workcamps in America. It also has 'volunteer exchanges' where US volunteers are placed abroad in exchange for receiving foreign volunteers into VFP domestic programmes. Both programmes are managed by partner organisations outside the US. For more information check out the VFP website **www.vfp.org** where you can join and receive a copy of the 2003 Workcamp Directory and 2004 Newsletter.

The International Volunteer Programme enables British and French people over eighteen to stay in California for six weeks, volunteering on various projects. Work is for eight hours a day, five days a week, and can include office work, working in homeless shelters, hospital assistance or after-school programmes for kids. The price is £900 for British, 1,350 euros for French, which includes a round-trip ticket London–California or Paris–California and rooms and meals. Contact International Volunteers Programme (IVP), 7106 Sayre Dr, Oakland, CA 94611 USA, website: **www.ivpsf.org**, for more details. The organisation also places American volunteers in France.

International Voluntary Service, the British branch of Service Civil International (SCI), runs programmes in the US. Most workcamps last around two to three weeks and there are also opportunities for longer-term voluntary placements lasting at least three to six months. These usually require previous volunteering experience. Current vacancies include helping at a Rudolph Steiner-inspired community for disabled people, working in a soup kitchen for homeless people and a wolf sanctuary in the remote mountains of Colorado. For more information and a copy of its directory, UK citizens can contact IVS South, Old Hall, East Bergholt, Colchester, Essex CO7 6TQ, Tel: 01206 298215, Fax: 01206 299043; IVS North, Castlehill House, 21 Otley Road, Leeds LS6 3AA, Tel: 0113 2304600, Fax: 0113 2304610; IVS Scotland, 7 Upper Bow, Edinburgh EH1 2JN, Tel: 0131 2266722, Fax: 0131 2266723; IVS Northern Ireland, 122 Great Victoria Street, Belfast BT2 7BG, Email: colin@ivsni.co.uk. Citizens of other countries should check the Service Civil International office of their resident country to see whether they organise workcamps to the US.

Concordia sends volunteers out to fifty projects in the US on workcamps lasting from two weeks to two months. Typical projects include taking adults with mental difficulties on trips, working on environmental projects in the Grand Canyon region and running soup kitchens in New York. Contact Concordia, Haversham House, 20/22 Boundary Road, Hove, East Sussex BN 4ET, Tel: 01273 422 218, Fax: 01273 422 218.

Involvement Volunteers places volunteers in programmes in the USA in conservation and community projects. For more information contact one of the following national offices: Involvement Volunteers, PO Box 218, Port Melbourne, Victoria 3207, Australia, Tel: 00 61 3 9646 5504 or 9392, Fax: 00 61 3 9646 5504; Involvement Volunteers – Deutschland, Matubadstr. 50, D-91056 Erlangen, Germany, Tel: 00 49 9135 8075, Fax: 00 49 9135 8075; Involvement Volunteers UK, 7 Bushmead Avenue, Kingskerswell, Nr Newton Abbot, Devon TQ12 5EN, UK, Tel: 01803 872 594, website: **www.volunteering.org.au**.

FINDING WORK ON THE SPOT
Under the visa waiver scheme, it is entirely feasible to turn up and look for volunteering opportunities as you travel around. There are, however, certain

points to bear in mind: the first is that, according to immigration rules, payment in the form of free board and food as offered in farm work, for example, can be classed as paid employment, which is strictly prohibited under the visa waiver scheme. The second is that finding projects as you go is difficult anywhere, particularly in such a huge country with a population of 285 million, and covering fifty states. The ideal scenario would be to have a good network system in place (i.e. family or friends who are resident in the US and can both ask around and help you out in a crisis), and to have a car, a mobile phone and plenty of money to back you up. While there are many conservation projects in the more rural areas, you may find it easier to find something if you head for the cities where the urban deprivation in places like New York can render many opportunities to help out in soup kitchens and hostels, etc. Take with you lists of indigenous voluntary agencies that you can phone on arrival. If you offer to turn up and help out on a less structured basis, some of them may not be so willing to turn you down.

You can also try the US voluntary brokerages to look for projects, although they might not allow you to register if you don't have the necessary visa. Bear in mind, too, that by offering your services for free, you may be taking work from locals, at least in the eyes of immigration. Given the US's strict approach to illegal work, there is sometimes a blurred line between unpaid 'voluntary' work and paid employment, an unclear distinction that could get you and your employer into trouble. According to US law, all employers are obliged to examine the documents of anyone they employ, and employing an illegal 'alien' carries a heavy fine. Being discovered working without the necessary documentation also carries a similar risk and you could find yourself deported and even banned from entering the States for another five years. Above all, if you intend to turn up in the States to volunteer on the spot, see it primarily as a holiday – that way you won't be disappointed if the right opportunities don't come along.

FINDING PROJECTS

The website **www.volunteermatch.org** promises to link volunteers to projects and also has links to other volunteer agencies. The GuideStar website (**www.guidestar.org/**) is the national database of US charitable organisations and carries details of volunteer opportunities in the United States, as does Network For Good (**www.networkforgood.org/index.html**). Also worth a look is **www.volunteersolutions.org**.

Hostels will sometimes exchange free board and lodging for work such as cleaning or running the reception, and you can check out their notice boards for advertisements for work. It is also the perfect place to meet fellow travellers who can often pass on rumours of other work opportunities.

Check out the local press for details of projects and keep an eye on the employment websites such as **www.coolworks.com**, which sometimes carry details of voluntary work.

VOLUNTEER BUREAUX AND ORGANISATIONS

The International Volunteer Programmes Association carries extensive information about volunteering both in the US and, for US citizens, overseas, as well as numerous links to other job-search websites and volunteering organisations. Go to **www.volunteerinternational.org**.

The Points of Light Foundation & Volunteer Center National Network engages and mobilises millions of volunteers who are helping to solve serious social problems. Contact: Point of Light Foundation: 1400 I Street, N.W. Suite 800, Washington, DC, 20005-2208, Toll Free: 1-800-750-7653, Tel: 00 1 202 729 8000, Fax: 00 1 202 729 8100, Volunteer Info: 1-800-Volunteer.

The Volunteer Centre of San Francisco (1675 California Street, San Francisco, CA 94109, Tel: 00 1 415 982 8999) has a Travellers' Volunteer Network (TVN), which places visitors and travellers on one-time events requiring little in the way of specialised skills or commitment. Typical events include planting trees at Golden Gate Park or serving food at a homeless shelter.

The following organisations also require volunteers:

Volunteers International, 10701 Main Street, Fairfax, VA 22030, Tel: 00 1 703 352 7550.

World Vision International, 919 West Huntingdon Drive, Monrovia, CA 91016, Tel: 00 1 818 303 8811.

YMCA of the USA, 101 North Wacker Drive, Chicago, IL 60606, Tel: 00 1 312 977 0031.

YWCA of the USA, 726 Broadway, New York, NY 10003, Tel: 00 1 212 614 2700.

SUMMER CAMPS

Despite not being classed as voluntary work *per se*, there are plenty of opportunities to work on summer camps for no salary except for a minimal amount of pocket money. Despite the demands of fitting into a tightly knit institution, these can be a fantastic way of experiencing American culture firsthand and come with a number of perks such as free return flights, pre-arranged visa and the luxury of independent travel for up to two months after the camp is over. Most camps need instructors to teach children a variety of skills, including archery, windsurfing, dancing, arts and crafts, music, drama, horse riding and sports, etc. Bear in mind that hours are long and some participants find it hard to fit in to such an institutionalised environment where you have to sleep in dormitories with kids and salute the flag every morning.

SUMMER CAMP ORGANISATIONS

The following organisations run summer camp schemes:

Bunac (16 Bowling Green Lane, London EC1R 0QH, Tel: 020 7251 3472, website: **www.bunac.org**) runs two summer camp programmes. KAMP is a low-cost programme that places staff in kitchen and maintenance positions in American summer camps for two months. Summer Camp USA places camp counsellors (aged 18–35) in US and Canadian summer camps. Camps last nine weeks and applicants receive free flights, salary, board and lodging and independent travel for a flexible period after the camp.

Camp America places people aged eighteen-plus in summer camps throughout America to work as Specialist Counsellors or Youth Leaders. Camps last nine weeks and positions available include childcare and specialist activities such as sports, watersports, music, drama and arts. Participants receive free board and lodging, pocket money, free London–New York return flight and up to two months' independent travel after the camp is over. For details contact Camp America, Dept. SJA, 37A Queen's Gate, London SW7 5HR, Tel: 020 7581 7373, website: **www.campamerica.co.uk**.

The Campower scheme, run by the same organisation and operating from the same address as Camp America, places students in kitchen and general maintenance work for the nine-week camp period. Perks are the same as for Camp America.

Camp Counsellors USA run a similar scheme, recruiting people aged between 19 and 28 to work in selected American Summer Camps. Applicants receive a free round-trip open return flight to the US, pocket money and after-camp travel. Contact UK Offices: Green Dragon House, 64–70 High Street, Croydon CR0 9XN, Tel: 020 8688 9051, website: **www.ccusa.com**, and 27 Woodside Gardens, Musselburgh, nr. Edinburgh EH21 7LJ, Tel: 0131 665 5843, website: **www.ccusa.com**. US Office: 2330 Marinship Way, Suite 250, Sausalito, CA 94965, USA.

Worldnetuk organises Camp USA. Contact Worldnetuk, Southern Office, Avondale House, Sydney Road, Haywards Heath, West Sussex, Tel: 0845 458 1551, website: **www.worldnetuk.com** for more details.

SOCCER COACHING

There are similar opportunities for unpaid soccer coaching. Providing you have the necessary training, you could find work for one of the many companies that recruit British soccer coaches to work on summer coaching schemes, based at children's summer camps all through America. The company Goal-line sends over expert soccer coaches to teach children in America and Europe. For more information, contact Goal-line Personnel Director, Goal-line Soccer Clinics, PO Box 1642, Corvallis, OR 97339, USA, Tel: 00 1 541 753 5833, Fax: 00 1 541 753 0811, Email: infoa@goal-line.com, website: **www.goal-line.com**.

The UK football magazine *FourFourTwo* carries adverts for soccer coach vacancies, and is a good first port of call.

VOLUNTEERS' STORIES

Alison Neighbour from Chepstow worked with adults with learning difficulties at L'Arche Irenicon, Massachusetts, organised by Gap Activity Projects. Her work involved teaching life skills such as house cleaning and maintenance, meal preparation, personal hygiene and laundry as well as assisting with outings. She says, 'Life in community was never dull, and each evening we would go bowling, roller-skating, swimming, to the YMCA, or maybe just relax with a bowl of popcorn and a movie. Often we had guests for dinner, so we could share our unique way of life with others. Always there was an excuse to celebrate, with a monthly birthday party, dances at the local club, and also some other more uniquely American rituals, including a Baby Shower for an ex-community member.

'The days were long, and sometimes it was tiring, but really it wasn't like a job at all, and the rewards I gained from knowing I had made a difference in people's lives were immense. Besides, it wasn't all work, and my weekly days away saw me doing everything from attending the legendary St Patrick's Day Parade in Boston to climbing mountains in New Hampshire and partying in Montreal (the greatest city in North America!).

'I kept a journal the whole way, which has given me something I can always look back on and remember the great times I had. My gap year has made me much more independent, as I got used to taking care of myself and having to care for others as well, putting their needs first. Although I had never considered working with disabled people before, I really enjoyed the experience, and learned a lot from my friends at Irenicon, which I would not have learned had I gone straight to university. I have a better idea of what I want out of life now, and more travelling is definitely part of the plan!'

CANADA

Canada has seen a growth of interest in volunteering in recent years and in 1998 hosted an international conference in voluntary work. Like the US, it has a good volunteering infrastructure with about 200 volunteer centres in Canada and more than 180,000 charities and non-profits. However, it also exercises a strict immigration policy and is highly vigilant in tracking down illegal workers. Work permits and visas are hard to come by, making turning up to find voluntary projects a difficult prospect. For short placements lasting no longer than three months (such as the three-week workcamps organised by Concordia) it appears that most people rely on the visa waiver that applies to many nationalities. For longer than that, however, it seems things are a little more difficult and you will have to negotiate your way through the irksome Canadian visa process. As in most cases, finding work before you go through one of the recognised organisations that organise projects here will undoubtedly make things less complicated.

VISAS AND REGULATIONS

In order to enter Canada for tourist purposes only (and not to work) most foreign visitors must have a passport, proof of intent to leave, and proof you have sufficient funds to support yourself during your stay. Citizens of Australia, Ireland, Mexico, New Zealand, the UK and the US do not need a visa, as long as you plan to stay for no more than ninety days. So far so good. In order to work legally in Canada, you must obtain an Employment Authorisation from a Canadian High Commission or Embassy before you leave your country of residence. In most cases this involves finding work before entering the country, which your future employer must prove cannot be filled by a Canadian citizen.

Once you have been offered a job, the Department of Human Resources Development Canada must normally provide a labour market opinion or 'confirmation' of your job offer. Once they have confirmed that a foreign national may fill the job, you apply to the Citizenship and Immigration Canada (CIC) for your work permit. Americans can apply for an Employment Authorisation at the port of entry to Canada.

In most cases, the same process applies to voluntary work – usually you will need a letter from the organisation agreeing to have you as a volunteer before you can even apply for the permit. However, people engaged in religious or charitable work are exempt from needing HRDC confirmation, as well as other skilled people who fill skill shortages such as technologically skilled workers, highly trained doctors, nurses and teachers, and construction workers. (For more information on skill shortages, contact the Canadian High Commission in your country.) If you are taking part in a voluntary scheme through a religious or charitable organisation, you also may be able to qualify for a special visa. This takes about a month to process, so make sure you allow plenty of time before you leave.

Commonwealth teachers may be able to arrange exchange placements – write to The League for the Exchange of Commonwealth Teachers, Commonwealth House, 7 Lion Yard, Tremadoc Road, London SW4 7NQ, Tel: 020 7498 1101, Fax: 020 7720 5403.

WORK EXCHANGES AND PROGRAMMES

The good news for students is that there are work-exchange programmes that in most cases allow for voluntary work. Most, apart from the Bunac scheme, require you to find work before you arrive.

The Canadian government runs official work exchanges for eighteen- to thirty-year-old full-time tertiary-level students wanting to work in Canada. The scheme requires that you fix up work before you arrive. Interested British and Irish students should check the website **www.canada.org.uk/visa-info** or send an SAE with a £1 stamp and marked SGWHP to the Canadian High Commission, Immigration Visa Information, 38 Grosvenor St, London W1K 4AA, Tel: 09068 616644. (Calls cost 60p a minute.)

Swedish and Finnish students should contact the Canadian High Commission or Embassies in their countries to find out more. Other participating countries tend to vary from year to year, so check with your Canadian Embassy first to find out if you are eligible.

Bunac runs a Work Canada Programme that enables students to go to Canada and fix up work once they are there. The scheme is open to gap-year students, providing they have an unconditional offer of a place at a university. Contact Bunac for more details (see chapter three on finding work).

Swap Travel run a Work Canada Programme in Ireland. For details contact UsitNow, 19–21 Aston Quay, O'Connell Bridge, Dublin 2 (Tel: 00 35 3-1-602-1667).

CIEE run an Internship Canada Programme (see the address in Voluntary Organisations and Gap-Year Section). This enables British and Irish full-time students and recent graduates (within a year) aged eighteen and above to do course-related work experience for up to one year in Canada. The programme costs £270 for two months, which includes assistance with obtaining visa, etc., support in Canada and advice on housing, tax, etc. The programme is also open to gap-year students with an unconditional offer of a university place. Applicants must secure a work placement before arriving in Canada.

FINDING WORK BEFORE YOU ARRIVE

Given the difficulty in obtaining permission to work legally in Canada, plus the limited number of Canadian organisations that will bring in people from outside the country to work for them, the best strategy is to secure yourself a voluntary placement before you arrive. UNA Exchange, Concordia, Earthwatch, Gap Activity Projects, Gap Challenge and Quaker Voluntary Action all organise voluntary projects in Canada. Alternatively you can try the following organisations:

Frontiers Foundation runs community development and social work projects in Aboriginal communities in Northern Canada. Volunteers should be over eighteen and are preferred to have a university degree and some experience working with young people. A minimum commitment of five months is required. The cost excludes flights to Canada, but does include all of the volunteer's travel costs within Canada and food and living expenses. It also covers medical insurance, a fifty-dollar-a-week living allowance for pocket money, and winter clothing that is adequate for a northern Canadian winter where temperatures fall to –40º and colder. Contact Frontiers Foundation/Operation Beaver (2615 Danforth Avenue, Suite 203, Toronto, Ontario, Canada M4C 1L6, Tel: 00 1 416 690 3930, Fax: 00 1 416 690 3934, website: **www.frontiersfoundation.org**).

Agriventure (**www.agriventure.com**), run by the International Agricultural Exchange Association, arranges working exchanges to Canada on farming and horticultural enterprises. Applicants must be aged between eighteen and thirty, have no dependants, be British citizens, have a full driving licence and have good practical experience within agriculture or horticulture or around the home. Programmes depart all the year around (apply two months minimum before departure). Programme costs start at around £1,700 and include return flights (and transfer to host family), full travel and work insurance, work permits, job placement, departure information meeting, seminar in host country and full emergency back-up through offices in hosting country. Programmes are also available to Americans, Canadians, some Europeans, Australians and New Zealanders through offices in their own country. See Voluntary Section for address.

Chantiers Jeunesse runs international workcamps in Quebec for people aged between sixteen and thirty. The camps are bilingual (French and English) and mostly last three weeks, although there are occasionally longer ones available. Chantiers Jeunesse also organises the International Exchange Program (IEP) offering young Quebecois the chance to take part in a workcamp in Europe, North America or Japan. The same programme allows youths from Europe, North America and Japan to come over to live in workcamps in Quebec. Contact Chantiers Jeunesse, 4545, avenue Pierre-De Coubertin, P.O.B.1000, Branch M, Montreal, Quebec, H1V 3R2, Tel: 00 1 514 252 3015 (Toll free: 1-800-361-2055), Fax : 00 1 514 251 8719, website: **www.cj.qc.ca**.

Maison Emmanuel recruits around thirty volunteers every year to help in the workshops and schools of its community with intellectually disabled adults and children. French-speaking skills are preferred but not essential. Contact Maison Emmanuel, 1561 Chemin Beaulne, Val-Morin, Quebec J0T 2R0, Tel: 00 1 819 322 7014, Fax: 00 1 819 322 6930, website: **www.maisonemmanuel.org**.

Travel Active (PO Box 107, 5800 AC Venray, The Netherlands, Tel: 00 31 478 551 900, Fax: 00 31 478 551 911, website: **www.travelactive.nl**) organises Work and Travel Programmes and conservation work in Canada for EU citizens (as well as other worldwide projects).

International Voluntary Service, Scotland and Northern Ireland, both place volunteers in projects in Canada. See Directory for contact details.

WWOOF Canada places volunteers on 400 farms and homesteads in Canada. WWOOF Canada, RR2 S.18, C.9, Nelson, British Columbia, VIL 5P5 Canada, Tel: 00 1 250 354 4417, Fax: 00 1 250 354 4417, website: **www.members.tripod.com/wwoof**.

FINDING WORK ON THE SPOT

A considerably more tricky option is to arrive in Canada and fix up your own voluntary projects. This is difficult but not impossible. Travelling through some of the more rural areas, for example, may introduce you to conservation projects, particularly if you are taking part in casual work such as tree planting or fruit picking in British Columbia. You can find out about voluntary opportunities by visiting Volunteer Canada, the national voice for volunteerism in Canada. Its website **www.volunteer.ca/volunteercanada** has lots of good information about volunteering in Canada and you can search for the addresses of your nearest centre. Volunteer Canada also runs the Volunteer Opportunities Exchange where people can advertise to take part in projects and link up with other volunteers across Canada. In all these cases, however, it is difficult to see how far you can get if you don't have Employment Authorisation and your best bet may be to look out for less structured opportunities and get involved with projects simply by turning up in person.

Contact Volunteer Canada National Office at 330 Gilmour Street, Second Floor, Ottawa, Ontario K2P 0P6, Tel: 00 1 613 231 4371, 1-800-670-0401, Fax: 00 1 613 231 6725, Email: info@volunteer.ca. The Vancouver office is Volunteer Vancouver, 301-3102 Main St., Vancouver, British Columbia V5T 3G7, Tel: 00 1 604 875 9144, Fax: 00 1 604 875 0710.

Also try Go Volunteers (**www.govolunteer.ca**), a new website collaboration between Volunteer Vancouver and four other volunteer centres in the Greater Vancouver area.

Canada Work Info Net has a volunteer Bulletin Board for Volunteer listings from across Canada. Go to **www.workinfonet.ca**. There are also Canada-wide opportunities posted on **www.charityvillage.com**.

If you are interested in social work opportunities you can always check out the Social Work and the Social Services websites (**www.gwbweb.wustl.edu/websites.html**) put online by the George Warren Brown School of Social Work at Washington University in St Louis. This listing features many sites that have links to other relevant sites, and some of these organisations will accept volunteers.

You can also try Youth Volunteer Corps of Canada, Bay 4, 1916 30 Avenue N.E., Calgary, Alberta T2E 7B2, Tel: 00 1 403 265 9822, Fax: 00 1 403 250 9480, Toll Free: 1-877-265-9822, website: **www.yvcc.ca/**.

It's always worth keeping an eye open on the employment websites that occasionally feature the occasional voluntary opportunity. Here are some to try:

www.seasonalemployment.com
www.summerjobs.com/do/where/jobtree/Canada
www.CoolJobsCanada.com

Action Jobs at **www.actionjobs.com** is a great website to fire your imagination and gear you up to the authentic Canadian experience. It covers some very physically demanding jobs such as in forestry and firefighting, as well as providing good solid information on jobs in summer, winter resorts and cruise ships.

The following websites have regularly updated job listings:

Canada Jobs: **www.canadajobs.com**
Canada Job Bank: **www.jb-ge.hrdc-drhc.gc.ca**
Net Jobs: **www.netjobs.com/index**
Canadian Employment Weekly: **www.mediacorp2.com**
For Students, Campus Canada Online: **www.campus.org/jobexchange**

It's also worth checking the newspapers, many of which carry job listings every day. Try the *Calgary Herald*, the *Globe and Mail* (Toronto paper), the *Montreal Gazette*, the *Ottawa Sun*, the *Toronto Sun*, the *Vancouver Sun* and the *Vancouver Province*. As usual, staying in hostels and checking their notice boards may find you projects.

SWAP offices (**www.swap.ca**) can be found in most major cities in Canada. They have a number of resources that are available to students, including job listings and helpful information. SWAP, Toronto Office, 45 Clarks St East, Suite 100, Toronto, Ontario M4Y 1S2, Tel: 00 1 416 966 2887.

SWAP, Vancouver Office, 60 rue West Hastings Street, Suite 710, Vancouver, British Columbia V6B 1P2, Tel: 00 1 604 689 2887, Fax: 00 1 604 689 8611.

USEFUL ADDRESSES

United States of America Embassy (and Information Service), 24 Grosvenor Square, London W1A 1AE, UK, Tel: 020 7499 9000.

United States of America Embassy, Visa Branch, 5 Upper Grosvenor Street, London W1A 2JB, UK, Tel: 020 7499 3443.

Canadian High Commission, Macdonald House, 1 Grosvenor Square, London W1X 0AB, UK, Tel: 020 7258 6600, **www.canada.org.uk**.

501 Pennslyvania Avenue, NW, Washington, DC 20001, USA, Tel: 00 1 202 682 1740, **www.cdnemb-washdc.org**.

Live and Work in the USA and Canada by Adam Lechmere, Susan Catto and Joshua White (published by Vacation Work Publications) is full of comprehensive information about living and working in the US and details many useful organisations.

DIRECTORY

PROFESSIONAL VOLUNTEERS

BESO (164 Vauxhall Bridge Road, London SW1 2RB, Tel: 020 7630 0644, Fax: 020 7630 0624, website: **www.beso.org**) is a development agency that offers professional expertise to organisations in the developing world. It sends volunteers abroad to give technical and managerial advice to small business and local industries.

British Red Cross Society (National Headquarters, 9 Grosvenor Crescent, London SW1X 7EJ, Tel: 020 7235 5454, Fax: 020 7245 6315, website: **www.redcross.org.uk**). International Red Cross and Red Crescent Movement is one of the largest humanitarian networks in the world. It requires professional volunteers in the following areas: medical health staff, prostheticists, relief workers, logisticians, programme managers, water/sanitation engineers, disaster preparedness and development specialists, information/press officers, finance/accountancy staff, organisation experts and telecommunications. Applicants must be at least 25 years old.

Catholic Institute for International Relations (CIIR: Unit 3 Canonbury Yard, 190a New North Road, London N1 7BJ, Tel: 020 7354 0883, Fax: 020 7359 0017, website: **www.ciir.org**) places skilled professionals with local organisations and some government departments in developing countries. Training and modest salary provided.

Concern Worldwide (52–55 Camden Street, Dublin, Ireland, Tel: 00 353-1 475416, Fax: 00 353-1 4754649; 47 Frederick Street, Belfast BT1 2LW, Northern Ireland, Tel: 028 90331 100, Fax: 028 90331 111; 248–250 Lavender Hill, London SW11 1LJ, Tel: 020 7738 1033, Fax: 020 7738 1032; Level 2, 80 Buchanan Street, Glasgow G1 3HA, Tel: 0141 2213610, Fax: 0141 2213708, website: **www.concern.ie**) sends international volunteers to less developed areas in the world in Asia, Africa and Central America. Professionals required include nurses, midwives, civil engineers, environmental health officers, foresters, teachers, accountants, mechanics, administrators, logisticians and agriculturists.

CORD Christian Outreach Relief and Development (1 New Street, Leamington Spa, Warwickshire CV31 1HP, Tel: 01926 315301, Fax: 01926 885786, website: **www.cord.org.uk**) is a relief and development organisation that places volunteers in refugee and community development areas. Professionals are required in healthcare, water and sanitation, agriculture and education. Volunteers should be over 21 years old and committed Christians.

Hands Around the World (PO Box 25, Coleford, Gloucestershire GL16 7YL, Tel: 01594 560223, website: **www.handsaroundtheworld.org.uk**) runs volunteer projects for caring, health and other professionals willing to share and encourage ongoing links and friendship. Placements last for two to six months.

International Health Exchange (IHE: 1st Floor, 134 Lower Marsh, London SE1 7AE, Tel: 020 7620 3333, Fax: 020 7620 2277) recruits and trains health workers for NGOs in developing countries.

International Service (Hunter House, 57 Goodramgate, York YO1 7FX, Tel: 01904 647799, Fax: 01904 652353, website: **www.internationalservice.org.uk**) recruits professionals for two-year placements with locally organised and managed initiatives in Bolivia, Brazil, Burkina Faso, Mali and the West Bank and Gaza Strip.

Médecins Sans Frontières (3rd Floor, 67–74 Saffron Hill, London EC1N 8QX, Tel: 020 7404 6600, Fax: 020 7404 4466, website: **www.uk.msf.org**) is a leading international NGO for emergency medical aid that provides medical relief to victims of war, disasters and epidemics in more than eighty countries. MSF recruits the following professionals: doctors, nurses, surgeons, midwives, anaesthetists, nutritionists, epidemiologists, lab technicians, mental health professionals, water and sanitation engineers, construction engineers and logisticians.

Peace-Corps (The Paul D. Coverdell Peace Corps Headquarters, 1111 20th Street NW, Washington, DC 20526, Tel: 00 1 800 424 8580, website: **www.peacecorps.gov**) provides training and field placements for qualified and experienced professionals willing to commit for around two years.

Skillshare International (UK Office: 126 New Walk, Leicester LE1 7JA, UK, Tel: 0116 254 1862, Fax: 0116 254 2614, website: **www.skillshare.org**) recruits development workers and healthcare trainers for projects in Africa and Asia.

United Nations Volunteers (UNV: Headquarters: Postfach 260 111, D-53153 Bonn, Germany, website: **www.unvolunteers.org**) sends professionals on volunteer assignments all over the world for peace-building, electoral or emergency relief operations. Most UN volunteers have degrees from technical institutions or universities and have extensive experience. The average age is 39 years old.

Voluntary Service Overseas (317 Putney Bridge Road, Putney, London SW15 2PN, UK, website: **www.vso.org.uk**) places volunteers on two-year assignments and some shorter secondments. It requires people with skills – from engineers to teachers, from fundraisers to social workers, from midwives to marine biologists – who will earn a local salary in the host country. Applicants should normally have at least two years' post-qualification experience. There is also a Youth Programme for 18- to 25-year-olds with a UK passport.

VOLUNTARY

Archaeology Abroad (31–34 Gordon Square, London WC1H OPY, UK, Fax: 020 7383 2572, website: **www.britarch.ac.uk**) runs archaeology placements worldwide.

The Across Trust (Bridge House, 70–72 Bridge Road, East Molesey, Surrey KT8 9HF, UK, Tel: 020 8783 1355, Fax: 020 8783 1622, website: **www.across.org.uk**) sends volunteers overseas on a range of projects.

Alliances Abroad (702 West Avenue, Austin, TX 78701, USA, website: **www.alliancesabroad.com**) organises customised programmes for individuals and groups around the globe who want to learn about other cultures by teaching, interning, volunteering or working abroad.

ATD Fourth World (48 Addington Square, London SE5 7LB, Tel: 020 7703 3231, Fax: 020 7252 4276, website: **www.atd-uk.org**) organises workcamps and street workshops in Europe aimed at tackling extreme poverty. Placements last for two weeks and take place during July to September.

Australian Volunteers International (71 Argyle Street, PO Box 350, Fitzroy, Victoria 3065, Australia, Tel: 00 61 3 9279 1788, Fax: 00 61 3 9419 4280, website: **www.ozvol.org.au**) sends Australian volunteers to take part in developing communities in Asia, the Pacific, Africa, Latin America, the Middle East and parts of Australia. Assignments are usually for one to two years.

Bridges for Education Inc (94 Lamarck Drive, Buffalo, NY 14226, USA, Tel: 00 1 716 839 0180, website: **www.bridges4edu.org**) sends Canadian and American students and graduates to teach English in Eastern Europe.

Bunac (16 Bowling Green Lane, London EC1R 0QH, Tel: 020 7251 3472, website: **www.bunac.org**) runs a wide range of paid work and travel programmes and a voluntary project on Volunteer Costa Rica.

CIEE (Council on International Educational Exchange, 52 Poland Street, London W1V 4JQ, Tel: 020 7478 2018, website: **www.councilexchanges.org.uk**) runs programmes in USA, Canada, Australia, Japan and China.

Camphill Village Trust (Delrow House, Hilfield Lane, Watford, Hertfordshire WD2 8DJ, Tel: 01923 856006, Fax: 01923 858035, website: **www.camphill.org.uk**) places volunteers on community projects throughout the world.

Christians Abroad (1 Stockwell Green, London SW9 9HP, Tel: 020 7346 5950, Fax: 020 7346 5955) requires volunteers to take part in international projects.

Concordia (Heversham House, 20–22 Boundary Road, Hove, East Sussex BN3 4ET, Tel: 01273 422218, website: **www.concordia-iye.org.uk**). The International Volunteer Programme organises workcamps for 16- to 30-year-olds. Projects last from two to four weeks and range from renovating old churches to assisting at a French film festival.

Council Australia (University Centre, Level 8, 210 Clarence Street, Sydney 2000) runs programmes across the world for Australian and New Zealand students.

Council International Volunteer Projects (CIEE: 7 Custom House Street, 3rd Floor, Portland, ME 04101, Toll-Free: 1-800-40-Study, Fax: 00 1 207 553 7699, website: **www.ciee.org**) runs more than 800 international volunteer programmes in archaeology, renovation, environmental protection and social work in over thirty countries. Projects typically last for two to four weeks.

Cross-Cultural Solutions (47 Potter Avenue, New Rochelle, NY 10801, USA, Tel: 00 1 800 380 4777/00 1 914 632 0022, Fax: 00 1 914 632 8494) sends volunteers abroad to provide humanitarian assistance in Brazil, China, Costa Rica, Ghana, India, Peru, Russia and Thailand. Volunteers must be over eighteen. No experience required.

European Voluntary Service (Youth Exchange: The British Council, 10 Spring Gardens, London SW1A 2BN, UK) runs a wide range of voluntary projects throughout the world for 18- to 25-year-old EU nationals. Camps run from 26 to 52 weeks throughout the year, and cover a range of causes including addicts, AIDS, animal welfare, heritage, inner-city problems and refugees, to name only a few. Skills required include anything from computers to journalism to catering to scientific work.

The Experiment in International Living (EIL): EIL Britain, 287 Worcester Road, Malvern, Worcestershire WR14 1AB, Tel: 0168 45 62577, Fax: 0168 45 62212, website: **www.eiluk.org**. US citizens should contact Federation International EIL Office, Worldwide Network of The Experiment in International Living, PO Box 595, 63 Main St., Putney, VT 05346, USA, Tel: 00 1 802 387 4210, Fax: 00 1 802 387 5783. Other nationalities should look at EIL website **www.experiment.org**.

Global Outreach Mission UK, 108 Sweetbriar Lane, Exeter, Devon EX1 3AR, UK, Tel: 01392 259673, Fax: 01392 491176.

Global Volunteers, 57 E. Little Canada Road, St Paul, MN 55117, USA, Tel: 00 1 651 407 6100, Fax: 00 1 651 482 0915, website: **www.globalvolunteers.org**.

Inter-Cultural Youth Exchange (Latin American House, Kingsgate, London NW6 4TA, UK, Tel: 020 7681 0983, Fax: 020 7681 0983, website: **www.icye.co.uk**) runs a wide range of volunteering placements in countries around the world.

International Voluntary Service, Scotland and Northern Ireland, both place volunteers worldwide. International Voluntary Service (IVS-Scotland), 7 Upper Bow, Edinburgh EH1 2JN, Tel: 0131 226 6722, Fax: 0131 226 6723; International Voluntary Service (IVS-Northern Ireland), 122 Great Victoria Street, Belfast, Co. Antrim BT2 7BG, N. Ireland, Tel: 028 9023 8147, Fax: 028 9024 4356; International Voluntary Service, IVS Field Office, Old Hall, East Bergholt, Colchester, Essex CO7 6TQ, UK.

i-to-i (1 Cottage Road, Headingley, Leeds LS6 4DD, Tel: 0870 333 2332, website: **www.i-to-i.com**) runs working holiday placements teaching English as a foreign language in Latin America, Russia, Africa and Australasia.

Institute of Cultural Affairs (ICA: PO Box 71, Manchester M15 5BE, UK, website: **www.ica-uk.org.uk**) organises the Volunteer Service Programme for community projects overseas.

Involvement Volunteers (PO Box 218, Port Melbourne, Victoria 3207, Australia, Tel: 00 61 3 9646 5504 or 9392, Fax: 00 61 3 9646 5504; Involvement Volunteers – Deutschland, Matubadstr. 50, D-91056 Erlangen, Germany, Tel: 00 49 9135 8075, Fax: 00 49 9135 8075; Involvement

Volunteers UK, 7 Bushmead Avenue, Kingskerswell, Nr Newton Abbot, Devon TQ12 5EN, UK, Tel: 001803 872 594, website: **www.volunteering.org.au**) places volunteers in programmes in the USA in conservation and community projects.

National Federation of City Farms (The Green House, Hereford Street, Bristol BS3 4NA, UK, Tel: 0117 923 1800, Fax: 0117 923 1900) places volunteers on city farms throughout the world.

Orphan Helpers (2 Eaton Street Suite 1000, Hampton, VA 23669, USA, Tel: 00 1 757 722 6940 or 6941, Fax: 00 1 757 722 6942, website: **orphanhelpers.com**) is an American Christian organisation that provides help and support to orphanages around the world.

Peace Brigades International (PBI Britain, 1B Waterlow Road, London N19 5NJ, Tel: 020 7281 5370, website: **www.peacebridges.org**) is a peace-seeking non-governmental organisation providing physical and moral support to peace activists whose lives are threatened by violence. It sends international volunteers to provide an international presence in war-torn areas throughout the world for one year.

The Prince's Trust (18 Park Square East, London NW1 4LH, UK, Tel: 020 7543 1365, Fax: 020 7543 1315, website: **www.princes-trust.org.uk**) sends volunteers on placements in Europe.

Quaker Voluntary Action (Friends Meeting House, 6 Mount Square, Manchester M2 5NS, Charity number 1083412, Tel: 0161 819 1634) runs short-term two- to three-week volunteer projects in Europe, Japan and USA from working with the disabled to environmental protection.

Service Civil International (SCI: USA – Main Office, 5474 Walnut Level Road, Crozet, VA 22932, Tel/fax: 00 1 206 350 6585, website: **www.sci-ivs.org/**) is a global peace movement with branches in thirty countries and works with similar organisations in about fifteen countries. SCI runs workcamps lasting two to three weeks as well as longer-term volunteer programmes in a huge variety of locations for volunteers with previous experience.

Sierra Club (730 Polk Street, San Francisco, CA 94109, USA, Tel: 00 1 415 923 5527) sends volunteers on wilderness trips combined with conservation projects.

Teaching & Projects Abroad (Gerrard House, Rustington, West Sussex BN16 1AW, Tel: 01903 859911, website: **www.teaching-abroad.co.uk**) runs a thousand voluntary placements in teaching, as well as medicine and journalism, in China, Ghana, India, Mexico, Mongolia, Nepal, Peru, Russia, Romania, South Africa, Thailand, Togo and the Ukraine.

Tearfund (100 Church Road, Teddington, Middlesex TW11 8QE, Tel: 020 8977 9144, Fax: 020 8943 3594) is an evangelical relief and development charity that works to tackle poverty in Africa, Asia, South America and eastern Europe. Applicants should be committed Christians.

The Time For God Scheme (7 Colney Hatch Lane, Muswell Hill, London N10 1PN, UK, Tel: 020 8883 1504, Fax: 020 8365 2471, website: **www.timeforgod.org**) places volunteers on a variety of programmes.

Travel Active (PO Box 107, 5800 AC Venray, The Netherlands, Tel: 00 31 478 551 900, Fax: 00 31 478 551 911, website: **www.travelactive.nl**) organises Work and Travel Programmes and worldwide voluntary projects.

Travellers Worldwide (7 Mulberry Close, Ferring, West Sussex BN12 5HY, Tel: 01903 700478, Fax: 01903 502595) runs teaching and work experience, conservation voluntary placements worldwide.

UNA Exchange (Temple of Peace, Cathays Park, Cardiff CF10 3AP, Tel: 02920 223088, website: **www.unaexchange.org**) sends volunteers to camps abroad for two to four weeks working on a range of projects including social, environmental work and play schemes. It also has a 'North-South' Programme in 32 countries in Africa, Latin America and Asia.

Volunteer For Peace (1034 Tiffany Road, Belmont, VT 05730 USA, Tel: 00 1 802 259 2759, Fax: 00 1 802 259 2922, website: **www.vfp.org/**) is a US-based organisation that sends volunteers on projects worldwide.

Working Abroad Projects (2nd Floor Office Suite, 59 Lansdowne Place, Hove, East Sussex BN3 1FL, UK, Tel & Fax: 01273 711 406, website: **www.workingabroad.c**om) runs a wide range of worldwide projects ranging from working with indigenous cultures to reforestation projects.

World Exchange (St Colm's International House, 23 Inverleith Terrace, Edinburgh EH3 5NS, Tel: 0131 315 4444, Fax: 0131 315 2222) sends volunteers on worldwide placements.

WorldTeach (c/o Center for International Development, Harvard University, 79 John F. Kennedy Street, Cambridge, MA 02138, USA, Tel: 00 1 800 4 TEACH-0 (483-2240) or 00 1 617 495 5527, Fax: 00 1 617 495 1599) sends volunteer teachers on placements throughout the world.

World Wide Opportunities on Organic Farms (WWOOF) (PO Box 2675, Lewes, Sussex BN7 1RB, website: **www.wwoof.org**) sends volunteers to organic farms throughout the world.

Youth Action For Peace (8 Golden Ridge, Freshwater, Isle of Wight PO40 9LE, Tel: 01983 752557, Fax: 01983 756900, website: **www.yap-uk.org**) sends volunteers on workcamps throughout the world.

Youth With A Mission (Highfield Oval, Ambrose Lane, Harpenden, Hertfordshire AL5 4BX, Tel: 01582 463216, Fax: 01582 463213, website: **www.ywam-england.com**) places volunteers on worldwide youth projects.

GAP YEAR AND UNDER-EIGHTEENS

Africa and Asia Adventure (10 Market Place, Devizes, Wiltshire SN10 1HT, Tel: 01380 729009, website: **www.adventure.co.uk**) runs unpaid teaching or conservation projects lasting for four to five months throughout Africa and Asia, followed by an exciting safari for school leavers or undergraduates aged between 17 and 24.

BSES Expeditions (Royal Geographical Society, 1 Kensington Gore, London SW7 4AR, Tel: 020 7591 3141, Fax: 020 7591 3140, website:

www.bses.org.uk) runs a range of arctic expeditions for young explorers aged sixteen to twenty.

Gap Activity Projects Limited (Gap House, 44 Queens Road, Reading, Berkshire RG1 4BB, Tel: 0118 959 4914, website: **www.gap.org.uk)** organises worldwide voluntary work opportunities for 18- to 19-year-olds including teaching English, caring for the sick, assisting on community projects, conservation work and outdoor activities.

Project Trust (Hebridean Centre, Ballyhough, Isle of Coll, Argyle PA78 6TE, Tel: 01879 230444) is an educational trust which sends 200 school leavers overseas every year. Projects range from teaching to development work, outward-bound activities, health and childcare. Placements last twelve months.

CONSERVATION

African Conservation Experience (PO Box 9706, Solihull, West Midlands B91 3FF, Tel: 0870 241 5816, website: **www.afconservex.com)** organises placements lasting from one to three months on game reserves in South Africa and Zimbabwe.

British Trust for Conservation Volunteers (36 St Mary's Street, Wallingford, Oxfordshire OX10 0EU, Tel: 01491 821600, Fax: 01491 839646, website: **www.btcv.org)** sends volunteers on conservation projects in the UK and overseas.

Coral Cay Conservation (The Tower, 13th Floor, 125 High Street, Colliers Wood, London SW19 2JG, Tel: 0870 750 0688, website: **www.coralcay.org)** sends volunteers to Fiji, Honduras and the Philippines for marine and rainforest conservation expeditions.

Earthwatch (57 Woodstock Road, Oxford OX2 6HJ, Tel: 01865 318838, website: **www.earthwatch.org/europe)** organises placements with scientists around the world conducting research into rainforests, endangered species, archaeology and restoration. Placements last from two days to three weeks.

Explorations in Travel Inc. (2458 River Rd, Guilford, VT 05301, Tel: 00 1 802 257 0152, Fax: 00 1 802 257 2784, website: **www.volunteertravel.com)** runs voluntary projects for people from all over the globe on conservation projects worldwide.

Greenforce (11–15 Betterton Street, Covent Garden, London WC2H 9BP, Tel: 020 7470 8888, website: **www.greenforce.org)** organises Work on the Wild Side conservation projects around the world in the Amazon, Africa, Malaysia and South Pacific. Placements last from ten weeks. No experience needed.

Trekforce Expeditions (34 Buckingham Palace Road, London SW1W 0RE, Tel: 020 7828 2275, website: **www.trekforce.org.uk)** sends people on eight- to twenty-week expeditions in conservation projects in South East Asia and Central America, concentrating on working in the rainforest and with local communities.

INDEX